Ignoble Displacement

Dispossessed Capital in
Neo-Dickensian London

T0306421

Ignoble Displacement

Dispossessed Capital in Neo-Dickensian London

Stephanie Polsky

Winchester, UK
Washington, USA

First published by Zero Books, 2015
Zero Books is an imprint of John Hunt Publishing Ltd., Laurel House, Station Approach,
Alresford, Hants, SO24 9JH, UK
office1@jhpbooks.net
www.johnhuntpublishing.com
www.zero-books.net

For distributor details and how to order please visit the 'Ordering' section on our website.

Text copyright: Stephanie Polsky 2014

ISBN: 978 1 78279 880 4
Library of Congress Control Number: 2014954854

A CIP catalogue record for this book is available from the British Library.

Design: Stuart Davies

Printed and bound by CPI Group (UK) Ltd, Croydon, CR0 4YY, UK

We operate a distinctive and ethical publishing philosophy in all
areas of our business, from our global network of authors to
production and worldwide distribution.

CONTENTS

Acknowledgments

This book is dedicated to my grandfather Eugene Polsky. When I was a little girl my grandfather used to tell me stories. The stories were about a place he had never been. Nonetheless he spoke of the characters that inhabited that place as though he knew them, as though they were relatives of ours. He spoke with a great surety and a humour that bound us up in this story, so much so that I nodded along with avidity. I felt certain it was his wish that I memorise these characters' names, their genealogy, the cartography of their movements, as though my life depended on it. For a long while it did and it would. It unlocked many doors to reference such figures. Then there was his finitude, which was for me the greatest locked door of them all, and no amount of accenting, meandering and avoidance could rectify that matter and so it was. When I was a little girl I imagined this was just our story; it was not. It was the story of an age; it was the story of an ignoble displacement... or perhaps more accurately a series of them. And so begins this second attempt at a passage. The stories he shared with me I present to you, dear reader, now in shared signature with 'The Inimitable' Charles Dickens.

I would like to sincerely thank Alison Alpern who came back into my life after so many years away to prompt me to write this book on a subject I had been made to know all my life.

Introduction

A Dickensian Narrative of Neoliberalism

We live in a time of great social, political and economic crisis that many date to the collapse of the global banking system in 2008. Many are finding it difficult to contextualise the hardships that have taken place in the years following on from those events. It is difficult to find the answers in our present media landscape, or in a political and intellectual climate that continues to laud capitalism as the winning economic system coming out of both World War II and the end of the Cold War, which has become over the last century synonymous with democracy itself. The irony is that in our times the majority of the world's people feel disenfranchised by both capitalism and democracy. How did we come to this historical juncture? What can we learn not just from history, but from our cultural artefacts that might tell us how we first came to conduct ourselves within a system of global finance capitalism?

This volume proposes that we reinterpret the writings of Charles Dickens to find the antecedents of our present situation with regards to capital, empire and subjectivity. This is the story of an age, the nineteenth century, where finance first becomes the stuff of a life for the average British subject and where capital or the lack thereof shapes whole destinies. Capital imagines a life built in its own image under the auspices of liberal governance, which insists on nature itself as the progenitor of the market. Such an age uniquely transforms Dickens, a political reporter, into a novel author capable of utilising his mental agility, his class motivation and his personal torment to inform on capital's excesses, its grievances, its ability to dispossess its subjects at will and, rarer still, its redemptive capacities. This becomes the story of our age, recast to mimic the contours of a post-imperial

1

Britain where capital has adapted itself over centuries to become once again the agent of social engineering. Whole classes of individuals are captured through its sophisticated stratagems for managing the flow of wealth and bodies that today no longer require direct management, but rather subtle invocation as neoliberal subjects tethered to the project of continuous self-improvement and self-generated value creation. Today failure is not an option, any more than the financial ruin of our Victorian yesteryear. What must be observed however is the way in which the prospect of failure has morphed into discourses around race, class, multiculturalism, immigration, austerity and postcolonial conflict that bear the unique markers of our age, yet at the same time find their institutional geneses in the spaces Dickens charts so assiduously in his narratives. It's there that we might find the vital clues that provide critical insight into the contemporary movement of capital, from its portent and modes of resistance to its most dire tendencies found not in the future, but in a past understanding we have heretofore largely neglected to revise.

The year 2012 marked the bicentenary of Dickens's birth. At this time it is relevant to consider the 'other' Dickens and to explore those aspects of Dickens's life and work that have been less subject to critical revision, reappraisal and transformation within contemporary cultural studies of his work. This book will aim to critically assess the 'Dickensian' cultural legacy of the Victorian age in the twentieth and twenty-first centuries with regard to the rise of free-market capitalism and imperial expansion, which form the backdrop of his canonical works. These themes, whilst certainly remarked upon in recent scholarship, are seldom examined with regard to the revolution in finance and wealth concomitant to his recurrent subject matters around gender, class, race, emigration, property and inheritance, and moreover, their intersection with trends in law, science, government and criminal apprehension taking place within that same era. This book will argue in particular that the continued influence of Dickens into the twenty-first century has everything to do with a trend towards neo-Victorianism that impacts all of our debates related to economic crisis, globalisation, consumerism, social justice, neoliberalism and neocolonial warfare. Dickens's work performs for us a past that can seldom be ignored in taking up all these questions and thus poses the opportunity to reassess these issues, in service to today's societal dilemmas. By focussing on Dickens's preoccupations within the space of Victorian Britain, we can foresee the implications of his thought to the shaping of attitudes that prevail today when considering the 'Others' of our own society and the 'Others' outside, which have held up the weight of global enterprise for the past two centuries.

At the heart of capital, and of the human forces that engage it, is the issue of the violence of society itself and what replaces society when it is combined with its surplus. Dickens feared that as time wore on, those considered surplus populations in the capitalist system would eventually face a systematic rejection, once the masses were no longer willing to tolerate the cost of them. The modern derivations of murder, suicide and mass killing as we have now come to know them are all branches of Victorian capitalism. These branches remain open and sign-posted in Dickens's writing for all those who care to look. Despite the interdependence between rich and poor that formed the cornerstone of liability that united all of Britain's citizens under a progressively capitalistic banner, it remained understood throughout the nineteenth century that poverty itself was nobody's fault, or even if it was it was in a very limited sense. It was unthinkable that such a condition should be in anyway considered a problem in league with the social classificatory system itself.

These same Victorian dynamics of class in an emerging global society play out everywhere in contemporary Britain, drawing once more on an incorrigible classificatory logic established during the nineteenth century to enact a neoliberal schema in which those who inhabit the under classes may be confined to a zone of economic illegitimacy. Their lives of intense hardship and poverty, according to this (neo)liberal logic, should not warrant care or valuation, because their dire condition comes to them as a result of their own actions. The contemporary lives of those subject to hardship and poverty bear an unmistakable resemblance to the lives of the characters portrayed in Dickens's novels throughout the nineteenth century. It is here that we arrive at a kind of historical reversal: a critical, historical, and legal moment in which a contemporary neoliberal Britain rejects the mid-twentieth-century ideal of providing a social safety net for all in favour of a liberal, conditional welfare regime backed up with increasing surveillance, moralising and punishment not witnessed since the Victorian era. Today the precarious existence of the poorest has become the precursor to criminality as individuals are reduced to an advanced status of marginality. It is these forces that make up the ills of our time and bring us back to an age where social category becomes destiny. The purpose of this book is to mark off paths of departure from the Victorians' legacy, through a re-acquaintance with their former representation preserved within the contours of Dickens's radical literary agenda.

From this standpoint, this book marks a major departure from traditional Dickensian scholarship, because it is about tracing a trajectory of capitalism through Dickens's writing and the conditions in society and in his personal dealings that reflect this development of capitalism from the Victorian era to the present day. Therefore it must be understood that this book is not in any way a strict literary or historical study of Dickens as such. Rather its object is to demonstrate how the recent financial crisis has its roots in nineteenth-century capitalism's liberal moral, economic and cultural legacies. This book explicitly draws out an underlying framework of capital subtending all of Dickens's narrative arrangements, emerging therein as the very substance of character in the Victorian Age. It also makes explicit the intersection of colonial themes into all of Dickens's ostensibly British-based novels, therefore allowing readers to more fully appreciate the intimate relations of metropole and colony that come to form the basis of numerous new transactional economies represented in the novels touched upon within this volume: *Oliver Twist, Nicholas Nickleby, Bleak House, Little Dorrit, Great Expectations, A Tale of Two Cities, A Christmas Carol, Our Mutual Friend* and *Edwin Drood*. It reveals the liberal, political and economic framework that literally reinvents Britain for the imperial capitalistic age through the naturalisation of new class and racial hierarchies based on colonialism that have re-emerged today in the guise of 'neoliberalism'.

This book argues that neoliberalism takes as it starting point the careful governance of such formations to promote a societal logic for the perpetuation of similar class inequities in the context of a contemporary postcolonial Britain. What we witness in the intervening era between the eighteenth century and the twentieth century is a progression in the understanding of the market from an arena of exchange in eighteenth century, to one of competition in the nineteenth century, and in the twentieth one of enterprise. As capitalism attempted to absorb all of these values, the outward consumption initially prescribed by liberalism over time evolved to become a prescription for inward consumption under the new terms of neoliberalism.

In the eighteenth century, classical liberalism identified labour as the critical original human infusion that both created and justified private property. Under the constraints of neoliberalism, any special status for human labour is done away with as are the nineteenth century's older distinctions between production and consumption rooted in the labour theory of value. What replaces such values in the late twenty-first century version of liberalism, by contrast, is an understanding of the human being as an arbitrary bundle of investments, skill sets, temporary alliances at the level of family, sex, race and so on. Under the new vestiges of neoliberalism there are no more classes in the sense of the older political economy, since every individual is both employer and worker simultaneously; every man should be an entrepreneur, making of himself the governable material of his own business, firm or corporation. As a rationale, neoliberalism has come to stand in for being itself and the market the template for the individual's own self-management. Therefore the only class that remains conspicuously visible is the one made up of those who fail to adhere to the new labour standard of self-enhancement and its related capitalisation.

The first chapter, '"Tomorrow" and Yesterday: The Peculiar British Property of Domestic Dispossession', explores the threat associated with the loss of shelter, whether it is on a material or ontological level, through a reading of Dickens's *Oliver Twist* and *Bleak House* and Elmgreen and Dragset's recent V&A installation 'Tomorrow'.

The second chapter, 'Bank Draft: The Winds of Change in *Little Dorrit*'s Domestic Economy', re-examines the representation of the market in Dickens's novel *Little Dorrit*. There we are able to not merely identify developments in the realm of contemporary finance capitalism proper to the age of the novel, but to unearth a new cultural imaginary within it that expressed changing ideas of moral probity and indeterminate identity, creditworthiness and the management of financial risks, and to consider its repercussions for the British subject both at home and abroad.

The third chapter, 'Cosmopolitan Fortunes: Imperial Labour and Metropolitan Wealth in Dickens's *Great Expectations*' looks at the spatial history of Britain's relationship to its penal colony, Australia. This is mapped by positing Magwitch's imperial labour as both central to the text, and part of a greater spatial history that crucially intersects with the linear biography of Pip's development in England.

The fourth and concluding chapter, 'Age and Ills: Dickens's Response to the Indian Mutiny of 1857 within the Present Context of Neoliberal Empire', addresses the ways in which Dickens's writings deal with a set of persistent anxieties and uncertainties that plagued the maturation of the British Empire within his lifetime. This chapter examines the parallel between the Victorian era of liberalism and its postmodern successor neoliberalism to map the ills of our present age, by bringing us back to a time where social category first materialises as biopolitical destiny.

In closing, the epilogue, 'Crony Capitalism and the *Mutuality* of the Market', provides a Dickensian critique of Prime Minister David Cameron's Lord Mayor's Banquet speech, delivered on 11 November 2013, which called for economic austerity to be enacted 'not just now, but permanently' in a political tone reminiscent of *Our Mutual Friend*'s Mr. Podsnap.

Whilst this book certainly references Victorian themes and their contemporary significance, its larger aim is to bring the political discourse of the Victorian era (which Dickens, as a public figure, played an enormous role in drafting) to bear on contemporary re-imaginings of the nineteenth century and their sustained impact in shaping twenty-first-century social, political and economic policies in Britain. These same relations still implicate themselves in the way we look at culture and capital, both human and financial, as we approach the twenty-first century in some senses as Neo-Victorians operating on registers of neoliberal and neocolonial enterprise that have their antecedents in the historical atmosphere of Dickensian London. Therefore, at a fundamental level, this book addresses the relationship between the themes of capital and empire in Dickens's novels and the confluence of global economy and liberal politics in the Victorian era that remain relevant to our understanding of our present global financial crisis and the

significance it has in maintaining a logic for neoliberal governmentality.

'Tomorrow' and Yesterday: The Peculiar British Property of Domestic Dispossession

In the autumn of 2013, The Victoria and Albert Museum commissioned leading contemporary artists Michael Elmgreen and Ingar Dragset to create a major site-specific installation in the former Textile Galleries entitled 'Tomorrow'. The setting already evokes a spatial and temporary reference to the British Empire, which is then mirrored in the central character of the exhibition: an elderly 75-year-old failed British architect named Norman Swann. Dragset explains in a video commissioned for the exhibition by the V&A that 'He had a lot of great ideas, he was quite visionary but he never got to realise any of his projects. He was a part-time teacher, probably at Cambridge. Visitors can see a lot of his models in the study that we install as part of his home. You do get a sense that this is a grand South Kensington apartment, all these things have trickled down through generations and now maybe the old architect living there might be the last person to sit on this from the family empire' (V&A, 'Elmgreen & Dragset at the V&A'). The idea that the British Empire might be coming to a close in 2013, rather than sometime in the 1950s or 60s, is an intriguing one. This is further spoken to by Elmgreen when he describes the audience for this installation as 'diverse, they come from many different backgrounds', tacitly referring to Britain's postcolonial social makeup. Their multifariousness for the installation artist is equated at once with the performance of labour on one level, and on another a bastardisation of the original rational intent of the architecture: 'Often your audience will create and elaborate on the artworks in a much more interesting way than you ever could do yourself – they make it wilder, more romantic, sentimental or perverse than your intentions were to start with'. This sets the stage for a drama of meaning to play itself out, often with results that undermine the order of things through an interpenetration of tastes and desires.

The V&A website describes the installation as a 'domestic setting that will appear like a set for an unrealised play' ('Elmgreen & Dragset at the V&A'). This play however must be in some sense stage-managed as evidenced by the provision of 'a script, written by the artists, made available for visitors as a printed book' prior to their entrance into the formal space. Though many visitors only take a cursory glance at this material, laying it down before commencing to explore the apartment, perch on the sofa and read Norman's books and magazines, it nonetheless speaks to an intention on the part of the artists to in some way maintain their script or rather inscription in the experience laid out before them and to mark them in some way upon entrance to this vaunted space. The choice of South Kensington to create the grand residence of a fictional architect in a series of five rooms within the museum is already overlaid with meaning, and then placed into further temporal relief through a careful 'domestic sequence of entrance hall, dining room, kitchen, study and bedroom, furnished with a combination of pieces from the V&A collection alongside replicas and the artists' own additions'. This potent combination of artefact and artifice says a great deal about the British Empire itself as 'the setting for a highly elaborate fiction' (Woodman). The objects point to a larger truth about empire. Despite its impressive holdings, the architecture that subtends its offering is only ever as good as the flawed and fragile individuals charged with its assembly. What we see then displayed in Swann's world is not solely of aesthetic interest, but is also useful as a means of detecting what will come in to reassemble these parts in the wake of the British Empire's formal dissolution.

Perhaps it is telling that we enter the exhibition space of 'Tomorrow' after passing the Devonshire Hunting Tapestries that were donated to the V&A 'in lieu of tax during the post-war dismantling of the old aristocratic system' (Jennings). Quite suddenly we find ourselves at the entrance hall of a grand Kensington town house, confronted as it were by another post-war period of English aristocratic austerity. The property we encounter, whilst superficially retaining its grandeur, also displays the look of decay – a bucket in the corridor catches the occasional drip coming through the ceiling making us perhaps subtly aware of other failings to come. What we confront next are an array of images that hang in the corridor mingled together in a grouping that speaks at once to nostalgia and loss: 'a photo of Ronnie Scott's jazz club next to one showing the moment Rhodesia initiated breakaway from colonial rule; childhood sketches; a military medal' (Jennings). The inhabitant seems to have difficulties in distinguishing his ardor for his male companions and their institutional settings as evidenced by a fake photo album we discover in the sitting room with holiday snaps reflecting his mutual interest in architecture and young men. One in particular is singled out through a series of postcards that appear in his study received from an 'acquaintance from Berlin recalling fond memories of their time together, but who is now seemingly upset Norman never replied' (Bradley).

As Kimberly Bradley mentions in her review, Norman's presence is portrayed totemically through 'a wealth of sculptures of horses ("They love their horses here, don't they?" Elmgreen observes); an OBE hanging on the wall; and perhaps most disturbingly through what presumably is a sculpture of him huddled in the frame of the fireplace, curled up in fearful despair with his face to his knees' (Bradley). His likeness is echoed in a portrait that hangs over the mantelpiece of that same fireplace, wearing an identical schoolboy uniform to his three-dimensional likeness below, equally melancholy and apprehensive. The theme of youth and its sorrows resonates throughout the house, existing as it were side by side with the torment of its present occupier: a living and aging man, the adult version of Norman Swann. Again it is not just the representation of young men that captures our interest throughout; it is also the way in which they become aesthetic objects and forms within themselves, trans-mitting through 'the carefully chosen library with books by Thomas Mann, Tony Benn and Jean Cocteau ... alongside tomes on queer architecture and copies of "Architectural Review"' a certain well-known structure of society which allows the very existence of Norman to become intelligible to visitors (Bradley). Norman's absent body is indeed riddled with meaning. The HIV medicine he takes to keep disease from ravaging his body is peeking out from the drawer, his pills reluctant objects in their own right competing, as it were, with his massive, unmade bed, a pillar of which is crowned with a golden vulture, looking over the sleeper perhaps lying in wait for his ultimate demise or rather in perpetual harsh judgment of his past actions in this position.

Norman's vulnerability, his propensity toward self-destruction, and his fractious life course are all meticulously plotted through Elmgreen & Dragset's arrangement of a number of set pieces: a dressed and decorated dining table broken into two denying the diner uncomplicated succor, a study populated with maquettes of his failed modernist social housing projects, an office where the unpaid bills that provoked Norman's departure are on view, an Evening Standard front page from the summer of the 2011 riots pinned to the wall, the headline: 'London's Shame'. Norman's lingering pre-occupations about discomfort encroaching upon the domestic environment are announced in the vacant drape of his Burberry trench coat, a discarded pair of his tatty slippers and a Zimmer frame concealed behind an elegant screen. The noise of a running shower and the drip through the ceiling together convey a sense of presentiment for the visitor. These perhaps are gothic reminders that this extraor-dinary new multi-room installation lodges within itself the historical insinuation of five vast Victorian spaces, which are being temporarily altered into these present quarters in aid of illuminating a greater historical legacy; one that at once shelters Norman's being and portrays Britain's own interiority.

Elmgreen & Dragset acknowledge as their inspiration for Norman's home 'the European interiors depicted by Dutch Masters and the Danish Golden Age' which equally portray the plenty that imperial enterprise afforded to these domestic settings (Himelfarb). Elmgreen asserts that their work, 'like artists painting interiors throughout centuries, is intended to imply psychology and social codes'. These codes support the act of trespassing into history's deepest recesses in the home. The fact that the owner of that property is an ambiguous one gives persuasive licence to the visitor to pass through. Norman's progressive bankruptcy gives the property a look of dereliction. It gives the visitor the initial impression that the owner has long gone, only to discover him curiously sonically embedded into the walls of the place. We never hear his voice, his version of events per se; instead his narrative is sustained through the script written by Elmgreen & Dragset. Within it are contained the heated discussions he has with former German lover Daniel Wilder and Daniel's present girlfriend Wendy, 'about how attached Norman is to the home and its contents, and how disappointed he is that the signs of decay point to the contrary' (Bose). Norman, like his belongings, is 'being tested against the perils of time' and found wanting. Conspicuously on the cover of the book is a tombstone emblazed with the word 'Tomorrow' and the impressed insignia of the V&A. Could this signal to us from the start Norman's demise, or indeed the untimely demise of our own 'Tomorrow'? Through Norman, Daniel and Wendy's conflict with one another, Elmgreen & Dragset are able to reveal personal histories as poignant in their own right, possessing of a dark humour that carries over to 'reveal the fragile, quivering heart of human avarice, ego and intellect behind various spatial and societal constructs' (Bose). The visitors for their part get to experience the crushing, private disappointment Norman embodies as a result of coming too late to the party of Empire, the loneliness of entrusting one's legacy to future generations for whom all biography will become the stuff of electronic entry and digital self-enhancement, a somewhat tragic missive sent from one dehumanising imperial architecture to another equally dehumanising neoliberal architecture.

One thing is for certain: the inherited and imperial wealth that empire provided is disintegrating, just like the institutions that house them, right before our eyes, giving way to new forms of wealth derived elsewhere beyond Britain and Europe and by a new money elite, who still wish to embrace for the time being 'the dust-sheeted dreams of a benevolent empire', to master its architecture and in some sense claim its power and influence for themselves as immediate cash buyers (Bose). Perhaps it is their time, this 'Tomorrow'. Perhaps it will become someone else's. Today the major shifts in society have their beginnings in political and economic will, as they once did in the nineteenth century when Britain was at the height of its empire. In Elmgreen's words, 'this rude, rough neoliberalism, new money from all over the world, and new parameters' appear superficially to clash with all the mindsets of old imperial Britain, which was brought about by a very strict class system and maintained a banal domestic architecture through aristocratic ministering of the state, leaving those less fortunate largely to negotiate the social structures they put in place with little optimism (Elmgreen qtd. in Bose).

During the Victorian era museums open to the public were designed to invite working-class individuals in to revere the spoils of empire in their best display, so that the hardships of their own environment could temporarily be offset in proximity to these riches. The V&A itself was established in 1852 (from the proceeds of the Great Exhibition of 1851) on the founding principle of making 'works of art available to all, to educate working people and to inspire British designers and manufacturers' (V&A, 'A Brief History of the Museum'). The air, light and space of such places would turn them into spaces of revelation. Many people visiting these type of institutions were anticipating being changed by what they saw, for these interior spaces to make them see things in a different light, to stimulate ideas and discourse and ultimately to act in the cause of breaking down the normal hierarchy in aid of another potential order. The museum as a structure, for Elmgreen & Dragset, is one that exists alongside other institutions such as 'prisons, social security offices, hospitals ... galleries and parks [to] act as means of social control' (Elmgreen & Dragset, 'The Welfare Show'). They see it as their job to enliven the theatrical, even filmic quality of all individually lived experience nestled within these institutions, by re-authorising these seemingly prosaic spaces and revealing their hidden, generative potential through novel exhibition.

In the case of 'Tomorrow', biographical and fictitious identities are made to connect seamlessly within the various strands of narratives defining this exhibition and indeed spacing out that identity-based logic to achieve full subversive effect. In 'Tomorrow', it is the personal detail, the exceptional circumstance and the disaffected atmosphere that are brought forth by the artists to interrogate what we consider common or universal about our age. The exhibition intimates, at least superficially, that it is possible to understand one's identity from one's belongings, but also that people can in a sense 'become' themselves through 'becoming' items in someone else's collection, allowing them to free themselves from the illusion that they are living their lives in assumed privacy, and instead realise that they have always in some sense been part and parcel of a larger societal apparatus. As subjects it is up to us to grasp the fact that what we are looking at are always already-staged interiors, our self-understanding coming to us through the windows of society, conventionally from the outside in. The spaces we occupy are equally invented for us to arrive at from a distance, our identities vaguely skewed to conform with the objects collected about us which themselves are slightly off, underlining the constructedness of the spaces we inhabit and in turn our own interior lives.

Elmgreen & Dragset's work implies that within society, some individuals replicate their personal narratives to function as miniature versions of the overall social hierarchy of the national space. However some cannot be employed for the roles they appear to be designed for, and some are broken and therefore cannot participate fully in the mechanism drawn up for them. Despite the apparent awkwardness of the design of such spaces and indeed subjectivities, outsiders are nonetheless welcomed in, if only to the extent that they are encouraged to imagine how life in these dwellings could be and what values the inhabitants share. The entry point for such dwelling assumes that one's life story is in some way based on one's possessions. Herein lies at once an institutional critique of capitalism, but also a social criticism that becomes a commentary on public shifts in power, aesthetics and priorities, and how they affect our most private ambitions and situations. It is these and many other recurring historical themes and overlapping subjectivities that populate this interior space, crowding it, forcing the visitor to devise meaning and decode themes within its narrative space.

In the case of 'Tomorrow', curiously, for a deal to be brokered to save Norman Swann from the burdens associated with his core identity, he must call up one of these very burdens: his former student, Daniel Wilder. Elmgreen explains that Wilder 'was never very intellectually gifted but has become a very successful interior designer of celebrities' homes and has found him a buyer', and has set to work remodelling the apartment for its new owners. 'So, unlike our architect, he's actually got something realized', adds Dragset. 'Though of course it's something dear Norman looks down on' (qtd. in Wrathall). Swann's disdain for

Wilder, presumed here to be a foreign interloper but nonetheless allowed to cash in on South Kensington, speaks to another theme Elmgreen & Dragset are keen to cash in on themselves in their choice of setting for Swann's tragic fall: 'the clash between old and new money' (Wrathall). As Elmgreen comments, 'Power is shifting in the world at the moment. Who are the rich in London? Not Britons. It's no longer the traditional upper class. It's mostly people who have moved here' (qtd. in Wrathall).

Tellingly, it is neither the traditional upper class nor their rich migrant counterparts whom Elmgreen anticipates as the audience for their installation, but rather the vast remainder of London's inhabitants who will flock to the exhibition 'to relax' amidst 'a nice welcoming environment with seating'; it is these people who will 'use' the installation, because '99 percent of the population in London have so little space' (Elmgreen qtd. in Wrathall). Elmgreen elaborates on their condition: 'They live in such shit domestic conditions that they enjoy just sitting on nice furniture in a big room. The reason people in London go to so many exhibitions is that they need to escape their tiny apartments. They go to get some space and air.' So in a sense theirs is a social housing project, if only one that remains temporarily open to this needy public. What is required of them in turn, according to Elmgreen's confident estimation, is that the public will respond as intended, becoming 'private detectives, sneaking into Norman's diary, his photo albums, his books, trying to figure out who he is and what's happened'. Beyond this mutual occupation, Elmgreen believes that 'all of us… are a product of our environments, controlled by the homes we live in and the objects we acquire. They are what influence, and perhaps limit, the narratives of our lives. How much happier and more productive might Norman Swann have been if he'd lived in the sort of Corbusian machine for living he dreamed of building? If there's a guilty suspect at this crime scene, in this story of an unfulfilled life … it's the house' (Elmgreen qtd. in Wrathall). This ominous remark implies that the 99 percent of the London population confined to their bleak manners are similarly destined to carry out this narrative of an unfulfilled life.

No one knows how long the rise in housing prices will continue, nor indeed when the housing market bubble will finally burst. In consolation to this fact the ordinary Londoner gets, for the time being, to sit on the present British aristocratic occupier's couches and leaf through his private collection of books, glance over a copy of *The Daily Telegraph* with the Duchess of Cambridge, the former Kate Middleton on the cover all amidst an array of ornate objects which refer in some way to Empire, including 'two antique revolvers, a sculptured fig leaf' used for the 'David' sculpture every time Queen Victoria would come to the museum, and 'a pair of ornate 18th-century candelabra with gilded Atlases holding globes aloft' (Donadio). Altogether they display Empire itself as in some sense a highly elaborate fiction staged at various moments to seeming perfection. The devil however is in the detail as a subtly displayed needlepoint reads 'Home is the place you left'. Norman Swann's domestic displacement was not a matter of straight-forward personal failing any more than today's would-be home buyer or renter are responsible for their own financial discomfiture in whatever relationship they have to dwelling in London property. Indeed at nearly every class level, the apprehensive desire to appeal for more competes against a bitter reality that at any moment they could be driven out by the vagaries of the market. The threat associated with the loss of shelter, whether it is on a material or ontological level, is explored time and again in the work of Elmgreen & Dragset. This is a means of surveying their obsession with both property and propriety and the necessity to subdue neoliberalism's worst tendencies to disenfranchise and drive out its domiciled subjects at will.

In reading such accounts, we find ourselves moving backward in time on the property ladder, to another narrative of domestic significance that resonates not a little with Norman Swann's scripted encounter with property: the Georgian London townhouse in Bloomsbury where Charles Dickens lived for two and a half years, between 1837 and 1839. The building, now the Charles Dickens Museum, reopened in December 2012 after a £3.1 million makeover based mainly on lottery funding, which was dubbed 'The Great Expectations Project', despite the fact that this particular novel was never penned at this house. Rather it was *Oliver Twist* and *Nicholas Nickleby* that were written here and this is also where Dickens finished writing *The Pickwick Papers* (J. Gilbert). The restoration, we are told by the current German-born curator Florian Schweizer was meant to result in 'a themed, atmospheric museum', and thus parallels in a significant way Elmgreen & Dragset's curatorial project (Nayeri). Here a script and a floor plan are provided to visitors entering the museum, who are encouraged at once to read a short narrative about Dickens, and imagine themselves briefly as inhabitants of a fancifully restaged Victorian home. Upon entrance, visitors are promptly greeted at the staircase by the silhouette of a twenty-five-year-old gesturing them to climb upward through his home. This is an apt gesture given that he himself strove upwards toward middle-class respectability by renting this house in 1837 for £80 per annum.

Much is made here of the interior of Dickens's home, but little is said of its exterior location. This property was not embedded in any of London's smart neighbourhoods of the time, but rather it was near the austere law offices of Chancery Lane whose grave manner is later intoned in his novels *Bleak House* and *Great Expectations*. It was also close to 'the squalid thieving dens that inspired the character of Fagin in *Oliver Twist*' (Nayeri). Despite these rather inglorious features of the borough at the time, Dickens felt secure against these darker elements of society, because 48 Doughty Street was situated on a portered, gated street, allowing Dickens to classify his dwelling as a 'frightfully first-class family mansion' (Nayeri). What was frightful about this property was how it managed still to relate to the residences of law and criminality that surrounded it, forcing upon Dickens awful responsibilities to avoid material commerce with either. Dickens's checkered financial past, based on his father's earlier confinement of the family at Marshalsea Prison for debt, meant that this house rental was only made possible through the relatively recent success of *The Pickwick Papers*. It was only through that influx of funds that Dickens was in a position finally to change his youthful circumstance. Schweizer comments that as a newly famous author, 'Dickens was able to step up the social ladder ... He was gladly accepted by the landlord, because Boz, his pen name, was a very strong currency at the time' (qtd. in Nayeri). Boz was not just the counter-signature for this home, it also functioned as its cash-book, substantiating the lives of so many others that dwelt here, including not only his wife, his new baby, his wife's sister and his brother but also a group of paid employees including a cook, a housemaid, a nurse and a manservant.

What remains intact of this home, for the visitor to explore, are the six rooms on three floors, three attic rooms and a basement. Inside the ground floor dining room, visitors are made aware of Dickens's reputation as a world-class society host, who regularly conducted lavish dinners worthy of his often-aristocratic companions. Blue China plates are displayed prominently on the dining table picturing regular attendees, including author William Thackeray, William MacCready and John Forster. These honoured guests 'dined on gold-rimmed porcelain, emblazoned with the socially ambitious Dickens's initials and the family crest' he invented: 'a lion holding a Maltese cross'. These items are displayed carefully inside a vitrine (Nayeri). A handsome portrait of a dashing young Dickens observes proceedings from above the fireplace mantle, looking every bit the Regency dandy. He is not alone in the display of a favourable likeness, with expensive portraits strewn about the place flattering the appearance of his wife Catherine and two daughters, Katey and Mary, who were both born in this house. The heart of the home not surprisingly is the drawing room. We are told this is the place where the Dickens family regularly performed readings, plays and recitals written by Dickens himself for the amusement of his rarefied guests, dedicated to that felicitous labour.

Equally preserved are the trappings of Dickens as a publically circulating writer. Up the stairs from this assemblage stands another vitrine, displaying Dickens's worn 'leather briefcase, a chain-mail money purse, a theater token and a silver matchbox holder' (Nayeri). Further upstairs, in the cramped study we are uncannily confronted with Dickens's leather-topped writing desk, which we are then given to imagine is the place where he tirelessly wrote *Great Expectations* and *A Tale of Two Cities*. A large bookcase contains his heavy leather-bound collected works, including pages of the *Oliver Twist* manuscript. 'The ink has gone brown, and blurry in parts. "Oh no they ain't!" reads one sentence' (Nayeri). The 'ain't' may refer to the fact that in many ways Dickens was no gentleman, nor a man blessed with domestic bliss within the confines of these walls. The higher we go in the house, the more cracks in the foundation of Dickens's domiciled past start to appear. The floor above is the preserve of Dickens's private life. We soon enter into the remarkably small bedroom he shared with Catherine. The room feels claustrophobic, and this sense of unease is underlined for the visitor through the display of letters and texts that all relate to his subsequent separation, and reveal Dickens's hatred of his wife's 'wicked mother', further scripting our knowledge of this now well-known separation narrative. These documents themselves mark a significant departure from the temporal scheme of this home, insofar as they relate to events that would take place many years on from this current habitation. Similarly, at the very top of the home are mementoes of Dickens's impoverished childhood, including a grille from the aforementioned Marshalsea Prison, which function as tangible reminders of the threat of sudden poverty and culpable debt that haunt the staging of this entire domestic tableau.

Dickens, as husband and father, in time became a comprehensive failure and indeed faced at the end of his life a similar crisis to Swann in terms of preserving the trappings of class ascension through his chosen profession. A foreshadowing of the tragic domestic breakdown of the Dickens family is perhaps even evident in this early household, which lasts less than three years. The fact 'that the clan decamped early owes much to the fast succession of two births, one miscarriage, and the sudden death of Dickens's beloved 17-year-old sister-in-law' in the back bedroom of the house, and speaks to the fragility of their domestic arrangement (J. Gilbert).

Whilst Dickens's image stands in relief at the foot of the stairs to guide us through these curious rooms and their contents, 'the picture is incomplete without sight of the letter, written to a friend by Dickens several houses later, when he built a wall across their bedroom, to shut out his wife' (J. Gilbert). But that was in the years to come: here at Doughty Street he at least partially manages to keep solvent such relationships. So the visitor is prompted to go further on with Dickens, despite the upheaval bespoken of by this artefact, at the prompting of the guiding pamphlet, designed to resemble one of Dickens's fictional instalments, to the café and gift shop where perhaps a less problematic consumption of Dickens remains possible. In the temporary display area adjacent to those, visitors may view costumes from the recent film adaptation of *Great Expectations*, released to the public in the same year as this restoration, in what amounts to an endless compulsion to rescript Dickens and in so doing reinstall colour to what would have been a life largely lived in the shadow of property and proprietary debt. Given the number of times Charles Dickens moved house, it's remarkable that only one of his houses still stands to be carefully requisitioned in this way. 'These events also dealt a blow to the future heritage industry since very little of the author's fingerprint remains on No. 48, reopened to the public after refurbishment … within a squeak of the end of the Dickens bicentenary' (J. Gilbert).

If Dickens were alive today he may well have been in the position of the fictional architect Norman Swann, confronting the dark side of the capital's housing boom, struggling against the tide of soaring prices and increased demand in the capital and left to fend for himself against the daunting spectre of homelessness as his problems became compounded by debt and the lack of reliable earnings to meet the burdens of his household. The deteriorating health of Dickens and Swann is mirrored in the breakdown of society respective to their times, it too failing in its obligation to provide reliable shelter. Today we find ourselves desperate to preserve our old neglected dwellings, while at the same time failing to recast our societal structure. Instead we tolerate those ignoble displacements that surely lie ahead for us as we continue to dwell under a banner of marketisation, whose character of labour is of course indebted to Dickens's signature observation; that the obsession with property comments on values beyond the purely proprietary. Material goods, in Dickens, are present to tell a story, and throughout his narratives find themselves 'becoming biographical containers, markers of lost lives, monuments to memory' (Traps, para. 2). As such, they should be understood as continuous with Dickens's miniature bourgeois mansion, 'the home he endeavours to preserve as a safe haven from the stresses of work', which instead becomes a prison house for his literary production and thus demands 'the suppression of feeling'. A feeling of resentment that the higher up you go can scarcely be contained and over time becomes its own object worthy of preservation within that same domestic space.

Whilst on the surface, Doughty Street may appear as a form of domestic retreat to the casual visitor, for Dickens it became a place of mourning that required if anything a hasty departure. The possessions Dickens chose to carry on his person are, in at least one significant way, superior to his domicile; as objects capable of accompanying Dickens to work, 'they let him recollect, at a touch, the perversely comforting narratives that somehow sustain him' (Plotz xv). Dickens's 'portable property bridges his public and private selves, bringing comfort to the workday by reminding him of the domestic life it enables, reminding him all the while that domestic life is itself made possible by work' (Traps para. 2). The character of that work is to create a 'Greater Britain' through his novels, at a time when the novels themselves were becoming implicitly and explicitly *national* portable property. For Dickens, like many of his Victorian-British counterparts, this requires an '*asymmetry* in portability, so that the flow of culture-bearing objects from core to periphery is not counterbalanced or interrupted by a flow in the opposite direction' (Plotz 2). 'The capacity of an imperium to sustain that kind of asymmetry' though 'a crucial component of its power' was itself a necessary fiction, as was the British Empire's 'ability to convince itself that its aesthetic objects could constitute and solidify identity on the move', requiring the whole of polite society to at once ignore its place 'in the global circulation of goods' and 'the counterflows of objects from its colonies abroad' that were nonetheless heading inevitably back towards their smart metropolitan homes to weigh on their foundations (Plotz 2). Their failure to recognise the gravity of their endeavour is one of the most important clues about the limitations of portability inherent to the very project of Empire. It is here that a series of displacements in Dickens really comes to the fore, from the core to the periphery, for tomorrow and yesterday, moving across boundaries found increasingly to be unsecured by the limitless flow of the marketplace, making complicated results of what at first appear to be simple impulses, which added together implicate us all and British identity as a whole with the ignoble distinction of being capital's first subject and Dickens one of its first mature authors.

The nineteenth-century domestic economy that Charles Dickens drew upon is an apt place to begin this study as what transpired there was nothing less than the story of an age. It was the story of an ignoble displacement, or perhaps more accurately a series of them, which precedes and gives shape to 'a global network of goods' circulating 'beyond the sanctity of the home' (Houston, *From Dickens to Dracula* 2). Whilst 'the professional, masculine sphere ... increasingly concentrated on national global finance', it held suspended within it a 'ghostly remainder' loyal to its previous local dwelling. During the 'industrialised Victorian period' a kind of dormant domesticity haunts all of its transactions, its movements; it's body politic (2). Moreover, it is the violence of the homestead that will inform upon the public as it comes to be shaped by certain norms of confinement proper to the intimacy and belongings of that place. What may be apprehended can just as easily be rejected out of hand. The spectre of dispossession is never very far from capital's pull and one must tread hard all his life to outpace it. Charles Dickens's own constant peregrinations began in childhood, when at the tender age of twelve he found himself forced to leave school to begin working ten-hour days at Warren's Blacking Warehouse where he earned shillings a week pasting labels on blacking pots by hand. The strenuous – and often cruel – work conditions made a deep impression on Dickens, who would remain terrorised throughout his life by how easily he was cast away at such an age from any form of societal protection, into a place of decrepitude and squalor. Whilst his fortunes would vastly improve, it was the character of poverty and its exposure through his many works that made the foreboding side of capital visible to the middle classes. Whilst many such readers were fascinated by the fate of the vulnerable figures created by Dickens's mind, most failed to receive much in the way of deeper insight into the character of the age that in reality housed or dispossessed all manner of individuals at the impulse of capital.

In the novel *Oliver Twist*, Dickens attempts to expose his readers to the dehumanising logics that accompany the Poor Law of 1834, which was largely influenced by the Malthusian population principle. From its point of origin, 'Oliver's existence is registered by the Poor Law and its administrators only in terms of the economic cost of his maintenance, a perspective that leads both experimental philosophers and Poor Law guardians to starve their "charges" in an attempt to reach the optimum, i.e., least expensive, level of material sustenance for them' (Klaver 80). The Poor Law nullified the paternalistic arrangement between rich and poor, which had been a holdover from feudalism, and authored in its place a new social contract predicated on the workhouse parish being the chief administrator of subsistence. Subsistence through it came in the form of the poor being 'means-tested', an individual's worth meted out on an individual case-by-case basis, premised on their ability to produce labour. Families were separated upon entry into the workhouse parish, wives from husbands, parents from children, atomised to the point where only their mouths and hands were of identifiable character.

Within this social schema, we find Oliver Twist, Dickens's famous mouthpiece of protest against such an abandonment of social paternalism. Oliver is a ward of the state, an illegitimate orphan born into the workhouse. Twice repeated, and today the subject of infamy in Dickens's work, Oliver's polite request: 'Please sir, I want some more', becomes the shorthand for a challenge against authority, which enraged his minders. So it was that Oliver was ejected from the workhouse, and hastened into the world of criminality, where ill fortunes are rewarded not with pathetic gruel, but rather moreish sausages. This is the delicious enticement, presented to him by Fagin, that is enough to induce Oliver into a tentative career as a pickpocket. Unlike the parish, Fagin's material largess is open to those who serve him:

> In a frying-pan, which was on the fire, and which was secured to the mantel-shelf by a string, some sausages were cooking; and standing over them, with a toasting-fork in his hand, was a very old shrivelled Jew, whose villainous-looking and repulsive face was obscured by a quantity of matted red hair. He was dressed in a greasy flannel gown, with his throat bare; and seemed to be dividing his attention between the frying-pan and a clothes-horse, over which a great number of silk handkerchiefs were hanging ... Seated round the table were four or five boys, none older than the Dodger, smoking long clay pipes, and drinking spirits with the air of middle-aged men. These all crowded about their associate as he whispered a few words to the Jew; and then turned round and grinned at Oliver. So did the Jew himself, toasting-fork in hand.
>
> 'This is him, Fagin,' said Jack Dawkins; 'my friend Oliver Twist.'
>
> 'We are very glad to see you, Oliver, very,' said the Jew. 'Dodger, take off the sausages; and draw a tub near the fire for Oliver. Ah, you're a-staring at the pocket-handkerchiefs! eh, my dear! There are a good many of 'em, ain't there? We've just looked 'em out, ready for the wash; that's all, Oliver; that's all. Ha! ha! ha!' (Dickens, *Oliver Twist* 137; ch. 8).

Oliver, like the pocket-handkerchiefs before him, will be bathed into the order of illicit wealth that plays no small part in sustaining the poor of society. Within this obscure domestic context, Oliver gets to have a restored family of sorts for a time, in the boys that become his brothers, the surrogate parents found in Bill Sikes and Nancy and even in Fagin who assumes the place of a wily grandfather or uncle. The proper alternative to this cosy arrangement from Malthus's point of view is that Oliver should have never been born, and that moreover his existence was a cruelty borne of the non-productive citizens who had no claim of right to partake 'in nature's mighty feast' (Dzelzainis 1). Malthus contends that the poor should not have children unless they can afford to support them, and thus we find ourselves once again mired within a vocabulary of prevention and deterrence when it comes to providing sustenance for the poor.

If the offspring of the poor do happen to exist, as Oliver plainly does, then such an offense should be rewarded with a lifetime contract of brutally enforced labour. Indeed, this is how the parish board of directors dealt with Oliver's 'impious and profane' offense to ask for more than his lot ever rightfully deserved. As a means of punishment they conclude 'that they will immediately advertise a bonus of five pounds, payable to anyone who will take him on as apprentice and thereby remove him from their care' (Dickens, *Oliver Twist* 31; ch. 3.). The gentlemen in question, who takes Oliver on as a chimney sweep, is notorious for his cruelty: 'As Mr. Gamfield did happen to labor under the slight imputation of having bruised three or four boys to death already, it occurred to him that the board had, perhaps, in some unaccountable freak, taken it into their heads that this extraneous circumstance ought to influence their proceedings. It was very unlike their general mode of doing business, if they had' (Dickens, *Oliver Twist* 35–6; ch. 3). As it was, the board members had no qualms about leaving Oliver to the chimney sweep's tender mercies; they merely endeavour to drive a harder bargain with him. Once Gamfield agrees to accept a reduced compensation for Oliver, they are happy to hand over the hapless orphan. 'Take him, you silly fellow!' concludes the gentleman in the white waistcoat ... He's just the boy for you ... [A]nd his board needn't come very expensive, for he hasn't been overfed since he was born. Ha! ha! ha!' (Dickens, *Oliver Twist*, 37; ch. 3).

This comment makes reference to these over-fed gentlemen's

blueprint for the ungainly provision of workhouse sustenance: 'They contracted with the water-works to lay on an unlimited supply of water; and with the corn-factor to supply periodically small quantities of oatmeal; and issued three meals of thin gruel a day, with an onion twice a week, and half a roll on Sundays' (Dickens, *Oliver Twist* 15; ch. 2.). Oliver himself is a product of factory farming of a sort. After being 'brought up by hand' by Mrs. Mann – fed a mixture of water and bread – in the workhouse of his birth for some months, the 'hungry and destitute' child is farmed out to a branch-workhouse nearby 'where twenty or thirty other juvenile offenders against the poor-laws, rolled about the floor all day, without the inconvenience of too much food or too much clothing' (17).

One of the novel's most powerfully affecting images is of Oliver immediately following his removal from the workhouse, greedily falling upon the scraps of a meal left untouched by a dog. Dickens remarks as his narrator: 'I wish some well-fed philosopher, whose meat and drink turn to gall within him, whose blood is ice, whose heart is iron; could have seen Oliver Twist clutching at the dainty viands that the dog had neglected. I wish he could have witnessed the horrible avidity with which Oliver tore the bits asunder with all the ferocity of famine. There is only one thing I should like better; and that would be to see the Philosopher making the same sort of meal himself, with the same relish' (Dickens, *Oliver Twist* 52; ch. 4).

Dickens closes the workhouse section of the novel with Oliver's furious assault on another boy who has provoked his rage by taunting him excessively about his dead mother, and his subsequent decision to run away from the man to whom he is apprenticed. Soon after, Mr. Bumble, the larger-than-life beadle who supervises parochial discipline and functions within the world of the workhouse, is called to the scene of Oliver's crime. He offers a 'practical philosophical' explanation for the young boy's violent outburst:

'It's not Madness, ma'am,' replied Bumble, after a few moments of deep meditation. 'It's Meat.' … 'Meat, ma'am, meat' replied Bumble, with stern emphasis. 'You've overfed him, ma'am. You've raised an artificial soul and spirit in him, ma'am, unbecoming a person of his condition … What have paupers to do with soul or spirit? It's quite enough that we let 'em have live bodies. If you had kept the boy on gruel, ma'am, this never would have happened' (Dickens, *Oliver Twist* 78; ch. 7).

Given this logic, Oliver literally has to steal away to fortify his humanity beyond the New Poor Law system, which would condemn him to more and more desperate levels of poverty and starvation. Having already lured him into a life of crime to mitigate his individual want, given time and fortune, they might draw him further still into the orbit of state sanction through bogus trial and subsequent incarceration. Ultimately it is Oliver's moral refusal to swipe a handkerchief from the elderly gentleman, Mr. Brownlow, that allows the path of destiny to fork in Oliver's favour. Despite Oliver's innocence, he is apprehended by the law and narrowly escapes conviction for the theft. Subsequent to that decision, Mr. Brownlow (the man whose handkerchief was stolen by the other two boys in Fagin's gang who escape apprehension) takes a charitable interest in him enough to bring the feverish Oliver back to his home to be nursed back to health. Even this act bears the mark of a certain class interest insofar as Mr. Brownlow sees a middle-class, relatable potential in the boy through Oliver's resemblance to a portrait of a young woman that hangs in his house. Oliver quickly strides into a middle-class mean when carefully tutored by Mr. Brownlow to be perceived as his (surrogate) grandson. His previous surrogate parents Bill Sikes and Nancy, however also have an invested interest in cultivating the boy's potential for their own gain, and thus capture Oliver and return him home to yet another would-be-familial figure in Fagin.

The working-class characters Mr. Bumble and Fagin have a great deal in common insofar as they recognise and operate upon the new liberal premise in which selfishness dominates society and each individual is out for his own interests. There is a hypocritical pretence in legitimate society within the institutions of government, law and religion that conceals within itself an illegitimate anti-society, represented by Fagin. This anti-society is, by comparison, honest in that looking after Number One is the openly avowed principle on which it rests. By contrast, those above it in legitimate society pretend they desire prosperity for all, while they progressively cut back the wealth of social institutions. Dickens's solution to all this is for private citizens like Mr. Brownlow to step forward and sacrifice for the greater good and in aid of the deserving poor. This however can quickly be converted back into the Poor Law principle where the poor are put to the test of their valour. Those found wanting once again might be discarded into the hands of criminal or state abuse. Dickens was correct in one respect; whatever the causes individuals make to end poverty, it is only when the spirit and administration of public law begins to reflect such compassion that a proper reform of society might become a reality.

Acting always from the periphery of society, Dickens's 'characters are devices' installed within his novels, 'not for the sake of plot', but rather for the sake of demonstrating 'a very particular type of construction, or should we say apparatus' within Victorian liberal society (Grossman 52). These characters are drawn through a series of affects, which establish in their own way a rhythm and time line, which allows a very particular type of social construction to come into relief. The outlines of such an apparatus become apparent, for instance, when we examine the subtle contours that make up Dickens's Jews: Fagin, Riah and Scrooge. We as readers are made to appreciate that when Fagin acts as a Jewish character, his hyper-visible

Jewishness forms the centre of an entire structure of anti-Semitism that had been concurrent with the rise of finance capitalism. By contrast when the Jew Riah acts as the moral manager of a money-lending establishment, his kinder portrayal announces a more progressive attitude towards the Jewish race in the latter half of the century within Victorian liberal thought. His more sympathetic features as a character can be in part accounted for by the slow but incrementally increasing presence of individual Jews within political, economic and cultural spheres in Britain as the century progressed. The character of Scrooge represents a largely assimilated and religiously converted Jew of high economic standing whose Jewishness has become all but invisible, but nonetheless persists in haunting the narrator's discourse about the evils of miserliness, complicating Scrooge's 'full' conversion into the Christian charitable mores of English society – at least until the very end of the tale when he decides to celebrate Christmas in munificent style. In this text in particular, 'Jewishness does not enter Dickens's text in mimetic form', but rather as a comportment that generates meaning (Grossman 52).

It is widely held by literary critics that the character of Riah in *Our Mutual Friend* was written as an apology to his Jewish acquaintance Eliza Davis, who wrote to Dickens in 1863 to complain about his character Fagin, whom she believed had 'encouraged a vile prejudice against the despised Hebrew'. In response to that charge, Dickens explained to her that his reference to the unseemly character of Fagin 'as "The Jew" [was] not because of his religion, but his race' (qtd. in Grossman 53, footnote 5). It is this comment that readily represents the inhospitable daily economy of anti-Semitism, more than an image or representation of a Jew in his novels ever could. It is not the anti-Semite who makes the Jew; rather than making him per se, he instigates him through narration. In Dickens's mind, the Jew becomes a Jew not through practice, but by ontology. In reality exactly the opposite is true: the Jew is both literally and figuratively enacted by Dickens for his own pleasure and that of his Victorian peers. Fagin could not be further apart in Dickens perceptions from his prosperous converted Victorian Jewish societal counterparts such as Eliza Davis, whom he had become acquainted with through her husband, when he had purchased Dickens's home in 1860. This category of Jew was highly differentiated from that of both unconverted Victorian Jews and poor Jewish migrants from the East within the classificatory schema of race in Victorian Britain. Whereas Fagin falls into the last socially dispossessed category, the first category, the converted Victorian Jew, as represented by Scrooge and indeed Davis herself, must face another form of dispossession altogether, insofar as they were required to isolate themselves from their former ethnic community and to accumulate considerable wealth before their racial difference could be rendered invisible within polite society. According to this same logic the second category, as represented by Riah, 'choose' to remain Jews, and thus forfeit a similar privilege of invisibility being extended to them. Instead, they 'retain their social and racial visibility within a classificatory schema, which practically prohibits most of them from sharing in England's economic and cultural prosperity' (Hadley 27).

Despite the sacrifice of their faith and community, Victorian liberalism was only prepared to tolerate a certain degree of Jewish exceptionalism based on the converted Jew's acquisition of private wealth. It actively sought to differentiate that wealth by classifying it as illicit, thereby denying these Jews full proprietorship over it. Indeed even this rarefied category of Jew could not fully distance himself from the association of his wealth with that of his poor brethren like Fagin, insofar as its acquisition was understood to be the product of illegal possession, and in effect stolen property. Such a distinction 'attests to this irrational but profoundly functional disassociation of Jews from property as well as propriety' (Hadley 27). In the way that Dickens performs him, 'The Jew' perfectly fulfils the implication of that functional disassociation. The Jew's inability to fully lay claim to either legitimate asset or moral integrity was wholly consistent with his religious impiety in the Victorian liberal imagination. It is for this reason that Dickens loved to theatrically portray Fagin in his wickedness. Despite making concessions to Davis in print, by altering roughly 180 negative references to 'the Jew' in *Oliver Twist* when it was eventually released in book form, Dickens remained passionately committed to the public derision of his Fagin character to the end of his life. 'Though his doctor warned him against it, Dickens added the character to his public readings in the late 1860s, and performed Fagin nightly, contorting his body and his voice, into what a reviewer called "the Jew Fence, crafty and cunning in his bitter vengeance." The performances raised his pulse dangerously high and probably killed him' (G. M. Levine 34).

One must question why Dickens wished to play such a high stakes game of portrayal when it came to 'the Jew' and the so-called nature of his 'wickedness'. Gary Martin Levine argues that his 'wickedness' was not the product of faith or character, but emerges instead as an effect of capital itself, 'because capitalism was a game of representation and misrepresentation, and in that game the shadowy Jew prospered, the Jew was wicked' (34–5). Yet as a misrepresenter himself within the capitalist game of representation at the level of class, Dickens never tired of playing the wicked Jew as an *artfully* racialised body.

In order to fully appreciate Dickens as a master 'misrepresenter' within the capitalist game of shadows, we must take into account the significance not just of race in the portrayal of Fagin, but also of class in his portrayal of Bill Sikes. Only amongst these characters are we as Dickens's audience able to witness for ourselves how capitalism's wickedness contours itself within the bodies it deems aberrant and worthy of such *dispossession*. In 1863, the same year of his correspondence with Eliza Davis regarding Fagin, Dickens prepared and rehearsed the brutal murder of Nancy by Bill Sikes from *Oliver Twist* for a public reading. 'In the novel Bill first pistol-whips her and then finishes her off with a heavy club. Dickens enacted Bill's roars and Nancy's screams with such fearsome reality he (or his advisers) decided the reading was too awful, although he eventually changed his mind, performing this acting out of violence in 1868 with bloodthirsty relish' (Johnston 95). In the case of both Fagin and Sikes, their societal dispossession must be taken up by a peculiar manner of temporary possession within Dickens's own bodily form. Within the Dickensian literary project moreover, it would seem that in order to achieve as it were a totalising encounter with their dire comportments, Dickens must vacate himself to the task, housing them within a narrative scheme that allows the full glory of their atypicality to come forward in his place.

George Levine asserts in his book *Darwin and the Novelists* that 'the project of the Victorian novel increasingly appeared to me as a cultural twin to the project of Victorian science; even the great aesthetic ideals of fiction writer-truth, detachment, self-abnegation, echoed with the ideals of contemporary science' (vii). Levine asserts that the organisation of *The Origin of Species* seems to owe a great deal to the example of one of Darwin's most frequently read authors, Charles Dickens. 'While Darwin rewrote for the nineteenth-century culture the myth of human origins, secularizing it yet giving it comic grandeur and a tragic potential, Dickens was the great mythmaker of the new urban middle class, finding [in] the minutiae of the lives of the shabby genteel, the civil servants, the "ignobly decent," ... great comic patterns of love and community and great tragic possibilities of dehumanization and impersonal loss' (120). Given the pervasiveness of their fame, Dickens and Darwin had to know each other's myths, the origins of which lay in an obsession with registering, documenting and describing atypicality. Both

Dickens's novels and Darwin's world bear the marks of Victorian design within their motifs of 'distortion, excess and clutter' (150). Within the design are variants, which bring what is aberrant into the fore of progressive development.

The problem with such a trajectory is that the results are irreversible, and in this sense allow for the crossing and recrossing of modern urban life to act as a breeding ground for change both positive and negative, and for the extremes of both lines to stray outside the bounds of convention. 'Mixing and denial of absolute boundaries become the condition of life in Dickens's novels and Darwin's biology' (G. Levine 150). For both Dickens and Darwin, knowledge of humanity was 'not attainable unless one learns to see the multiplicity of the variants that lie beyond the merely typical' (150). At the same time, both men struggle to resist installing a redemptive line for humanity in exploring such patterning, the ideal they prescribe, in superimposing a morality to such co-joinings, is what allows violence and death to subtend the structure of their mythological worlds. It was that tendency that allowed for very telling re-enactments of their theories.

We know that the desire to accomplish such re-enactments eventually cost Dickens his life. That such action was in a sense motivated by Darwinian ideals, with their emphasis on the survival of the fittest and the articulation of the view that progress requires the actual elimination of the unfit renders this determination on the part of Dickens – to prematurely expire for the sake of his literary creations – all the more troubling as a prospect. 'By making death a creative force in nature – a vision taken up far more readily outside science than within it – Darwin may indeed have unwittingly helped to unleash the whirlwind of hatred that is so often associated with his name' and indeed consonant to Dickens's portrayal of these aberrant characters (Bowler 564–5). More ominous still is the way in which the economic world is twinned with the natural one, in a way that places emphasis on 'inheritance at the individual level' and on 'artificial selection' at the societal level that all but guarantees the persistence of a principle of class elimination held over from Malthus (565). Darwin picked up his enthusiasm for Malthus's principle of population at an early stage in his career and worked with it throughout the next several decades. 'If we follow Adrian Desmond and James Moore, the selection theory was a product of the pessimistic atmosphere of the 1830s, not the more comfortable 1850s', therefore Darwin's thinking was not merely articulating the laissez-faire ideology of his time in a way that anyone else could have done, but rather retrofitting it to conform with the prior logic of Malthusianism in a particular way that was a regressive, not progressive, measure (563).

As a consequence of his epoch-making *Essay on Population* (1797), Thomas Malthus was accused by a number of critics, including Dickens, 'of setting population increase against economic well being', and 'of viewing a populous nation as one on the brink of disaster' (Gallagher 50). Catherine Gallagher points out that 'by ignoring the complexities of Malthus's argument as well as its polemical situation inside the debate over the perfectability of man, his humane critics', including Dickens, 'saw in his essay only a devaluation of human life and accused him of trying to found the wealth of nations on the death of babies' (50). Moreover, 'the alleged zest with which he described the positive checks to population (death by starvation, infanticide) scandalized many reviewers, who characterized Malthus' as a an ungodly individual who prefigured 'death, physical misery and vice' into the basis of economics, thus instituting a negative bio-economics in the equation of life, wherein human well-being was cast as a balance against resources and consumption that could only be levelled through 'the devastation or prevention of life' (50).

Whilst social critics could readily identify the belief that the entitlement to consume should be linked to the ability to produce within Malthus's critical work, they failed to appreciate that this same principle was at the heart of Darwin's evolutionary model. Despite the fact that his work was deeply indebted to a Malthusian economics, Darwin did not face detractors in the same way as Malthus did in his lifetime. However the principle through which their work is joined remains resonant in contemporary biology as well as economics, which together continue to conceive life and its worth in fragile balance with resources and consumption. Darwin openly 'acknowledged his debt to Malthus, confirming in his autobiography that reading the *Essay* in October 1838 had been pivotal in the development in the evolutionary theory set out in *Origin of the Species* (1859)' (Dzelzainis 3). It is quite possible that Darwin had read Dickens's critique of Malthus in *Oliver Twist*, published in 1837, the same year coincidentally that Queen Victoria came to the throne. She too seemed, at the time, to align her thinking not with Dickens's literary conclusions, but again with Malthus's economic ones. Marx noted with some mirth that 'it is remarkable how Darwin rediscovers amongst the beasts and plants, the society of England with its division of labour, competition, opening up of new markets, "inventions" and Malthusian "struggle for existence." It is Hobbes' *bellum omnium contra omnes* [war of all against all]' (Marx, *Das Kapital* 381). For Marx it is also remarkable how Queen Victoria, owing to Malthus, founds her society of England similarly along the lines of economic individualism, a characteristic which would then emerge as the hallmark of Victorian capitalism and indeed would come again to reassert itself in the late twentieth century as Thatcherism.

Rather than simply demonstrating how individuals might become ensnared by the vagaries of nineteenth-century capitalism, Dickens demonstrates how individuals themselves exist as a mode of production. In order for that modality to reveal itself to readers, he must construct his characters as unwieldy assemblages composed hastily from 'quirky phrases, strange body tics, irrational desires and affections and highly partial histories' (Colebrook 83). Their awkward appearances make evident that character itself is not a single unified field and a body that houses certain distinguishing features, but rather that all of us are no more or less than 'collections of randomly gathered affects' (83). Claire Colebrook provides the example of Miss Havisham in *Great Expectations* as one of Dickens's more memorable composite characters comprised disjointedly of a 'hatred of men, a rotting wedding cake, a decaying body, a memory of loss, a darkened room and a desire for revenge' (83). Through her comportment it is possible to apprehend that our selves are the products of events and histories far greater than the confines of an individual body and that, moreover, our personal habits and preoccupations have their basis in the events of life shaped by encounters with the outside world. What distinguishes our trajectory from the others that surround us is the singular fashion in which we respond to those happenings. Therefore, no one can be like us; our expression in comparison to theirs represents nothing short of the appearance of another possible world. Miss Havisham's appearance therefore cannot be apprehended as merely the representation of a human life that we all assume and acknowledge. Rather Dickens's literary creation of her in all her marvellous affect is in aid of opening another world to his readers. This ability for worlds to open up through the intersection of characters within the space of an event means that no singular event 'leads to a simple fatalism in which individuals are simply caught according to a predestined path' in Dickens's writings (Hammond 1). Rather with each new event that emerges within the trajectory of a character's life, another set of possible responses reveals itself. 'For example, Dickens makes clear that if Pip had reacted to his good fortune differently, if he had been less proud, then the final resolution of the novel would have been very different. Being caught within events beyond one's control does not therefore, for Dickens, remove the necessity for acting ethically (this is the mistake Pip makes), rather it necessitates such action' (1).

Theodor Adorno picks up on this ethical device in Dickens's novels that cleaves to its narrative edge. Adorno refers to its presence as 'embedded in the work, perhaps without the author clearly knowing what he was doing' (171). It nonetheless allows his writing to 'contain a fragment of the dispersed baroque' within itself, acting as a placeholder, 'a strange ghostly presence in the nineteenth century', for an era that otherwise has no cause to be maintained (171). Amidst the poverty, despair and death that are all too recognisable as the fruits of a bourgeois world in Dickens's fictional work, there are outlines of a completely different sort of view of the world, where 'the traces of human warmth and kindness in individual human relationships [that] reconcile one' point beyond themselves – to an alternate reality (171).

This world is prelapsarian by capitalistic standards, insofar as a middle class has yet to emerge, nor has the autonomous individual in his splendid isolation. Rather, he remains 'a bearer of objective factors, of a dark, obscure fate and a starlike constel-lation that overtake the individual and permeate his life but never follow from the law of the individual' (Adorno 171). The law it follows instead is one of objective meaning, wherein the human being is made to demonstrate the world, rather than represent it. There is no room for psychology within such a landscape, where a life space is struggling to remain open amidst the corrupting influence of exchange value. In the battle between subjectivity and illustration, Dickens's characters remain inten-tionally flat. They are uncapturable because they *spread.* The surface puts such characters back in touch with their 'impersonal and preindividual singularities' and 'literally releases them like spores and bursts as it gets unburdened' from the ego self which 'had imprisoned' the named subject (Deleuze 244). In this pronominal state, neither active nor passive, their role is not to reify subjectivity, but to cleave to events in their purest form. In this way it reverses subjectivity upon itself, creating in its wake a spectre of phantasm that presents itself as just so much alliteration in Dickens's act of naming them throughout his work.

His critics routinely indict Dickens as an author 'for lacking credit or credibility, for breaking this or that fictional mimetic law, for tangling up his plots and making promises he could not keep' (Bowen 35). The biggest transactional case against him however is reserved for his very name. 'Dickens's characters, like his plots, are self-divided and proliferating, his rhetoric excessive, his forms unstable ... they can be taken home or sent to wander the streets' (36). Whatever scenario is played out there is something remarkable in the impossibility in Dickens through his own narratives to be either 'quit of debt or to lay all the ghosts safely to rest' (36). Instead something very powerful happens elsewhere to manipulate the currency of Dickens's own name, which gets floated about for rhetorical advantage, in 'syllables and phonemes ... free to be hunted and crushed into new combinations, uses, and shapes in a continual linguistic perversity which begins with the mad errancy of the name Charles John Huffham (or Huffam) Dickens' and continues on into 'the overnaming of his own queer name [that] does not end with Dickens's characters and signatures, even with everything we could call "Dickensian"' (38–9). At the pinnacle of his literary career, Dickens was beyond proper names altogether and became himself a noun: The Inimitable. The term utterly transformed Dickens, translating his comportment in the world into 'the sense of [an] event' and 'releasing an incorporeal double of himself that is purely superficial' (Deleuze 13). This in turn lends itself to an unreality, which is then communicated through language to a general understanding and to his reading public. This allows his readership to move in two directions at once, insofar as its understanding of him moves in a similar fashion. Charles Dickens and the Inimitable together occupy the position of both subject and noun, creating as it were 'a personal uncertainty' that 'destroys common sense as the assignation of fixed identities' (Deleuze 5).

Dickens emerges from this destructive event as a character of *speech*, doubled over in his diligence to the task at hand, persistent in the way in which he assails his readers through the device of language, laying into them in such a way as to mould and twist them to the point where they are tempted to fragment just beside the characters he is illustrating before them. Dickens's novels, what Henry James refers to as 'their ply', 'surpass and defy imitation itself, going further to reveal the protean, exorbitant, impure, vulgar affirmation that is the spark of being itself' (Bowen 43). Dickens implores his readers to heartily embrace their misfortunes, his novels convincingly demonstrating how they might learn to embody their perfection and brilliance. There is a claim of redundancy in Dickens's plots and yet 'nothing more can be said, and no more has ever been said: to be worthy of what happens to us and thus to will and release the event, to become the offspring of one's own events and therefore to be reborn, to have one more birth, and to break with one's carnal birth – to become the offspring of one's events and not of one's actions' (Deleuze 150). Such plots figure everywhere in Dickens's writing where someone is reborn into society, and in some cases must face destruction as the cost of such a venture. This is no matter. At the end of the day what is tested and tested to the limit is the power to imagine oneself differently and to amass affect in such a way as to unseat reality, or indeed probability, for a time and allow conjuration alone to take precedent.

Dickens conjures 'an idiom and mannerism' from the past in order to inform it again through what he terms 'fancy,' the flight of which he defended in many of his works (Bowen 22). The right to fancy for Dickens was a political right, and his natural constituency for this party were what he calls 'pleasurers', i.e. 'those people who take pleasure but also add to it, just as Dick

Swiveller will add to life when he promises to become a "liverer"' in *The Old Curiosity Shop* (Bowen 27). The liverer cannot be separated out from the livery in Dickens, who 'took great interest in the farcical nature of political and historical processes, the politics of old wardrobes, and the multiple hauntings of the present by the past. We are not free from such hauntings, farces, and old clothes today, and have seen in recent years how effective some varieties of political tyranny and folly have re-animated themselves and found new spirits to haunt, new figures to dress' (28). Adorno discerns that the individual in Dickens is coerced constantly by the surrounding bourgeois social reality, and given over to revolt when the mythical powers of capital demand too great a sacrifice, and sometimes even the greatest sacrifice of all – death. Amidst all the horrible desire that bourgeois capital extracts from us, remains our humanity. It alone promises freedom in a way the tether of greed for acquisition in capitalism never can grant an individual. Capital is time bound, whereas the space of the human figure knows no history, 'until it [is] shattered … by the industrial fumes of the city' (Adorno 175).

Through that shattering of the self, capital brings a unique type of malady to human beings, wherein their very existence is doomed to dwell in a kind of a 'negative eternity', wherein what was emblematic about the sympathetic nature of humanity has been subsumed into what Dickens refers to as 'a constantly unchanging air of coldness and gentility … Life has become craven, a replica of itself where it is hard to distinguish "the city" from other Hell spaces of the bourgeois world' (176). All of these domains have in common a world wedded to objects that provide at once the gravity for human beings, but also the burden of their undoing insofar as there is a contest between the object world and the individual, where the odds are stacked against the individual who remains in life beholden to belongings and in death beholden by dispossession – even of his bodily form. Here too there is cost extracted.

There is however a singular hope extracted by Dickens and this has to do with a revaluation of the poor useless things of this world. Their persistence points the way towards the recovery of this lost rejected world of the pre-bourgeois where what is discarded, what is sacrificed, might still make the transition into worth. Not in the form of reification, but rather of dissolution. The human being in this case tries to dissemble the bourgeois object world around him that threatens to engulf his identity and repurpose it to complement his own subjectivity. The extension of his power through a fantasy merger with such items allows him to become conversant with the things denied appearance within his own life. In this way he is able to emigrate, to escape temporarily the bounds of bourgeois society.

Gilles Deleuze apprehends that there are so many coupled characters in Dickens because his narrative 'is a question of movement', which can only be answered through a process defined on the basis of a dyad' (154). Dickens's 'paired characters have on one hand everything they need to be happy together... then something happens that shatters them like an old plate or glass' (154). A great deal happens to them in between, 'confronted as they are by war, financial crash, a certain growing older, depression, illness, the flight of talent' (154–5). In order to cope, Dickens's characters must double themselves; view their own identification at a distance, in order to give themselves the chance of going further than anyone thought possible. In Dickens's writing things always could have been otherwise and might still be if lived in other times.

Dickens is careful to give us access to these other pathways; even if inevitably the worst sorts of things get actualised in his narratives, these can be reversed provided the techniques of social alienation are themselves sent packing, and a revolutionary means of exploration is brought to the fore instead. This is the piousness we experience in Dickens not as religiosity, but as pure faith. Faith in the idea that events will be able to be relived and recovered for their own sake at the surface of society, and no longer be confined to the depths of secret and shared miseries. This is why destruction, and most importantly, self-destruction are so crucial to Dickens as the shattering of individuals allows for something truly miraculous to happen, for them to intertwine with other lives, other pathways out from the limit of movement they formerly acceded to; thus transfigured they take on a course of risk and endurance few know the outcome of. Dickens was in the business of creating new bodies, that would last the test of time and be made up of substances and co-joinings we had yet to imagine, we his faithful readers for other times, who remain scarcely aware of his writing as a kind of liberation theology for industrial times.

Dickens's ideal profession is not writer, but actor. In his books he casts himself not as a silent author, but as an offstage narrator. Dickens as a writer holds himself in the place of the actor, insofar as he 'maintains himself in the instant in order to act out something perpetually anticipated or perpetually delayed, hoped for and recalled' (Deleuze 150). Importantly, the role played by Dickens 'is never that of a character; it is a theme (the complex theme or sense), constituted by the components of the event, that is, by communicating singularities effectively liberated from the limits of individuals and persons' (150). What Dickens and his surrogate characters perform is something that opens up the space of the impersonal and preindividual to readers in such a way as to connect them temporarily with the notion of events not as that which befalls us, but rather what we conjure for ourselves in terms of our own self-expression, our own will. To be able to release events without recourse to a judgment of them will allow us to recast ourselves in part – to exist comfortably in liminality, in the mobility of the instant in which understanding can once again be reformed.

What thwarts the advent of such an understanding is 'the

inequality feeding down from the top of the income distribution' that 'is probably linked to a whole range of negative consequences for society, from higher rates of mental illness and incarceration and family breakdown to alcoholism, drug abuse and suicide', which come to hound whole classes of individuals (Lanchester). Just at the moment Dickens's characters endeavour to spread themselves outward, they are confronted with a counter-swell, a ripple-out effect of poverty. Subject to a rapidly industrialising Britain, the Victorian working classes find the quality of their labouring situations to be temporary, transient and devoid of meaning or progression. This precarious relationship to work engenders within them a hedonism, a need for escapism and intoxication that intensifies individuating and sexualising forces within them, making them that much more apt to equate courting risk with maintaining a feeling of vitality.

Dickens is fascinated precisely by those who *have not*, and his fascination is not in their appearance but in their disappearance, often unsettlingly so. What is he signalling to us about the state of a mankind in which so many are trodden under the wheels of the new labour? And what great house could shelter such a population to mitigate such savagery? Perhaps with Dickens it is too early to let on. A man who died from overwork for fear he would become an inadequate provider for his brood, Dickens regularly expressed his concern about the circulation numbers of his work. 'He calculates the economic return he can expect as a result, this at the same time he seems to be literally grinding out articles, speeches, and readings, as well as fiction' (Houston, *From Dickens to Dracula* 87). Dickens places himself on the artistic treadmill, describing himself in literal circulation during the act of writing, walking about in a strenuous manner in order to invest his novels with literary momentum.

The popularity of Dickens's work had much to do with the similar, characteristic impatience founded in his serial reader, who tended to care as much for the welfare of Dickens's characters as they did their own, if not more so. And hence the attendant worry that came from such preoccupation. His most loyal readers belong to the class of the excluded, who read each instalment with a smouldering impatience, vying to catch a glimpse of their own interests being expressed in some small way. As time wears on, these figures are less and less subject to the fortuitous winds of change. By the narrative's end they often find themselves confronting bitter outcomes.

Through serialised literature the public learnt to suffer from things that did not actually occur right alongside those that did. In writing these instalments, Dickens is kept out of his own conspiracy even as he is its central actor. In the act of representation, Dickens reproduces the cacophony of characters who construct our reality, and at the same time installs a subtle level of apprehension through which we may begin to fragment and dissolve that reality. We are all the while engaged in a community that is produced out of our own conspiratorial and interpretative means. This delusion has grave consequence for our political reality insofar as a nominal authority colours deeply every relationship we have, intimate or mundane, in the world we craft meaningfully around ourselves. At the same time we constantly misrecognise those around us. Instead of trying to correct this, Dickens points the way forward to profiting from such encounters: not to see the worth of people, but to value them for aspects of their character we simply forgot to register as important at first glance. This is not a redemptive view of them, but an inhabitable way of being in the company of others, however temporarily, beyond the usual stratagems of power and authority.

In order to understand this we have to go back a century before Dickens as an author makes his appearance, to castigate capitalism's contemporary, dire derivations. Just a century before his novels were written, capitalism was still in its infancy, born and built up through the institution of slavery, which used free and stolen human labour to gain its advantage. In the eighteenth century, it would allow for profit to transform itself in remarkable ways, lifting margins from a standard 10–30 percent into a 1000 percent profit. It was suddenly possible for countries and individuals to amass enormous wealth. The fact that the riches that poured forth were garnered from the miserable abuse of other humans treated worse than animals or inanimate tools, both abroad and domestically, was a fact seldom dwelt upon by those with the most to gain from it. At the time of Dickens's writing, slavery of one kind or another had foreshadowed capitalism's rise for the better part of three centuries.

The emergence of Britain's financial institutions, including trading houses, insurance companies and banks, was not solely the product of Britain's thriving overseas trade and empire, but more accurately were made possible mainly because of the Atlantic slave trade. 'The expansion of overseas trade, especially in the Atlantic, relied on credit, and bills of credit (like modern travellers' cheques), which were at the heart of the slave trade' (Walvin). The giants of contemporary British banking all had their start in collusion with the triangular trade. Financial institutions including Barclays, Lloyds, Rothschild & Sons, Barings and even the Bank of England itself were deeply implicated in cultivating their stores of capital from the labour of enslaved people. While at one level the merchants and traders in London, Bristol and Liverpool acted as the immediate financiers of the slave trade, at another level it could be argued that the Bank of England's wealthy City members, from the governor down, were its greatest indirect financial beneficiaries as men whose fortunes had been made wholly or partly in the slave trade from the fees and interest they earned from merchants who borrowed money for their long voyages. It was their combined wealth that enabled Britain to stabilise its national finances, thus enabling the state to wage its major wars of the eighteenth century. 'These wars were aimed at securing and safeguarding overseas possessions, including the slave colonies, and to finance the military and naval means that protected the Atlantic slave routes and the plantation economies' (Walvin). Such wars continued throughout the centuries as finance capitalism emerged as the key mechanism of modern statecraft.

The institution of slavery was an essential precursor to capitalism insofar as it put into motion a series of profound, interrelated economic changes that would become critical to its rise, including 'the seizure of new lands; the expropriation of millions of people and their redeployment in growing market-oriented sectors of the economy; the mining of gold and silver; the cultivating of tobacco and sugar; the concomitant rise of long-distance commerce; and finally a planned accumulation of wealth and capital beyond anything the world had ever seen. Slowly, fitfully, unevenly, but with undoubted power, a world market and an international capitalist system emerged' (Rediker 43). The slave ship itself was a precursor to a number of key mechanisms of societal enclosure for the property-less working classes that remain present in our contemporary world, including the factory and the prison. At the same time, it allowed Britain in particular to break out of national economic limits and to take its 'place in the larger "arithmetic" of empire' (44–5). Portrayal of the horrors associated with the slave trade ran counter to the promotion of commercial interests, as well as the safeguarding of the national psyche. Therefore those who stood to indirectly profit from it had a vested interest in devising a complex system of representation to shield themselves and their countrymen from its grimmest realities.

To ensure its acceptance, slavery's coarse appearance had to be cultivated to look the part of legitimate commerce through the appropriate accoutrement of 'graphs and tables, balance sheets and statements of corporate philosophy' to allow those who dealt with it to 'remain busily and safely in the realm of the abstract', comforted in the knowledge that what they were doing was considered by state and society to be both a wholly lawful and laudably profitable endeavour (Rediker 12). The pervasive torture and terror associated with their gains remain nonetheless both materially and abstractly consequential to our understanding of the rise of global capitalism. The unthinkable violence, terror and death that shadow its legacy persist throughout the centuries; just as the apparition of slavery remains lodged within the liberal hierarchies of race and class. Dickens's writing flounders to stave off capitalism's worst tendencies, while at the same time anticipating a return of its impulses toward slavery, in the event that its fortunes desert it, and in the dire belief that a contravening of the basic rights of humankind alone might revive it. Indeed his writing anticipates a return of its impulses toward savagery against its competitors at home and abroad as the nineteenth century wore on.

If Victorian-British society is a restraining force against capitalism's worst inclinations, what can be said of the excess, bursting forth beyond its pallid wall? In short what can be said for enterprise if it so mingled in its fortunes with the blood and body of humankind? What of those who are dead without being aware of it, written off as inferior souls, only to rise up of an instant and unleash misery on another at the slightest offence? We want that assailant to be a rogue individual whose solution is equally singular. We seldom wish to question the whole structure that invented him. Nonetheless, in this difficult enquiry we must not cede to the standards of our enemies. We must instead face something altogether more daunting: to push phrase and appearance to their very limit, to distort them so that all men know and recognise a valuable immaturity in their initial judgments of worth. By refusing to embrace so easily their bondage and indeed to make of themselves something noteworthy beyond property and propriety, they become that much more able to parry shock and to move aside from hastening judgment. It is only then that they might be in a position to ask what value there is for humanity away from category, away from emotion, away from the constraint of kind itself. Individuals, real and imagined, tangible objects and fictional constructs, give their lives to the institutions that house them. It is around their narratives that we shape tomorrow.

In order to critically revisit the Victoria and Albert Museum in South Kensington or 48 Doughty Street in Bloomsbury we must familiarise ourselves with a London grammar proximate to their common, mid-Victorian origins. The first word of Charles Dickens's epic novel *Bleak House* (1853) is also its first sentence: 'LONDON'. There he starts as he means to go on, choosing an agrammatical pathway as a means from which to assemble his capital built boldly of letters, displaying his 'LONDON' as a blunt instrument, a shard, a scrap, seized in the midst of its verbless stasis. 'London's streets, Dickens's justly famous opening description tells us, render progress impossible, and dogs and horses are caught in the mud as in the paragraph's grammar. While on first glance, London's foot passengers appear to be in motion, following "tens of thousands of other foot passengers [who] have been slipping and sliding since the day broke," their apparent progress is again impeded by Dickens's refusal to give the sentence a main verb: they are continuously in motion, yet going nowhere in particular' (Heady 312). The Londoner bears a characteristic verblessness about him; we find his progress impeded on the heels of just such an omission. We find him apparently dallying, even as he is slipping and sliding in legion with his anonymous others, through a mired thoroughfare underwritten by yet another agrammatical pathway he must drag upon his tread: CAPITAL. Indeed within this perpetual human motion, Dickens shows, as the movement of money through London's banks, they take on an archaeological portent in the midst of their 'adding new deposits to the crust upon crust of mud, sticking at those points tenaciously to the pavement, and accumulating at compound interest' (Dickens,

Bleak House 17; ch. 1). This layering of detritus upon London's streets will eventually generate philanthropic real estate in the capital as an asset class worthy of inclusion in any providential, if somewhat mishandled, portfolio bearing the ostentatious stamp of progressive economics.

Here we only need a set of actors to play out the conclusions of such an investment, a twinned pairing worthy of representing the audacious display of quintessential modernity that is Victorian London. At one end stands Crystal Palace and at the other Bleak House, and what is left to index amongst these edifices is the stuff of Dickens's loaded narrative equation 'of mud with money', one refracting upon the other, suggesting that the faultless lens through which liberals would wish to see the national coming of age in Victoria's time is one fouled by the genealogy of 'the national inheritance' gathered from 'a murky tangle of circulated and recirculated cash' (Heady 312). The liberal narrative of tidy financial gain thus remains dogged by the spattered footprint of that following, which makes any straightforward construal of capital a futile exercise. The source of the upset, Dickens leads us to believe, is the London slum that is a victim of aristocratic liberal governance that makes itself one with the progress of capitalism resulting in nothing short of the creative destruction of the fortunes of the landed gentry, and in the same allegiance fails to recognise that the distortion of land values holds direct consequence for the lower classes.

London becomes the site of a significant disturbance within the traditional wealth make-up, the quintessence of the poor's involvement with both a prior feudalism and present capitalism wrought by the parliamentary hash made in the hatching of the two together. The flow of capital now causes the corruption of the aristocracy to flow downward to its former serfs and present labourers, propagating its gains through just so many unrecognised somewheres. Though the aristocracy may be willfully unaware of the geography in which the urban pauper lives, or the squalor he carries about him on his person, their lack of under-standing has nonetheless produced acts of class violence perpe-trated routinely against him without apparent reprisal. As Sir Leicester Dedlock recalls with favour, we have had no revolution here. Despite that fact, every order of British society carries within itself the taint of this active forgetting, this disavowal of the least by those who appear to have the most. This is the source of the British nation's long progress towards decline.

It is these circumstances that laid the legislative cornerstone for 'the landmark 1834 New Poor Law [that] was, for all its centralizing features, an attempt to strengthen local government, abolish the largesse of the Old Poor Law, and institute laissez-faire. In the words of its framers, the act was "intended to produce rather negative than positive effects": to deter pauperism rather than to treat it' (Goodlad, 'Beyond the Panopticon' 541). The deterrent of choice was a call to simply move the destitute along, out of sight of their societal betters. If they could not be compelled to disappear from the streets quietly into an orphanage or a workhouse, then as a last resort they must be shut up somewhere, and thereupon be treated no less as a source of revenue. In this way the poor were forcibly obliged to become financially generative to justify their necessity whatsoever in being. Bentham envisioned his new-fangled Panopticon prison as a privately run enterprise, not a public institution: 'I would farm out the profits, the noprofits, or if you please the losses, to him who, being in other respects unexcep-tionable, offered the best terms' (Bentham qtd. in Goodlad 543). If the invention of the profit-making Panopticon teaches us anything, it is that power, however ubiquitous, does not circulate equally.

The question becomes: when is a prison a house and at what level does it serve such recognition for all its societal engineering? Bethnal Green's philanthropic architecture responds with every mean, patronising, sentimental, brutal or humane social assumption about the housing needs of the Victorian urban working class, bearing reference in its design to both the prison and the museum. This was an imperial age that sought to populate its collection of species and artefacts through expansion of its proprietary holdings both outwards and inwards, the value of which was directed from the colonies toward the metropole. The most brutal and barbaric of London's parish districts were classified at this time as 'internal colonies' (Poon 114). Summoned from these environs the poor were disaggregated into two orders: the deserving and the undeserving poor. Those of the former category would be deemed tameable creatures that would greatly benefit through time spent in certain forms of social confinement, so that they might subsequently be trained to conform to civilised ways of living.

The Victorian middle classes, who viewed themselves as pioneers in such undertakings, made it their business to not only sociologically register the lower classes, but also to appeal to the aristocracy to philanthropically fund the construction of shelters for those individuals amongst them found worthy of cultivation. The new housing for the deserving poor would be rent-based to generate funds for their maintenance. It was the newly formed housing trust's responsibility to make sure these new building projects were kept financially solvent during, and long after, their initial construction. With this financial objective in mind, the target consumers for this new philanthropic housing were the steadily-waged lower-middle class and upper-working class, as opposed to those who were old, sick, unemployed or casually employed. That class of individual could not be redeemed and therefore was left to dwell in the pre-existing private slums that continued to skirt these newly built structures.

It is here that we finally arrive at the grounds of Columbia Square, Dickens's very own philanthropic housing project in Bethnal Green, funded by the banking heiress Angela Burdett-Coutts. Initially in 1853 Dickens and Burdett-Coutts tried to set up a model house in Westminster, a kind of show house in which landlords could see how to improve their properties for the greater health and happiness of their tenets and their own peace of mind. The private landlords in attendance failed to be impressed by this benevolent endeavour, and Burdett-Coutts's appeal to install sanitary facilities also failed, 'even though she promised to meet any costs that exceeded a modest estimate' (Lewis 248). Their intractable disregard for the comfort of their poor tenants was something that later motivated the design and construction of Dickens's and Burdett-Coutts's philanthropic housing scheme Columbia Square.

Columbia Square was named after the bishopric of British Columbia, founded by the baroness in 1857. Alongside its adjoining Market there was 'a large foul colony of squalor and misery, consisting of wretched low tenements – or more correctly speaking hovels – and still more wretched inhabitants; the locality bore the name of Nova Scotia Gardens, and its surroundings in fact were formerly one of the most poverty stricken corners of the whole of the East End, and doubtless one of those spots Charles Dickens refers to in his "Uncommercial Traveller" when he draws attention to the fact that while the poor rate at St. George's, Hanover Square, stands at seven pence in the pound, there are districts where it stands at five shillings and sixpence' (Thornbury 506). In Britain the poor rate was a property tax levied in each parish, which was used to provide relief to the poor. It was collected under both the Old Poor Law and the New Poor Law. The same tax exists to this day to provide relief to the poor as Council Tax collected by the council, the modern-day successor to the parish, to issue support services to the local community. Similarly the richest boroughs will collect a larger sum of council tax than their poorer neighbours and thus the 'poor rate' or individual budget to provide social services faces a similar variant to its Poor Law predecessor. St. George's, Hanover Square was located in the wealthy parish of Mayfair, whereas the district where Colombia Square was to be erected was located in the poor parish of Bethnal Green. Their respective poor rate revenues reflect this discrepancy in wealth.

Bethnal Green's poverty during the Victorian era is so wretched that it must in some senses be excised from the whole of London. It must be isolated and identified into a distant colony, hence the dissimulating nomenclature of Nova Scotia Gardens or Columbia Square, which act to distance it developmentally and geographically from the greater London metropole in the imagination of those able to dwell in superior conditions. Indeed such conditions must be imported in from elsewhere and the land approached as terra nova. Before this can take place a sophisticated operation of sanitation must be enacted and 'the whole of the seat of foulness ... cleared away' (Thornbury 506). What needs to happen in Columbia Square is two-fold: the creation of a structural paradigm for civilisation, and the importation of a working-class population to fill in for the paupers presumably transported to other less salubrious parts of the parish, who were the prior source of its 'foulness'.

Columbia Square put in place four large blocks of model lodging-houses to be 'occupied by an orderly and well-behaved section of the working class population of the district' (Thornbury 506). These flats were not pitched at the 'undeserving poor', but those with a regular income from their trade. By contrast, none of the philanthropic housing schemes of the day were designated to shelter London's poorest residents. These philanthropic housing schemes were erected on the basis of profit making, and their facades literally bore the signature of the nation's wealthiest inhabitants. At the centre of Columbia Square stood a large gothic tower whose side bore an inscription of the name Angela Burdett-Coutts, reminiscent of Bentham's Panopticon structure. Burdett-Coutts, as its founding philanthropist and present heir to the Coutts banking fortune, expected her tenets to mimic her spirit of industriousness and condition of prosperity relative to their lower station in life. 'Incomes ranged from sixteen to thirty shillings a week among occupants working as charwomen, shoemakers, clerks, policeman and fireman' (Lewis 256).

In Columbia Square 'rent was collected assiduously and failure to pay one week's rent resulted in eviction ... it was vital that tenants were in a position to pay weekly rents or else their tenancies would be forfeit' (Lewis 2). Tenets were dealt with strictly within these 'model dwellings' that were intended to take on 'a similar role to the prison, as a tool for the moral education of the poor' (Lewis 258). Good behaviour and good prospects on the outside were similar grounds for considering release from Columbia Square as they might be with any prison reform scheme. The dwellings were designed with the intention that occupants would not become permanent residents, but rather that would function as a sort of halfway house on the road to becoming capable of maintaining private sector accommodation.

Comfort or familiarity was therefore not a value on the premises. Sanitation and circulation by contrast were pressing concerns:

> In an effort to prevent miasmas, [Columbia Square] had permanently open windows at both ends of the corridors, positioned doors and windows in the flats so as to produce maximum draughts and used doors that do not fit too close. These permanently opened windows and doors would obliterate any notion of privacy, or security. Similarly to reduce the risk of infestation there was no plaster on the walls nor wallpaper, just stock bricks coated with two-coats of well-sized distemper (Lewis 257).

The lack of plaster or wallpaper would enforce a sense of nominalism and transiency amongst the inhabitants as distempered surfaces can be easily marked and discoloured, and cannot be washed down, and therefore are only suitable for residences conceived of as temporary accommodation. Despite these most unpleasant features of dwelling, the buildings themselves endured in their place for over a century through many generations of discomfited inhabitants.

Blame for this design can be laid at the door of the architect Henry Darbishire. When the original plans were drafted by Charles Dickens in 1852, Burdett-Coutts wholeheartedly supported his recommendations to construct flats that would be able to provide gas, water and drainage and 'a variety of humanising things you can't give them so well in little houses' (Lewis 250). Dickens, having experienced the ill effects of subletting first-hand, counselled Burdett-Coutts 'on the necessity of including a clause in the lease prohibiting this because it led to unsanitary conditions of overcrowding and greater profits on the part of unsavoury landlords that ought have been their due for the size of the properties they had to let' (Lewis 250). When Darbishire became involved in the construction of Columbia Square, years later in 1863, this concern was interpreted in practice in a far different manner than was Dickens's original intention. At that time the subletting prohibition was enforced solely to exclude anyone who could not afford the rent without it; this was a means of deterring London's poorest residents from attempting to live there. This policy was much more in keeping with Henry Darbishire's principles than Dickens's, which were, by contrast, extremely class- and cost-conscious.

At the Peabody Estate, which Darbishire also had a hand in designing, rents had to be paid in advance and a reference was required from an employer. These conditions were put in place to dissuade the casual labourer from seeking refuge there. Respectability was something Darbishire demanded of his tenants both at Columbia Square and at the Peabody Estate; 'no washing was to be hung up to dry in the flats, no dogs were allowed and tenants were encouraged to be in bed by 11pm and no children were allowed to play in the corridor or on the stairs' (Lewis 257–8). There was a strict code of social control to be applied to philanthropic housing tenants. Darbishire approached these tenants as members of another society far apart from his own: 'The working man is a Nomad, so much so as the Arab of the desert, the nature of his employment compels him to wander from place to place like an unquiet spirit' (Darbishire qtd. in Lewis 258). This statement both orientalises the workingman's character and robs it of material situation. Darbishire never questions the nature of the work, nor the employer for setting such conditions upon the worker, but rather assumes his mecuriality is an inborn characteristic. Therefore, the best that can be hoped for by those who undertake to improve his home is to improve his habits and tastes from the time he takes possession of it so as to alter his comportment positively prior to his next unscheduled departure.

Darbishire's lack of concern for those pedestrian to his architectural projects made it possible for him to design bleak, prison-like structures, which deterred trespassers/visitors and at the same managed a fixed return on investment to keep them financially solvent. The Columbia Square buildings were indeed so bleak that Burdett-Coutts insisted that they be ornamented to make them less imposing. This decision cut into her profit margin, reducing it to just two and a half percent. This move was publically criticised by Darbishire, who had originally designed Columbia Square for a return of five percent profit. Her contemporary philanthropists such as Peabody, Waterlow and Rothschild expressed no such concern for the beauty of their new architecture, but rather focussed their attention on utility and profit in their similar ventures. All of them had in common a desire to house the striving, industrious poor, bearing a distinction between them and their idle, thriftless and mendicant brethren. These poor individuals would be offered no opportunities to secure a similar quality of shelter. Indeed, in the minds of this philanthropic class, if they were deserving of anything, it was further social censure.

Meanwhile, tenants who could not meet their rent requirements via steady employment were quickly evicted, while on the other end of the spectrum no one could be thrown out of these philanthropic buildings for earning too much. As a result of this policy these charitable housing trusts over the course of time established an aristocracy of a sort amongst the working classes, especially as the quality and space of these tenement houses improved into the next century. The flats themselves became hereditary, passed down like a peerage amongst the best of the poorer families. In this way such housing stock not only immunised them from the contaminating influence of the surrounding slums, but also civilised them in a way that might be habituated through the generations privileged enough to live in these dwellings. Philanthropic housing strove to intervene on the detail of private life, and to alter it according to liberal ideological design, while at the same time concealing the appearance of poverty's indignities through its foreboding prison-like facades.

An article in *All the Year Round* praised Columbia Square when it was completed in 1862, although there is no evidence that Dickens ever visited it. 'By this time his separation from his wife had ended his close association with Miss Coutts' (Schlicke 481). Such a separation was foreshadowed in the situation of Columbia Square itself, which caused visitors to 'plod through dirty thoroughfares … by the side of sordid alleys to [reach] that substantial oasis of comfort and luxury Columbia-square' (Lewis 248). Columbia Square's tentative entry into class ascendency was similarly impossible to reconcile with its surroundings, as was the cockney Dickens's friendship with the heiress Burdett-Coutts. In both instances, their values were too disparate from one another to endure based on the flawed founding inherent to their original design. And yet today's housing crisis forces us to revisit such a relational geography amongst the classes and the cause of their proximal depreciation over time, in a way that takes into account the delicate choreography of class relations at play in the founding of its construction. The material it reveals will say a great deal about London then and now, and the national inheritance we reckon with when we endeavour to plot the stuff of our long history of urban habitation.

This desire to clean up the appearance of poverty necessitated that the very poorest of society disappear from public scrutiny all together. The slum housing Dickens christens 'Tom-All-Alone's' in *Bleak House* stands in for 'a whole invisible nether world of poverty and despair lying unnoticed in the midst of the midcentury prosperity of which it is a perhaps necessary byproduct' (Herbert, 'The Occult in *Bleak House*' 105). The upper-working class, as represented in the figure of Mr. Snagsby, live in close proximity to slum dwelling without ever having the faintest suspicion of its existence. When he sees it for the first time he finds himself in a state of terror and disbelief:

> Mr. Snagsby passes along the middle of a villainous street, undrained, unventilated, deep in black mud and corrupt water – though the roads are dry elsewhere – and reeking with such smells and sights, that he, who has lived in London all his life, can scarce believe his senses. Branching from this street and its heaps of ruins are other streets and courts so infamous that Mr. Snagsby sickens in body and mind and feels as if he were going every moment deeper Down into the infernal gulf (Dickens, *Bleak House* 321; ch. 22).

The invisibility of such a massive rookery, which includes within it Tom-All-Alone's but is scarcely limited to it, 'is largely a function of what Dickens evokes so powerfully in this and other novels, the all-enveloping secrecy of a modern city' (Herbert, 'The Occult in *Bleak House*' 105). This secrecy is cultivated not by the poor themselves, but by the literate, morally virtuous and well-heeled classes that dwell above them, pleading ignorance of the conditions which subtend the workings of their contemporary lives. The darkness in which this problem is allowed to dwell in no way diminishes it as the property of the age for Dickens, who lays responsibility for the misery of the poor at the door of the court, the clergy, law, parliament and industry.

Tom-All-Alone's is a piece of inner-city real estate that has devolved into a dense slum as the funds for its upkeep become consumed over time by legal costs related to the interminable law suit of Jarndyce and Jarndyce. Tom Jarndyce's middle-class heir is John Jarndyce, who describes Tom-All-Alone's as the 'true' Bleak House, there sitting consonantly 'in that city of London' as 'some property of ours' (Dickens, *Bleak House* 111: ch. 8). That is to say that the existence of Tom-All-Alone's forms some part of 'a large inheritance' brought together by the 'world of fashion and the Court of the Chancery' to produce 'a deadened world ... its growth sometimes unhealthy for want of air' (Dickens, *Bleak House* 24; ch. 2). John Jarndyce recognises the evil of that world even as he tries to wrap his wards in cotton wool and various refinements. Poverty takes an appointed place amongst them based on the principle of costs, and in the name of progress. Costs are the only power on earth that will get anything of value out of the condition of poverty, or will register it as anything beyond an eyesore and a source of heartache. COSTS. Another agrammatical pathway is found leading to 'a street of perishing blind houses, with their eyes stoned out; without a pane of glass, without so much as a window-frame, with the bare blank shutters tumbling from their hinges and falling asunder; the iron rails peeling away in flakes of rust; the chimneys sinking in; the stone steps to every door (and every door might be death's door) turning stagnant green; the very crutches on which the ruins are propped, decaying' (Dickens, *Bleak House* 111; ch. 8). Such costs belong to Jarndyce and Jarndyce, Tom and John, Generation and Generation.

Through such sad partnership, Bleak House becomes a cipher to describe 'every form of gloomy housing … which emblemizes the state of Victorian society'; a limited world made stagnant by the 'compound complexity' of architecture parallel to the crafting of a liberal state narrative (Kelley 253). Although the British are rushing toward larger worlds through the expanding project of imperialism, their progress at home is impeded and their fate sealed within the walls of 'Bleak House', which was not of society but nonetheless in it, for 'its master was and it was stamped with the same seal' (Dickens, *Bleak House* 111; ch. 8). Coutts, Waterloo, Peabody, Rothschild, 'these are the Great Seal's impressions, my dear all over England – the children know them!' (111). This younger generation feels itself encoded by the progress of industrialisation and the social control it instigates upon the working classes. That disciplinary bearing becomes the signature of their dwelling, and the regimented design of these new streets the strict hallmarks of their age. Those privileged developers who stand above them seek to occlude the real meaning behind these new dwellings and the costs extracted in their wake.

In *Bleak House* the bitter consequence of this practice of self-deception is portrayed as lying elsewhere in housing schemes of a far different nature: in the rookery where 'Jo lives – that is to say, Jo has not yet died – in a ruinous place, known to the like of him by the name of Tom-All-Alone's' (Dickens, *Bleak House* 232; ch. 16). Tom-All-Alone's is described by Dickens as 'a black, dilapidated street, avoided by all decent people, where the crazy houses were seized upon, when their decay was far advanced, by some bold vagrants, who, after establishing their own possession, took to letting them out in lodgings' (232). Vagrants not philanthropists run this vile housing venture, promising instability to its inhabitants forced to dwell in these miserable, tumbling tenements, and yet there is connection here to the ruling elite insofar as 'these ruined shelters' which 'have bred a crowd of foul existence' bear in their 'every footprint' the stamp of a government run by the likes of 'Lord Coodle, and Sir Thomas Doodle, and the Duke of Foodle, and all the fine gentleman in his office, down to Zoodle' who in Dickens's estimation have little wherewithal to 'set right' these deplorable conditions, though by dint of their aristocratic class's predominance in law and legislation they were 'born expressly to do it' (232–3). As for Tom-All-Alone's,

> this desirable property is in Chancery, of course. It would be an insult to the discernment of any man with half an eye, to tell him so. Whether 'Tom' is the popular representative of the original plaintiff or defendant in Jarndyce and Jarndyce; or, whether Tom lived here when the suit had laid the street waste, all alone, until other settlers came to join him; or, whether the traditional title is a comprehensive name for a retreat cut off from honest company and put out of the pale of hope; perhaps nobody knows (233).

The existence of Tom-All-Alone's within Chancery, and the whereabouts of Tom, are features of understanding that must be isolated for the benefit of the reputation of the greater good being enacted:

> Much mighty speech-making there has been, both in and out of Parliament, concerning Tom, and much wrathful disputation how Tom shall be got right. Whether he shall be put into the main road by constables, or by beadles, or by bell-ringing, or by force of figures, or by correct principles of taste, or by high church, or by low church, or by no church; whether he shall be set to splitting trusses of polemical straws with the crooked knife of his mind, or whether he shall be put to stone-breaking instead. In the midst of which dust and noise, there is but one thing perfectly clear, to wit, that Tom only may and

can, or shall and will, be reclaimed according to somebody's theory but nobody's practice. And in the hopeful meantime, Tom goes to perdition head foremost in his old determined spirit' (Dickens, *Bleak House* 632; ch. 46).

The debate around Tom's source of punishment belies the capacity for reprisal that his most unnatural fouling by society must naturally bring forth:

> There is not an atom of Tom's slime, not a cubic inch of any pestilential gas in which he lives, not one obscenity or degradation about him, not an ignorance, not a wickedness, not a brutality of his committing, but shall work its retribution, through every order of society, up to the proudest of the proud, and to the highest of the high. Verily, what with tainting, plundering, and spoiling, Tom has his revenge (632–3).

Tom-All-Alone's casts a shadow upon the national glory at the same time that the British elites are casting an Empire in which the sun would never set upon its dominions. Within such ambition there is no place for Tom and therefore it must be that its recognition never adequately dawns 'upon so vile a wonder as Tom' (Dickens, *Bleak House* 632–3; ch. 46). Nonetheless 'Tom has his revenge' (633). Kelley notes that 'Tom's disease spreads that revenge to every level of the social scale and lords and ladies bow to a presence they had refused to recognize' (Kelley 259). Tom's fundamental displacement from the register of domestic life, reveals a great deal about Victorian's society's understanding of homelessness as a type of ravaging dereliction. The concept of homelessness in 'its larger and more subtler senses and variations', must then necessarily include within it a 'whole series of representations of middle-class families whose existences and homes are destroyed' by a variety of personal, ideological, legal, and social failings 'that seize hold of those responsible for keeping and maintaining homes and families together' (Marcus 96). This spectre of homelessness functions as part of a grouping, which contains within itself 'the dramatizations of certain kinds of intact middle-class domesticity and home-endorsing doctrines, sentiments, and behaviors that are both destructive in themselves and serve as pretextual disguises for the exploitation of others' (96). What encompasses them all is 'the greatest of [Dickens's] bleak houses, England, whose windows to human suffering are misted over by the pettifoggery of an archaic parliamentary and legal system bogged down in tradition and technicalities, whose foundations are embedded in the mud of the past, and whose door to change is stubbornly rusted on its hinges' (Kelley 254). The cause of such decay is a selfishness that not only is characteristic of parliament and the Chancery, but exists as a value 'that permeates each decadent level of Dickens's society. The society of Victorian England, then, is the bleak house which Dickens is intent on describing' (Kelley 254). Dickens builds his case through layering upon one another a succession of physically and spiritually desolated houses. Through his vivid descriptions he allows Chesney Wold, the crumbling fortress of the aristocracy, to become proximate to Tom-All-Alone's depilated tenement for the poor. Closely interspersed in between the two major edifices of the narrative are a great number of houses occupied at every level of Victorian-British society carefully bricked together to illustrate its many wrongs:

> Where the windows at Chesney Wold are blind to the world outside, the blindness to hope in Tom-All-Alone's is found within and without the frameless windows. The aristocratic lands are pock-marked with rain, but the disease in Tom-All-Alone's is so real and so widespread that the very houses seem to be ill and can only stand upon crutches. Dickens unites the

parallel between the internal rottenness of the Dedlock estate and the external festering of the London slum by the similar weather which links them both to the fruitless philosophy of Chancery (Kelley 258).

The barren quality of both Chesney Wold and Tom-All-Alone's make them two of the bleakest of Dickens's bleak houses; but there are many others dispersed throughout the novel which continue year upon year to reside in their stagnant predicaments while at the same time refusing to address them. 'The Jellyby's house is a prime example of Chancery-like chaos resulting from a refusal to see actual problems and the desire to create romantic theoretical ones. In the same way that parliament refuses to deal practically with Tom-All-Alone's, letting the slum run to greater and greater ruin, Mrs. Jellyby refuses to see the confusion of her own household, let alone that of the London slum, preferring to spend her time and energy, and the time and energy of her eldest daughter, on a little-understood state of affairs hundreds of miles away in Africa' (Kelley 259). The needs of the Empire were often used as a foil to deflect attention away from the neglected domestic sphere. Its systematic neglect could and often did lead to violent ends as was the case with Tom Jarndyce, who blew out his brains over the frustration of Chancery proceedings. It is he who christened Bleak House and gave it the right to stand for all the bleak houses Dickens was to introduce into the novel as a monument perhaps to his legal confinement there, which appeared to be without end: 'day and night he sat poring over the wicked heaps of papers in the suit, and hoping against hope to disentangle it from its mystification and bring it to a close. In the meantime, the place became dilapidated, the wind whistled through the cracked walls, the rain fell through the broken roof, the weeds choked the passage to the rotting door. When I brought what remained of him home here, the brains seemed to me to have been blown out of the house too; it was so shattered and ruined' (Dickens, *Bleak House* 111; ch. 8).

Bleak House then is a precursor to Tom-All-Alone's where Tom presumably spent his last days in Chancery attending the case and making it the place of his eventual self-destruction amidst its mouldering. The aristocratic Tom Jarndyce is the cause of the deterioration of his private property, which in time transforms itself into 'Tom All Alone's' slum. Such decline was managed through financial neglect concurrent with the rise of capitalism and its new apparatuses for generating 'cost'. John Jarndyce recalls ruefully 'when my great Uncle, poor Tom Jarndyce, began to think of it, it was the beginning of the end!' (Dickens, *Bleak House* 111; ch. 8). Perhaps his middle-class brethren also realised that entanglement with such issues could lead to a no-go and like John sought to avoid having anything to do with confronting the thorny case of wealth distribution at all costs. Such avoidance, the novel argues, does little 'to suppress or conceal the underlying causes of social conflict; on the contrary, its representation of Victorian society demonstrates the ways in which class discourse serves to circumscribe popular agency and thus promote public discord' (Vanden Bossche 27). John Jarndyce's benevolence appears to be the repaying of a personal rather than a more general social obligation. 'Dickens seems to be saying that little progress can be made in the curing of society's ills if the task is left only to those directly involved, and that not until concerned but uninvolved men enter the fray can the general blanket of fog be lifted and the way made clear for the new Bleak House' (Kelley 268). Thus his home, the future and final Bleak House, 'suggests the duty of every individual, aristocratic or otherwise, to share the suffering of the poor or oppressed by helping to alleviate it with the tools he has' (268). Today that duty still remains to be taken up by those with the greatest power in British society. Those who dwell in both council and private housing must rely on outside resources to enable and perpetuate their shelter.

Michael Rosen described conditions for current council tenant occupants today in his editorial for *The Guardian* written on 14 January 2014. He writes that the current situation eerily parallels the heartless policies imposed on residents 150 years earlier at Columbia Square:

> It's more of the same: with poverty there often comes a disruption of place. Migration, war and developers do a lot of disrupting. You leave your home, or your home is destroyed. If you don't move, the person who owns it can move you. There aren't many paintings or statues for you to commemorate this. The up side of this is that you live for now. The down side is that it all seems to confirm that your life is of less value than people with big country houses.

Rosen contends that conditions have diminished within his lifetime as the housing policies of the 1960s have made way for a new generation of thought with regard to sheltering the poor that emerged in the 1980s. The Housing Act of 1988 introduced renters to a new form of tenancy agreement. The assured shorthold tenancies, which are still in use today, last a minimum of six months with a minimum of two months' notice required by either the tenant or the landlord for vacation of the property; termination of the agreement prior to that time period requires a court order. When this new type of tenancy agreement was introduced it took control of council housing out of the hands of local authorities, which prior to the Act were one of the biggest direct providers of housing. 'Right to Buy' and other policies, such as the right for tenants to opt for management of their properties by an 'approved landlord' rather than the council under the Housing Act 1988, were intended to transform them into agents able to intervene in their own housing conditions. Putting such power into the hands of private landlords, however, has considerably diminished the role of local government in the

management of council housing, and afforded greater parliamentary control over the terms of tenancy.

Rosen accuses the current Conservative government of further
compromising this relationship of the tenant to local government
and indeed usurping council power, to seize authority over those
'who live in council housing to cut their standard of living'.
Rosen is referring to the 'Bedroom Tax' and its negative impact on
the stability of living conditions amongst poor residents. Rosen
refers to the situation of his son's passing, wherein he was able to
preserve his room during the period of grief. Rosen argues that
with the introduction of the Bedroom Tax, poor and grieving
families similar to his may soon be denied this choice out of
financial necessity. The penalties they would pay to maintain this
additional room in their homes would amount to a levy on the
grief of the poor. The proposal to quickly reabsorb the bedrooms
of those who've recently died back into benefit assessment for
him amounts to an affront on the quality of life for poor families.
Rosen asserts that 'rich people are using the power they have to
force poor people to do things that they, the rich, never would or
could force on themselves'. He maintains that 'the rationale that
this is "good for the economy" is a lie to conceal something
simpler: by transferring wealth from poor to the rich, it's good for
the rich. If that means being cruel, so be it. They are working to
the rule that death is the great unleveller' ('Bedroom Tax Plans')

Rosen's description of council housing as a class of asset
management distorted to reflect its elite government administration resonates with Dickens's chapter in Bleak House,
'National and Domestic', which likewise refers to the economic
parlance that animates the commonplace figure of the house as
nation and nation as house. This liberal cliché is evoked, for
example, in the January 1852 Punch cartoon 'Mrs. England
Setting Her House in Order', which depicts Queen Victoria as a
housekeeper instructing the prime minister, Lord John Russell, to
pay a 'bill' (Vanden Bossche 7). The concept of government as

national housekeeper was revived as neoliberal rhetoric when Margaret Thatcher said 'in an interview for the magazine *Women's Own* "there is no such thing as society. There are men and women and children and there are families"' (Littler 63). As it had been in the era of Queen Victoria, 'this phenomenally atomised view of society was made to seem familiar and unthreatening by figuring Britain as a household' (Littler 63). In the contemporary version (with Thatcher in charge in Victoria's place), balancing the household budget once again allows the general public to believe that national expenditure operates in much the same way as household's to monitor their private spending. Women in particular were receptive constituencies to this notion because they had traditionally been denied access to power beyond the domestic sphere. Unfortunately their situation of power, particular amongst the lower-middle classes and upper-working classes, hadn't improved significantly from the Victorian era through to the Thatcher era in Britain.

The source of both Victoria's and Thatcher's largely unprecedented political power was drawn in part by the cadre of wealth established before their respective rule. In the case of Thatcher the importance to her success of her husband's wealth is something she barely acknowledged. She preferred instead 'to dwell on her humble roots as grocer's daughter and to imagine that her achievements were attributable to drudgery and discipline' (Littler 67–8). Those who did not exhibit aspiration to achieve similar levels of class ascendency as she was able to, in her view, were simply lazy and undisciplined, their unfortunate condition first and foremost a product of their of moral failure. Thatcher painted herself as 'the working-class girl … welcomed into the protective arms of Victorian respectability' as a working-class body made good by careful measure (Hadley 27). As a working-class girl, Thatcher's 'only true road to moral superiority was found in her capacity to disappear from public view as such' and instead to assume a former identity as being Dennis's 'homey wife' (Hadley 31). On the occasion of her next transformation into a politician she had to assume yet another guise, not as the average man, but as the male entrepreneur. 'Thatcher's recent biography charts her admiration for and emulation of men that influences her own sense of personal development. In this instance, her admiration for robber barons forms a productive substitution, for the entirely different sort of baroness she is to become towards the end of her life' (Hadley 25, footnote 42). Thatcher thus ultimately wished to purchase her place at the table of nobility with the political capital she earned at times through disreputable means, by selling out the needs of her former working-class community.

Today that legacy is handed down to her successor in Conservative Government David Cameron, who plays upon her former rhetoric of 'hard work' as a means of de-articulating the voices of the poor forced to address his cuts to the social safety net through purse-tightening within their households. This at a time when the '96% of benefit claimants who will be penalised' by the Government's new Bedroom Tax 'cannot be rehoused' (Dugan). Despite this reality, Conservative Work and Pensions Secretary Iain Duncan Smith is quick to blame the issue on low-income families themselves who are responsible for making other low-income 'families wait and wait for a house that is big enough, while other households on benefits are allowed to live in homes that are too big for their needs, at no extra cost' ('Britain Cannot Afford the Spare Room Subsidy'). He contends that 'many working families cannot afford the luxury of having spare bedrooms' like their richer societal counterparts presumably can. Similarly, 'Government cannot afford to pay for bedrooms that are not needed' except of course for their rural peers who must maintain local properties in the home constituencies that are rarely inhabited by Government ministers who nonetheless are able to claim them on expenses without penalty. The constituents they represent on the other hand must one way or another shell out cash as penalty for their flagrant disuse of space.

Liam Byrne, the shadow Work and Pensions Secretary, said: 'This hated tax is trapping thousands of families, forcing vulnerable people to food banks and loan sharks, and there is now a serious danger it could end up costing Britain more than it saves as tenants are forced to go homeless or move into the expensive private rented sector' (qtd. in Dugan). For these people their choice remains between slum-dwelling and involuntary entrapment into a benefits system that subjects them to conditions barely above mere survival, with no means with which to further bargain. We are reminded here of Harold Skimpole's argument in *Bleak House* against state welfare, which follows the logic that if the poor were allowed access to generous state benefit, they would demand to be fed by society's golden spoon. Today we return to such punitive attitudes towards the poor as undeserving of our care, based on their lack of contribution to the product of national wealth. Why should these individuals merit shelter and sustenance? Today the richest areas of Britain seek to purge themselves of their poorest residents; feeling like Skimpole, they no longer wish to share the national cost of caring for them. These residents are turned out by cost of living pressures to reside in lower-rent council districts where they figure its someone else's problem, now leaving the most deprived areas of the country to somehow pick up the whole social bill they have left for them. Skimpole's reasoning can therefore be read as a template for the Conservatives' current position on the benefits system:

> At our young friend's natural dinner hour, most likely about noon, our young friend says in effect to society, 'I am hungry; will you have the goodness to produce your spoon and feed me?' Society, which has taken upon itself the general arrangement of the whole system of spoons and professes to have a spoon for our young friend, does NOT produce that

spoon; and our young friend, therefore, says 'You really must excuse me if I seize it.' [...] 'In the meantime,' said Mr. Skimpole cheerfully, 'as Miss Summerson, with her practical good sense, observes, he is getting worse. Therefore I recommend your turning him out before he gets still worse.' (Dickens, *Bleak House* 443; ch. 31).

As for Skimpole himself, as a close friend of John Jarndyce, he is shown throughout the novel to be in the habit of seizing the spoon for himself. Routinely sponging off the wealth of his friends, Skimpole is able to partake in the spoils of elevated society with no contribution whatsoever on his part. Not surprisingly, Skimpole takes up regular residence at Bleak House, alongside the other financially dependent 'wards of Jarndyce', making a case if ever there was one for the longstanding 'wealthfare' system of property administration and the competitive disregard toward those subject to privation. Such attitudes reify the societal malady satirically discerned in the narratives created by Elmgreen & Dragset as well as Dickens. Such work is dedicated to exploring the strong political seam running through Britain's social and economic architecture and the changing perception of our traditions and architectural spaces, as well as our political ideas, as those structures begin to deteriorate in the wake of neoliberalism. Liberal governance, despite its prevalence over the past century, can no longer be taken for granted as the foundation for society, nor its former institutions further recognised as constants in European society. One of its key features, the welfare state, has been eroded 'by forces related to the international globalized economy and communication and financial systems', so much so as to appear increasingly as a remnant of the past (Elmgreen qtd. in Moore). As a direct consequence, 'we're dealing with a disappearing Europe, exemplified by Britain with its shrinking Empire, and also European history, which doesn't seem to have the same impact or legacy anymore'

(Dragset qtd. in Moore). The European family, absorbing the harsh consequences of the global financial crisis, looks itself to be breaking apart with those who depend upon it for their welfare made to survive under ever more precarious terms.

Dickens's writing was often preoccupied with the breakdown of families, which unravel before the reader despite, or indeed because of, the characters' best intentions. Elmgreen & Dragset replicate Dickens's narrative scenography in their 'Tomorrow' exhibition, insofar as our first encounter with the story is through the registered absence of the parents, a deficiency felt strongly by the child. We first encounter the young protagonist, Norman Swann, thinly clad in a school uniform, 'sitting, cradling his knees in the clean fireplace/proscenium stage, echoing a naked boy decorating a fig leaf-shaped ashtray nearby, upon which rests his Father's abandoned cigar' (Elmgreen qtd. in Moore). The abandoned position of the child suggests there is no lineage to appeal to for comfort, as even their ancestral portraits appear to have vacated this scene of hereditary habitation. In their place stand a maid and a butler, working-class figures painfully inadequate to the task of filling the space left open. This awkward situation only serves to further separate Swann from his place at the table once worthy of its ornate, French-Victorian ormolu clock; today it stands aside boxes waiting to be loaded for the removal men, their arrival signalling nothing so much as a frightful new era of dispossession. It becomes clear to us that this contemporary story about Europe is the story of a family made different by its systematic breakdown. This catastrophic event is reflected in the breakdown of the Swann family.

In the universe generated by Elmgreen & Dragset, an elderly version of Norman Swann stands as its failed architect, the last living member of his family, who must play the role of a false 'avatar' against his real-life predecessor, 'the noted Victorian architect, Richard Norman Swan' (Dragset qtd. in Moore). In our non-fictive universe, there was a young man, Charles Dickens, who as author can be said to be the true avatar amongst the noted Victorian writers of his time. Many similarly lauded persons visited his apartment in Bloomsbury. He, in contrast to Swan, was the first living person his family to build up the family name. Coming from this divergent set of angles between them it is possible to chart the tragi-comic mores of English society, the flaws of Modernist utopianism, changing community values, the ambiguities of sexuality and London's frenzied property market, which together have come to inflict so much personal injury over the centuries. In the twenty-first century we find that what shelters us is a very corporate building, and for those experiencing the feeling of dislocation in the capital, this discomfiture will be even stronger than the establishment that has become Dickens's writing. Institutionally, it has the effect of pulling us into anachronistic future, into an abstract virtual space, where the New World of finance capitalism still bears the impression of an Old Europe, which in itself is full of fictional landscapes and settings, mythologies and stories that continue to inform upon what is happening now. This is the hallmark of an age where liberal imperialism is making its whereabouts known to the neoliberal authority of globalisation.

Bank Draft: The Winds of Change in *Little Dorrit*'s Domestic Economy

In Dickens's work people tend to resemble their homes, and the home of all homes is the bank. In his novel *Little Dorrit*, the architecture of such an arrangement is subtly drawn out in his portrayal of the bank as the feature that subtends all residence in nineteenth-century Britain. Dickens sets his novel in 1825 to correspond with the first modern economic crisis, the Panic. The financial crisis was generated by over-investment in shares that became inflated well beyond their material value as assets. This phenomenon intersected with a fiction of a sort insofar as newspaper journalists handsomely paid to promote speculative investment through 'money market' columns, which falsely contrived the information about the viability of the ventures. Investment in this fiction was further driven by 'a system of easy credit, where confidence was further mediated by a vastly increased number of country banks and a widespread dependence on paper bills' (Esterhammer 1). At the time the London capital market was producing a bewildering array of new financial assets for customers to replace the high-yielding government debt now being retired from the Napoleonic wars. 'This left the London private bankers and their corresponding country bankers – as well as their customers in agriculture, trade and manufacturing –foundering in the resulting confusion' laid on by the introduction of this new asset class (Neal 54). Therefore, what distinguished the financial mania of the early 1820s from earlier bubbles is that it was caused not exclusively by speculation, but rather by the rapid diversification of possible investments one could make and the lack of real understanding about their soundness. Those who stood to lose the most from the crisis were individuals who were new to the market and thus were at the mercy of stockbrokers to direct their shares. When a crash resulted from massive over-extension of capital the pain was shared out amongst the country banks and smaller investment firms, as well as their customers, as a consequence of their channelling vast sums of private capital into diverse and uncharted investments.

Dickens's first fictional engagement with the Panic of 1825 was written between 1838 and 1939 when his family were residing at 48 Doughty Street. His novel *Nicholas Nickleby* was written simultaneously with *Oliver Twist*. The mood of the former is considered to be remarkably lighter, but nevertheless begins with a tragedy when Nicholas's father, a country gentleman, is ruined by the Panic. When the bubble finally and inevitably burst, 'four stockbrokers bought villa residences in Florence, 400 nobodies were ruined – and one of those was Mr. Nickleby' (Dickens, *Nicholas Nickleby* 12–13; ch. 1). Mr. Nickleby dies shortly thereafter from grief related to this financial failure, the once favourable prospects of the Nickleby family consumed by the speculative mania that had gripped the whole of the country. Mr. Nickleby's quick demise leaves Mrs. Nickleby, daughter Kate and son Nicholas to attempt to survive with no economic wiles to fall back upon. They soon find themselves swindled once more by another stockbroker, the nefarious Uncle Ralph, who sends Nicholas to be a school master at a horrid Yorkshire academy foreshadowing *Hard Times*, and retains his sister to be summarily prostituted to entice capital from one of his wealthiest investors. By novel's end Uncle Ralph is himself ruined, losing £10,000 as result of his own ill-fated speculative investment. Mr. Nickleby's benevolence and unwitting judgment are revived when Dickens formulates the later character of Arthur Clennam, another gentleman 'nobody', who despite his best intentions is led astray into speculation. There are plenty of real-life fraudsters waiting to take advantage of those occupying a similar position of financial naïveté to these two fictional gentlemen. Dickens commenced writing the novel in June of 1855. Within weeks 'the ancient banking-house of Strahan, Paul & Bates spectacularly folded, after which the owner, Sir John Dean Paul, was sentenced to fourteen years for fraud', providing Dickens with ample fodder for his critique of market capitalism (Douglas-Fairhurst). The following year it was discovered that 'John Sadlier, MP, a Junior Lord of the Treasury' and someone considered in his time to be a financial genius, 'was plundering the Tipperary Bank until it too collapsed, with debts of £400,000' (Douglas-Fairhurst). These events portended more financial turmoil to come. In 1857 Britain would experience a financial crisis more severe and more extensive than any that had preceded it. 'In the last three months of 1857 there were 135 bankruptcies, wiping out investor capital of £42m' (Economist, 'The Slumps that Shaped Modern Finance').

Though the novel *Little Dorrit* was written and serialised between 1855 and 1857, the inferences it makes to the Panic of 1825 would nonetheless have been vivid to Dickens's readers. The Panic would have remained embedded in the public's imagination because it was understood as one of the defining features of the century, in much the same way as we may well view the financial crisis of 2008. In a similar fashion, it left many amateur investors financially ruined in its wake. In the late 1810s, Britain experienced a dramatic escalation in both its domestic productivity and its per capita prosperity. During this period, rapid mechanisation and the availability of cheap labour accelerated and extended the processes of industrialisation. Abroad Britain took advantage of emerging markets, in particular in South America, seizing on the recent decolonisation of the Spanish Empire to increase its outlets for both production and trade. South America paid for goods imported from Britain in gold and by the early 1820s this contributed heavily to Britain's financial growth. Britain's trade with South America soon became circular insofar as British loans to the governments of Colombia, Brazil and Argentina helped to finance an increase in mining for gold.

Direct British investment in these operations brought in more profits as well, in the form of gold. In 1821, the Bank of England began to convert that gold into paper money to be used as currency in trade with other nations outside of South America. Britain's reserves of gold and paper currency, as well as the expanding confidence of British enterprise, allowed London to emerge as Europe's main financial hub, quickly becoming the place where foreign governments sought funds. 'The rise of the new global bond market was incredibly rapid. Debt issued by Russia, Prussia and Denmark paid well and was snapped up' (Economist, 'The Slumps that Shaped Modern Finance'). This new transfer of international fortunes through London meant that the Panic of 1825 did not only cause widespread bankruptcies and unemployment for hundreds of thousands, as the British economy went into a period of recession, it also caused recession in the economies of continental Europe, with bankruptcies of major banks in 'Germany, Italy, Amsterdam, Saint Petersburg, and Vienna. The financial crisis extends itself further to Latin America' as overseas loans from Europe are abruptly cut off triggering a major fiscal crisis in its newly independent nations (Kaminsky and Vega-Garcia 3).

Then-Prime Minister Liverpool spent much of 1824 warning bankers against overtrading. He told them explicitly that his government would not spend Treasury money to rescue them should their cavalier actions result in an overheating of the market. Privately he was aware that a crisis was highly likely, and knew that it was of vital importance that 'the banking system of London not collapse under the weight of speculation and the popping of all those stock company bubbles' (DeLong). Liverpool was both the First Lord of the Treasury and Prime Minister of His Majesty George IV. He had very close ties to the Bank of England and was already starting to devise provisions to bail out the banks with Bank of England Governor Cornelius Buller and his deputy John Baker Richards. Whilst the Parliament itself might refuse to appropriate funds to prop up the failing assets, the Bank of England could be more conciliatory because of its desire to preserve the fortunes of its global investors. At the end of the last century, it had begun to emerge as an institution of enormous authority with a scope far greater than that of national politics. At the dawn of the new century, Parliament remained populated by feudal landlords who looked upon the stock-jobbing financiers of London with disdain. These financiers however did not need to answer to the British public, nor have to follow to the letter government policy and thus were in a position to operate with considerable autonomy in the running of their vast enterprise. The Bank of England wielded such authority because it was 'the bank for the entire British Empire' (DeLong). The fortunes of the whole of Empire rested with its monetary policies.

The Bank of England was controlled by a small number of aristocrats in much the same way as the British Parliament. At the time the Bank of England was not a central bank but a public, for-profit bank with loyalties to its shareholders, the British government, and its correspondent commercial bankers. The crisis was precipitated when the Bank of England raised the lending rate to protect its investors, instead of lowering it to protect the public, initiating a credit crunch. Conversely it was only when it eventually reversed its policies and lowered the lending rate that the crisis was brought under control, but at the cost of additional, unnecessary failures due to its initial delay to act. When it did, the cash reserves the Bank of England produced literally overnight to secure the British economy amounted to £400,000 in bank notes; in today's currency that figure corresponds to roughly £2.5 billion in collateral; a massive sum to maintain orderly markets and financial stability in a crisis. This event marked the advent of the modern relationship between liberal governance and central banking that would come to dominate economic policy until World War I with the semi-private Bank of England routinely called upon to purchase private banks' toxic assets, to print banknotes to increase the money supply, and to lend out its reserves when crisis ensued.

After the market crash of 1825, the market economy began to be perceived as a distinct entity that had the power to reshape the fates of individuals as well as communities, and the market to which they ultimately owed the whole of their existence and subsistence. After the Panic of 1825 private banks fell out of favour with industrialists and traders who had suffered direct losses from the bank failures under the private banking system, an entity largely controlled by the aristocracy. Joint-stock banks were touted as more stable entities that would promote their assets 'to benefit local and regional economies and industries' (Newton 1). Joint-stock banks traded on the fact that they had a broader and 'therefore more stable capital base due to their ability to issue shares' (1). The new joint-stock banks possessed relative advantages over their private predecessors in that they were able to extend credit to businesses on a far greater scale than the private houses. The ability of joint-stock banks to issue stock was the decisive factor in the larger scale of their operations and in their competition against private banks. Many private bankers soon realised that future business prosperity lay with joint-stock banks and amalgamated with them for this reason. During this process of amalgamation, many private banking families ascended to the highest rank of these new joint-stock institutions. Thus the distribution of wealth remained largely in the purview of old private-banking families, despite their new corporate valance, and banking, if anything, increased its sway in the affairs of ordinary individuals.

Dickens would have been just thirteen years old when this economic crisis hit in 1825. He would have recently resumed his schooling after being forced into manual labour to support his family in the previous year when his father was briefly imprisoned for debt. His situation was representative of the changeable fortunes associated with the expansion of middle-class society, whose pursuit of money, social identity, respectability and status were similarly subject to the perils of their diversification and their private prospects speculative in various ways and to varying degrees. Dickens's adolescence intersects with another crucial cultural transition taking place in 1825. This was the first year that 'the traditional market for vellum-bound epics and triple-decker novels was eclipsed by cheap reprints and serial publications' (Dick). The rise of these new print formats would insure Dickens's widespread commercial success as a writer in later years. This historical development also 'signals the end of what we might call the Romantic ideal and the emergence of an existential malaise in English literature that persists in Victorian writing and beyond', of which Dickens became the paramount progenitor (Dick).

As a mature writer Dickens sets nearly all of his novels in the early period of his life, the 1820s. Through him the older city of his youth is at once immortalised and reanimated. There is something preternatural in Dickens's pre-Victorian schema, as within the space of his novels, the living and the dead, the old and the new lived precariously together with Dickens as their raconteur striding amongst the subjects of the present and the recent past. Dickens writes, 'the old time never grows older or younger with me' (qtd. in Ackroyd 873). In his novels, 'it remains as it was, always present and always being invoked' (Ackroyd 873). This invocation and its modern refrain together manufacture a fictional London whose Victorian mooring comes to it at a distance in both a spatial and temporal sense to inform its preoccupations. The protagonist of *Little Dorrit*, Arthur Clennam, returns to London in early 1825, only months in advance of the Panic. Arthur's twenty years in China date roughly between 1805 and 1825; he leaves as a young man of 20 and returns at 40, middle-aged (Xu 56). The East India Company was in its final phases as a trading company during much of the period that Arthur resided as a trader in China. By the 1820s the East India Company was already starting to be perceived as a declining commercial entity. By 1824 its future as an enterprise was hotly contested by London shareholders. The Clennam family's merchant status in China would have been wholly dependent on the East India Company who held a monopoly trade in China. Because it was solely in charge of setting the price of their company's manufacture, its declining status would have been of great concern to the family. Arthur's father was sent out to China shortly after Arthur was born, therefore Mr. Clennam would have been in China 'from about 1786 to 1825' (Xu 56). 'Since almost no manufactured goods were sold to China there is no indication that the Clennams had a factory in Britain, they could be selling either India cotton or opium' (56). Arthur's guilt concerning their business in China suggests that it was likely that over time the business was forced to switch from the former to the latter to maintain itself as a commercial entity both in China and in London.

The ambiguity of the Clennam's enterprise there, in terms of propriety, corresponds to the moral haziness that surrounded 'the smuggling of literally tons of opium into China, whose ports were not open to that commodity', by the British merchant class (Çelikkol 126). In the public's imagination, the fictional Clennams certainly would be understood to be a part of the British merchant class and thus affiliated in some way with these operations. 'Little Dorrit's contemporary audience would be familiar with the history of the opium trade, because the second opium war was taking place as Dickens was composing Little Dorrit in 1857' (Çelikkol 126). As with the first opium war in the second war Britain demanded that China open up its ports to importation. Britain's unrelenting force was deemed necessary in view of the fact that 'the opium trade created their first major accumulations of capital – without which none of the rest that followed would have been possible. The great British merchant houses, banks and insurance companies that had their roots in the Asian trade, all had a start in opium' (Trocki 9). The management and exploitation of opium as a commodity served as a template to reconfigure labour, fiscal relations and the imperial state itself to complement the activity of profit-making and mass consumption.

Dickens made allusions to the economic and social relevance of opium dating back to his earliest novelistic work, *The Pickwick Papers*, and those allusions extend through to his last unfinished novel *Edwin Drood*. In between we have mention of these substances in practically all of his novels including *Oliver Twist, Hard Times, Bleak House, Little Dorrit* and *Our Mutual Friend*. The fact that in all of the novels the engagement with opiates is by prominent characters demonstrates at once the commonality of its usage, but also something far more profound: that 'there is no outside to the far-reaching tentacles of free market capitalism' (Çelikkol 125). Opium did not just provide relief from pain in a general sense, but in a specific one, insofar as it was seen as the anecdote to the unrelenting pressure of capitalism on its subjects at home and abroad. The Britain that Arthur returns to is the same 'dark and depressing place of his childhood', where 'everything was bolted and barred that could possibly furnish relief to an overworked people' (Dickens, *Little Dorrit* 28; bk. 1, ch. 3). It is no wonder that the masses sought relief elsewhere, in the lure of financial liquidity and the intake of casual narcotics.

In the nineteenth century, finance capitalism was for the most part a highly unregulated, laissez-faire enterprise. The City of London stood at the epicentre of a vastly concentrated financial system, which produced a regular cycle of booms and busts, creating in their wake tumultuous events in the lives of the individuals who invested their fates and fortunes within it. Thanks to the industrial revolution, this early part of the nineteenth century was characterised by rapid advancements in banking, credit and company formation. These advancements later contributed to 'a second, more profound financial revolution in the mid-nineteenth century' (Wagner, *Financial Speculation* 20). Not only the individual, but also his sphere of influence, was deeply implicated in what we now refer to as finance capitalism. As a system of credit it transformed the British subject's understanding of 'management' as pertaining 'to the control of the house, the original meaning signified by Greek *oikonomia*' into something pertaining 'to the public sphere of the country's economy' (14). In this new era, domestic affairs became deeply enmeshed in financial ones. Investment acted as the article that bound them together and choreographed their domestic arrangements to fall in step with the pace of overseas expansion. Plots around investment and speculation emerged together to reconstruct the foundations of fiction in the Victorian era, recasting the novel itself to complement these new formations experienced in the lives of the new, aspirational middle class.

With the rise of capital as a measure of middle-class wealth, the public's esteem for landed wealth plummeted. In response to this change in values, writers began to abandon providential inheritance plots in favour of financial plots that allowed them to 'explore matters involving personal agency and individual will, like financial temptation and fiscal responsibility' (Poovey 52). Literature's use of the stock market reflected developments not merely in the realm of contemporary finance capitalism, but well beyond it to form 'a new cultural imaginary that expressed changing ideas of moral probity and indeterminate identity, creditworthiness and the management of financial risks, the experience of instability and the contesting strategies to consider its repercussions at home and abroad' (Wagner, *Financial Speculation* 6). Its figurative scope had to keep pace with Britain's constantly expanding market for its products abroad, which in turn propelled its bourgeoisie subjects to establish their fortunes literally across the entire surface of the globe. Suddenly it was possible for Britons to establish their households abroad and establish intimate contact with foreign cultures all for the sake of the market. Capitalism's ideal subject and audience were understood as one entity; a harried middle class goaded by the prospect of economic triumph and dogged by its uncertainty. Members of this emergent class were coping on one level with the loss of a stable home or fixed community, and on another grappling with the emotional fragility attendant to the new reality of their becoming socially and geographically mobile in the cause to obtaining and maintaining their newfound wealth.

Mary Poovey maintains that Dickens was able to garner a unique perspective on this new readership and its needs because he was 'the most famous financial journalist' of his era (45). This fact is largely unknown to modern readers, because of 'the anonymity and co-authorship of many of the articles in *Household Words* and *All the Year Round*' which make it difficult 'to see the interest Dickens took in exploring financial topics' (45). Nonetheless his financial articles 'helped make the financial system imaginable as a system' to Britons whose primary experience of finance was probably limited to transactions with country bankers (46). One way to make that system intelligible to readers was to locate them within financial plots, wherein a variety of characters – including ones like themselves – could engage with this new reality. *Little Dorrit* sits amongst a number of narrative plots in this mid-nineteenth-century period, which concern themselves with the exploitation of a naïve, well-meaning, but nonetheless misguided amateur speculator. Finance capitalism was imagined at the time as a sort of infernal machine that consumed speculators, using intentional misrepresentation and deliberate financial fraud, falsely promoted as investment, to pray upon those taken in by financial mania.

There was a moral dimension to all of this, insofar as those who fell prey to the lure of speculation often did so to the forfeiture of their investments in work and home. The speculator is therefore imagined to give over his constant attention to his money, suggesting that he has no others apart from himself to invest his interests. 'In this way, the speculator turns out to be a strangely unified figure, and the Victorian discomfort about him reveals the undesirability of such unity in Victorian ideologies of identity' (Jaffe 159). Speculation eventually becomes a byword for villainy, and 'in the case of the villain, it is not the actual name but the body that conquers space' (Çelikkol 134). This realignment of the body towards a speculative economy impacts the affective economy insofar as the love story in *Little Dorrit* is deeply ensnared in the world of economics. It is commercial rather than romantic preoccupation that drives the plot forward at 'all levels – import-export, petty shopkeeping, banking, and high finance, contraband trading, entrepreneurship, rent collecting, debt and bankruptcy law, manufacturing, investment, business cycles, unemployment, accountancy' – these together form the affective choreography of *Little Dorrit* (Çelikkol 196). All of the individual destinies can be mapped in the novel as the products of economic functionality. Moreover, what appear to subtend Dickens's own novelistic imagination are none other than the laws of political economy relating to primitive accumulation, suggesting that material gain has become the marker of societal validity, overtaking morality and spirituality as seemly forms of social capital.

Aligned with this economic determinism is a world that reflects back to itself a sense of resignation for its inhabitants, whose hopelessness comes from the fact that God has been replaced by Society, represented here mainly by the Circumlocution Office, which 'demands submission and even worship but fails to provide any spiritual fulfillment' (Higbie 133). This situation easily led to a feeling of '"total infidelity," a sense that there is nothing worth believing in' (133). The mind wearied in such a way tends to see the world as a prison. In *Little Dorrit*, Arthur Clennam adopts such a carceral perspective.

Arthur is not alone in being infected by the nihilism of the market and its attendant features of risk. On one level the principal economic institution in *Little Dorrit* is not the bank, but rather the debtor's prison. It is in this sense that it competes with the bank to become the source of the novel's dominant imagery. The debtor's prison portrayed in the novel as the Marshalsea prison in South London holds particular resonance within the novel because it is one of the main sites of traumatic memory from Dickens's own childhood. The Marshalsea becomes a sort of magnetic force field within the novel, drawing characters from afar into a particularly menacing orbit where they must confront the persistent threat of never having enough money. This threat pervades not only a heterogeneity of bodies, but also of spaces, whose contiguity is attributable to capitalist expansion, and the integration of new investors and consumers into the global market, which exists in microcosm in the London of *Little Dorrit*. 'Dickens not only focuses the action of the tale relentlessly upon the locale of the Marshalsea, but, in addition, he symbolically transcribes the unconscious life of this outwardly prosperous society as a constellation of different living quarters, from Bleeding Heart Yard to the mansions around Grovesnor Square, all of which, as a number of critics have observed, uncannily reproduce the image of the debtor's prison' (Çelikkol 198).

Acquaintance with such detail can only be the province of someone with intimate and equal knowledge of both repressive milieus. Dickens shares in common with Little Dorrit the need to temper the perception of the institutional violence visited upon the working class to suit the prejudices of a middle-class audience. At the same time, through the use of images of personal suffering he is able to elicit a series of cultural interactions that unsettle that understanding. It is Little Dorrit who is required to make the rounds to a variety of middle-class homes, including those of the Clennams, the Casbys, the Merdles and the Gowans in what amounts to an act of rhetorical circumlocution, in order to both elucidate and conceal her ambiguous origins within the debtor's prison. Through such encounters we are made keenly aware of the pressure exerted upon her from these families to abstract the hardships of her historical circumstances, in order to garner acceptance within their present society. The fact that Little Dorrit's actions in a sense originate in Dickens's own life experience speaks to Dickens's apprehension that a portion of that sentence remains to be served.

During his father's imprisonment for debt in the Marshalsea prison in 1824, Charles Dickens was lodged elsewhere. The remainder of his family (like the Dorrit family) dwelt there together for three months. Despite the short duration of John Dickens's imprisonment, the omnipresent shadow of the Marshalsea prison looms over Dickens's imaginative life for the whole of its duration and the spectre of imprisonment haunt nearly all of his mature fictional outputs. This 'probably owes something to his father's melodramatic pronouncement that "the sun had set upon him forever"', relating his reputational demise to his former occupation as an imperial naval clerk following his release (Suchoff 58). In this same breath he was invalidating the legitimate labour his son had performed outside the walls of the prison, at Warren's Blacking Factory, not only to materially support the family, but equally to maintain the public fiction of its minimal propriety. The gift that John Dickens gave to his son Charles was that he could identify himself as someone who had never technically crossed the gates into carceral habitation. This fact offered him little comfort, knowing that he was fundamentally subject to the same ruling passion that led to his father's financial ruin, the desire to grow richer and get on in the world. When this passion morally and materially negates itself through the vagaries of the market there is little public sympathy available to it. 'Even the high minded Arthur Clennam, one of the few capitalist heroes in Victorian fiction (where an ethic of Christian spirituality and self-denial nominally prevails), is prone to such dreams, as his disastrous plunge into high-risk speculation testifies' (Herbert, 'Filthy Lucre' 198). John Dickens's desire to come up in the world from the lowly pay grade of naval clerk and provide for his growing family corresponds with the fictional characters in *Little Dorrit* whose imaginative lives are predicated on aspirations of financial gain and social mobility.

Related to these aspirations was 'society mania', described by Dickens in *Little Dorrit*, as 'a perfect fury for making acquaintances on whom to impress their riches and importance' (511; bk. 1, ch. 7). In the novel, Mr. Dorrit was just as affected by it as his elder daughter Fanny; indeed it had seized almost every member of the House of Dorrit, though their falling under its influence was hardly an exceptional case. This particular fury caught hold of a great many characters who were in a position to acquaint themselves with elevated society. Beneath societal mania resided its exact converse, societal abjuration, 'a stringent system of avoidance and repression that expresses itself in the form of panicky dread of indelicate references to money matters, or of even indirect contact with the taboo element of poverty' (Herbert, 'Filthy Lucre' 199). It is this element of poverty that appears throughout the novel as an object of disavowal, a condition that requires constant deflection through a fixation on financial acquisition and the display of wealth in order to keep rank, as it were, with society's betters. Behind this façade of striving lies a terrible foundation of struggling, making the architecture of wealth precariously proximate to the base structures of poverty and financial crisis. In capitalist society their relation to one another therein materialises as irrevocable. In *Little Dorrit*, the foundation and design of these new commercial arrangements are made immediately apparent in Dickens's portrayal of the newlywed home of Pet and Henry Gowan in Venice:

> On the first floor of the house was a Bank – a surprising experience for any gentleman of commercial pursuits

bringing laws for all mankind from a British city – where two spare clerks, like dried dragoons, in green velvet caps adorned with golden tassels, stood, bearded, behind a small counter in a small room, containing no other visible objects than an empty iron-safe, with the door open, a jug of water, and a papering of garlands of roses; but who on lawful requisition, by merely dipping their hands out of sight, could produce exhaustless mounds of five-franc pieces. Below the Bank was a suite of three or four rooms with barred windows, which had the appearance of a jail for criminal rats. Above the Bank was Mrs. Gowan's residence (Dickens, *Little Dorrit* 491; bk. 2, ch. 6).

The home of this newer generation of Britons has at its heart a space of enterprise that extends the reach of British authority to any commercial centre of note, in this instance Venice. The labour it produces is homosexual in nature, insofar as man and wife no longer occupy the centre of productivity in the home, but rather more substantially do two officers of the law, their filiation is at once British, but also foreign, insofar as their mysterious offspring comes out in the shape of the five-franc piece. Much like its co-habitants above, the Gowans see no differentiation between their lives in London where everyone knows everyone, and this temporary accommodation, as both are fueled by the capital in one or another formal manifestation. That such dealings are subtended by confinement and criminality are truths seldom got at, at the surface, and even from the height that the Gowans occupy, above the Bank, their presence is a mere detail or trifle as compared with the business going on below. And yet fashionable Society 'is no less a prison or forcing-house than the … gaol itself', which forms in the home's darkened foundations (Ackroyd 757–8).

For Dickens, Society, the Bank and Mrs. Gowan represent three aspects of one narrative and a singular design for maintaining Britain's aristocratic status quo. Dickens has no sympathy for Pet Gowan within the scheme of this arrangement, insofar as she seems quite blind to the intricate financial netting holding her precariously in place. She is the mistress of the home, but by no means its master. In the context of the evolution of capital in the nineteenth century, she is Pet to Mrs. Clennam's guard dog, in terms of domestic agency. She lacks her ferocity, and it is ferocity that is required in response to this dawning age, in England and English society. Perhaps not surprisingly for Dickens it is the morbid worship of riches and title that undermines the middle-class household and its affectionate bonds, making of them something incomprehensibly perverse in service to a subterranean cultural logic, which puts the desire to make aristocratic connections before every other consideration of need. In *Little Dorrit*, the Meagles's plot is designed to demonstrate just such an outcome when Mr. Meagles chooses to give his beloved daughter Pet's hand in marriage to the brutish aristocrat Henry Gowan, over the affable merchant banker Arthur Clennam. Arthur's matrimonial rejection as a suitable match is due to a recent financial decision. He has chosen to sever ties with his family's banking and trade business, the House of Clennam, over concerns about the moral probity of its accumulated fortune largely amassed abroad in China. Mrs. Gowan, mother to Mr. Henry Gowan, the soon to be husband to Pet Meagles, understands the aristocracy's susceptibility to the wiles of commercial fortune derived from similar ambiguous forms of commercial trade:

'Why, don't I know my son, and don't I know that this is exactly the way to hold him?' said Mrs Gowan, contemptuously; 'and do not these Miggles people know it, at least as well as I? Oh, shrewd people, Mr Clennam: evidently people of business! I believe Miggles belonged to a Bank. It ought to have been a very profitable Bank, if he had much to do with its management. This is very well done, indeed' (Dickens, *Little Dorrit* 137; bk. 1, ch. 26).

Mrs. Gowan's contempt for the match stems from her disgust regarding the diminishing fortunes of her own aristocratic kind at a time when the 'Miggles' of this world who know very well how to manage their fortunes are in the ascendant. Their ability to manipulate money allows them to manipulate society and those not aware of their growing influence will soon find themselves easily overtaken by these financiers. 'It is very knowingly done indeed, and seems to have taken YOU in completely' (Dickens, *Little Dorrit* 137; bk. 1, ch. 26). Mrs. Gowan's remarks also suggest that her son Henry Gowan has been similarly caught unawares and manipulated these shrewd investors who seek to bank on his family's reputation in society. Henry believes that quite the opposite is true, that nothing has changed and that the despite the middle classes' recent incursion into society the only territory worth considering in this country remains situated with the aristocracy, the Barnacles and the Stiltstalkings of this world. Indeed, regardless of the financial pretences of a family like the Meagles, when it came down to it anyone who was not related in some meaningful way to 'John Barnacle, Augustus Stiltstalking, Tom, Dick or Harry Barnacle, or Stiltstalking, had to be nobody, simply because there was no one else but the mob' (Dickens, *Little Dorrit* 314; ch. 26).

Gowan's perspective is far different to Clennam's, in that he does not assume the superiority of the company around him, nor does he entertain the possibility of any obstacles that would separate him from obtaining a place at any table he wished to join with, of any rank or calibre, without the slightest bit of hesitation. His credit-worthiness does not fluctuate, because he is an artist, an amateur, a dabbler, but first and foremost an aristocrat, for whom the concept of profit is an abomination and the concept of earnings little more than an irascible con. Gowan assures

Clennam that he is not 'a great impostor', though his pictures are 'not worth the money'. He assures him that the bargain one strikes with him is a finite one in comparison to men who must rely on the market for their livelihood, who as a result are forced to see everyone around them instrumentally, as a potential 'buyer' of the fruits of their labour. This truth applies to 'painters, writers, patriots, all the rest who have stands in the market' (310). The more money this individual acquires from his buyer, the greater the expectation that this buyer will become a source of revenue in the future: 'give almost any man I know ten pounds, and he will impose upon you to a corresponding extent; a thousand pounds—to a corresponding extent; ten thousand pounds—to a corresponding extent' (310). For Gowan, great success comes at the price of great imposition, in the contemporary world of capitalism. Gowan's feinted enthusiasm for it bears one final chilling, sarcastic refrain: 'What a jolly, excellent, lovable world it is!' (310) This economic lesson that he gives to Clennam reveals that the complement of the capitalistic world is none other than the patrician world of the Circumlocution Office, which by contrast had no stands in the market or price to their influence, and thus had no personal investment in the endeavour of others. Their freedom from the burdens of labour allows them to share amongst themselves the task of 'balancing' the political economy, to suit their light-handed authority, which in turn 'reduced everything in the wide world to the same light weight', tilting pressure once again towards the middle class to produce the principle for such gestures to be maintained (Dickens, *Little Dorrit* 310; ch. 26).

Gowan muses, 'though I can't deny that the Circumlocution Office may ultimately shipwreck everybody and everything, still, that will probably not be in our time—and it's a school for gentlemen' (310). It therefore is not Clarence Barnacle who turns out to be the 'most agreeable and most endearing blockhead' in *Little Dorrit* (310). Rather it must be Arthur Clennam who is the 'accountable Blockhead' who is summoned forth by Dickens ('Nobody, Somebody and Everybody' 119). It is he who manages to spend the whole of the narrative victim to a kind of social and financial amnesia, based on his wholly unpractised and unused identity as an English gentleman. Henry Gowan, to the contrary, will always be a gentleman, because the shipwreck that is surely coming to Britain and indeed has come in the form of crash after crash, crisis after crisis, will never unbalance him, as he is already well-aware and surefooted in his understanding that his chosen labour is largely ornamental and thus practically valueless. Nonetheless, and fortunately for him, his schooling as a gentleman remains priceless in guaranteeing his future wellbeing on balance. Society will overlook the deficits of its own, but rarely, if ever, the deficits of those outside of it.

Dickens writes in a letter to John Forster on 27 April 1855 that the aristocratic class that rules Britain, not only refuses to take responsibility for its botched affairs in war-making abroad, but equally for its conduct towards its ailing population at home. It wilfully refrains from acknowledging the 'enormous black cloud of poverty in every town which is spreading and deepening every hour, and not one man in two thousand knowing anything about, or even believing in, its existence; with non-working aristocracy, and a silent parliament, and everybody for himself and nobody for the rest; this is the prospect, and I think a very deplorable one' (qtd. in G. Smith 147). Arthur Clennam is amongst this population that is unable to recognise the reality of poverty in Britain, even as he progressively forms an attachment to the Dorrit family and in particular Little Dorrit. It is he who stands powerless as a middle-class individual before the ubiquitous class of patricians in the civil service. These individuals have become legion through their ontological allegiance to the operational structure of finance capitalism. The Barnacles are often described as 'colonies' or 'shoals'. They operate as a 'school', which in Arthur Clennam's opinion is 'a very dangerous, unsatisfactory and expensive school for people who pay to keep the pupils there' (Dickens, *Little Dorrit* 310; bk. 1, ch. 26). The people who pay for such schooling are middle-class 'Somebodies' like Arthur Clennam, because it is ultimately their taxes that fund the government misadventures of the patrician class. Dickens uses a 'crustacean metaphor to depict "the Barnacles" mode of operation as a sort of multitude without an organizing center and without individual agency, but capable of acting and reproducing en masse in a parasitical manner. Another implication of course is that such a decentralized collective mode of operation makes the Barnacles all the more difficult to criticise or resist' (Knezevic 129). The Barnacles and their ilk managed any number of dubious political ventures, including commercially driven warfare, through a system of 'false pretence' and 'general swindling' (Dickens, 'Nobody, Somebody and Everybody' 118).

His subsequent article, 'Nobody, Somebody and Everybody', which appeared in *Household Words* on 30 August 1856, registered what he identified as a shameful decline in responsibility at all levels of society, evident in both Britain's core institutions and the individuals charged with their preservation. Those in charge of the nation's governance were responsible for its deterioration, which if extended over the course of time might someday bring about 'the national death of us' ('Nobody, Somebody and Everybody' 118). Administrative reform, therefore, was indispensable for the future prosperity of the nation and the empire. Dickens maintained that in order for such reform to take place, a vacuum in middle-class power must be acknowledged, because it was that deficiency in power which prevented political reform from taking place with any real force across the class structures of society. At present the middle class in its vacuity has come to stand in for the incapacity of Somebody to intervene on the activities of Nobody. Dickens writes in his article,

I don't want Somebody to let off Parliamentary penny firecrackers, against the evils that need to be stormed by the thunderbolts of Jove. I don't want Somebody to sustain, for Parliament and Club Entertainment, and by the desire of several persons of distinction, the character of a light old gentleman, or fast old gentleman, or debating old gentleman, or a dandy old gentleman, or a free-and-easy old gentleman, or a capital old gentleman considering his years. I want someone clever at doing business, not evading it ... I want Somebody who shall be no fiction; but a capable good determined workman (118).

For the time being however that Somebody referred to here is not clever enough for the job and as an entity has fallen prey to a type of crude organism, a Barnacle, that collapses the material boundary between commercial and organic structures and in so doing reconfigures the middle classes as mere accessories to its central operation. By contrast, even loose Barnacles such as Henry Gowan are able to attach themselves at will to the market; Gowan establishes his union with Pet Meagles as something that takes place within the world of commodities and allows him to sponge off her family to their financial impairment. In similar fashion, a Barnacle starves the nation by attaching itself to the structures of government, to the structure's detriment. It then proceeds to foul its organisational structure and parasitically feed its wealth outward from an intricate point of attachment, to support the growth of its own privately motivated enterprise. The extreme ineptitude inherent in the world of government is driven materially by the financial system, which serves as a kind of biopolitical engine in the novel pervading society, shaping characters' personalities and destinies, and involving them, in the end, with a struggle for survival.

The Barnacles with their hands seemingly at idle nonetheless manage to generate a fractious world, which cracks through the surface of the text of *Little Dorrit*, seeping into the narrowest of syntactical spaces in the novel. It establishes itself as an undertone through Dickens's consistent use of the indefinite article to describe the Barnacles as a means of attaching blame to '.a' Nobody. Dickens uses this indefinite Nobody to describe the failure of the Crimea campaign through its dispersed parts: 'When Nobody was shown with these few weeks to have occasioned terrible misery and loss in the late war, and to have incurred a vast amount of guilt in bringing to pass results which all morally sane persons can be understood to be fraught with fatal consequences ... My Lord's impaneled course cried there is no impostor but Nobody; on him bring shame and blame' ('Nobody, Somebody and Everybody' 117). Therein Dickens accuses this same Nobody of being at the heart of all public disaster in the United Kingdom and Ireland. The sound of this accusation ricochets within the financial system only fall back onto Arthur Clennam as Somebody, a representative of the middle class, whose individual resistance to Circumlocution is rendered as weak and futile. That same expression is echoed in Arthur's earlier description of himself 'as empty, citing "the void in my cowed heart everywhere" ... and it is this very emptiness that allowed him to be swayed into conspiring with his own eventual financial demise. He is both a "Fool", as Mrs. F's Aunt repeatedly emphasizes, and an everyman – an empty vessel waiting to be filled up' (Jarvie 107).

What in the end is Nobody's Fault is the way England's empty bodies tend to fill in with the material for the nation's production to continue as it is, as well as take on the commodified appearance of their labour. 'By combining separate acts of labor into unified and marketable commodities, capitalism magically performs its own metaphoric transformations of dismembered laboring bodies into reified products' (Novak 22). Therefore Dickens's techniques in summoning the appearance of his characters in the novel allow the reader for a time to remember their own bodies and reflect on their own serialised production from diverse fragments generated in the open market. *Little Dorrit* is at one level a biting criticism of aristocratic entitlement, and the informal, amateurish culture of the British civil service throughout the nineteenth century. On another level, it cannily identifies the middle class's collusion with the patrician political culture that led to a perpetuation of crises in identity and self-worth on both an individual and national scale during that same period. Knezevic maintains that in the nineteenth century, 'the fortunes of many who had any measure of disposable capital were made or lost in banking and speculation, causing rapid bumps up or down the social ladder, which entailed all sorts of difficult questions about class identity. In a society so profoundly structured by a class hierarchy and its attendant forms of class mobility, it is less than surprising that the typical novelist hero is most often caught between classes – orphans and children of the impoverished middle-class parents, governesses, bankers and (less often) writers and artists' (40). One class that did not appear to fall prey to such insecurity was the patrician class who under-stood that the precariousness inherent to a system of finance capitalism played an integral role in maintaining their monopoly on political power.

In *Little Dorrit*, Dickens is keen to demonstrate that the Circumlocution Office was mainly staffed with members of one aristocratic family, the Barnacles; however it was not their only public domain, rather they 'were dispersed all over public offices, and held all sorts of public places' (Dickens, *Little Dorrit* 310; bk. 1, ch. 26). Dickens emphasises their ubiquity as a means of shattering the spell of middle-class amazement at the reach of a patrician power system when tied to the mechanism of finance capitalism. This sort of novelistic revelation suited Dickens's own political project of generating an autonomous middle-class public sphere. This undertaking was a formidable one, because by mid-century finance capitalism had come to formulate itself as nothing less than the arbiter of social mobility. In so doing, it only served to reify the existing class system as the main component in the social construction of Englishness. Dickens in writing *Little Dorrit* is not outside of the system he is attempting to represent, nor does he reject finance capitalism outright in either the narrative or indeed his person conduit as an investor in the stock market. Nonetheless, 'by putting the financier speculator Merdle in the spotlight', in tandem with the Barnacle family, 'Dickens presented the practices of finance capitalism as a moral and political drama, and Merdle ultimately as much of a crook himself as victim of a specific social and political regime' thus implying that anyone not belonging to the patrician class was potentially its casualty (Knezevic 39).

Indeed, Merdle as much as anyone else fell victim to a much larger conspiracy than mere fraud, through 'the irresistible colonization of the state apparatus by the Barnacles ... accompanied by their attitude of entitlement towards the business of government' (Knezevic 15). As their stock persistently rose and indeed expanded in value, 'the social achievements and attitudes associated with the middle class faced a future of constant devaluation' (16). For this to happen there must be collusion on a grand scale between the political society and the civil society; the middle-class's failure to recognise its part in this greater scheme of complicity meant that it was handicapped in its attempts to build up an effective civil society in order to challenge the patrician monopoly of political power. This middle class subservience to the patrician monopoly of power is challenged through two crucial partnerships that emerge at the end of the novel between Clennam and Doyce, but also Clennam and Little Dorrit, which are formed significantly after Clennam's disastrous decision to speculate and his consequential financial ruin. These functional partnerships are 'meant to extol the virtues of industry and industrialization, in contrast to the moral pits of speculation and finance capitalism' (16). They also point the way towards the power of the industrial engineering and the manufacturing sector to pose a challenge to the patrician political system at mid-century. Dickens's task here was to show the Barnacles for what they were, merely hangers-on to static vessels, at a time when others in their natural form were able to transport themselves or at least parts of themselves through more innovative, transient forms of commercial merger.

As Sussman and Joseph point out, it is no coincidence 'that Daniel Doyce, the mechanical genius of *Little Dorrit*, is a fictional version of Charles Babbage, any more than Mr. Merdle, the fraudulent financier of *Little Dorrit*, is a fictional version of the real life Irish financier John Sadlier' (627). Both characters come to represent archetypes of their age, ranging from 'the congruence of the human psyche with the mechanical' to 'the equivalence of the human body with the financial' (621). The fictional Daniel Doyce, however, unlike Babbage summons the foresight to leave London and go to St. Petersburg, where not only is he able to have his machine function, but is equally able to profit from it. Dickens writes passionately about Russia as an imperial rival to Britain, which may retain 'a certain barbaric Power' but nonetheless is able to obtain and indeed maintain 'valuable possessions on the map of the world' (Dickens, *Little Dorrit* 672; bk. 2, ch. 22). When the occasion arose for the need of 'the services of one or two engineers', it made certain 'their ingenuity perceived to be wanted' (672). Russia outpaced Britain insofar as its imagination extended to the possibility of a workforce crafted, as it were, 'out of the best materials they could find at hand' and furthermore grasped the value of investing 'in the adaptation of such materials to their purpose' (672). Russia, rather than Britain, located itself at the forefront, and thus was boldly willing to refashion 'the conception of ... purpose itself', and in turn allowed 'this Power, being a barbaric one', to energetically unleash its capital in a way that would quite naturally appear belligerent to an entity similar to the 'Circumlocution Office'.

Indeed the real British bureaucracy of the time routinely engaged in 'stowing away' its great objects, cataloguing them, 'with characteristic ignorance', making certain that its most decided actions corresponded to 'the great political science' of the status quo (672). The Russians, by contrast in Dickens's estimation, 'were regarded as men who meant to do it, engaging with other men who meant it to be done' (672).

By travelling to Russia with his invention Doyce is able to circumvent the machinery of the Circumlocution Office in London. The machinery of government no longer clings to him, but instead his yolk is now harnessed to the mast of global profiteering where labour is now routinely apprehended as an intellectual property. What the characters in the novel cannot explicitly reference, but Dickens's readers can infer, is that the present war with Russia in the Crimea will likely be lost because of bureaucratic incompetence. It is this same incompetence that is preventing British soldiers from being adequately equipped to fight. The British government is unable to confront the fact that victory hinges on one concern above all others: how the conception of purpose itself can be refashioned to keep pace with the rapidly intellectualised and imperialised conditions of industry. Setting his novel 30 or 40 years in the past allows Dickens to draw out the trajectory of that imperative, which leads to the inevitability of this contest. It is useful to recall that 'despite the general feelings of rivalry between Britain and Russia, in the early decades of the nineteenth century, a handful of British engineers went to Russia to work' (Philpotts 444).

Doyce's being one of them is polemical insofar as he was a mechanic before he was an engineer. His 'complex class locations and the tenuous relations between mental and manual labor' distinguish Doyce from his contemporaries, and 'clearly link' him 'to the emerging figure of the professional' (Kuskey 149). Dickens's participation in the cultural construction of this figure relies on his own process of becoming a professional writer.

Professionals who performed intellectual labour possessed a kind of capital, which produced a novel relationship to acquisition in the form of the stored labour of knowledge. This nascent form of labourer was able to subvert the relationship between economic and social class on a number of levels: firstly if he did not look or act like a wage labourer, it became harder to determine if he relied upon a wage or salary; if he did not ostensibly possess a great deal of financial capital, the fact could now be dissimulated through the appearance of what we would now call cultural capital. This emergence of the professional comes into direct contest for recognition with another emerging economic and social class, the imperial merchant, for whom a differential in capital represents connection to an entirely divergent space of manifestation, engineered to mingle labour not with the intellect, but rather to merge it into licit and illicit economic and social enterprises abroad.

Tamara S. Wagner describes the novel *Little Dorrit* as centring around 'a paradigmatic episode of disappointed return' on the part of Arthur Clennam that in time will result in agony on a much grander scale ('Imperialist Commerce' 4). The literal collapse of the House of Clennam and its related networks of power finds its beginnings in a novel geography that merges the fortunes of the East with contemporary London. Dickens's mapping of this territory creates confusion insofar as commercial imperialism is treated very much as a prosaic operation. It brings what is far away closer to hand, insofar as in Dickens's novel 'work places abroad stand exposed as at once fairly indistinguishable from those located at the empire's financial centre', the City of London (4). For all their banality, they are nonetheless disconcerting and alienating environments which foster ambiguity because of their remarkable likeness to one another. Dickens's readers must face a startling fact: that 'Red tape, as the main output of the infamous Circumlocution Office in Dickens's *Little Dorrit*, encompasses the globe' (4). Such red tape becomes a kind of Mobius strip; having the property of being non-orientatable, this entity quickly becomes functionary to formulating a continuous loop between home and colony. Moreover, it allows for a reconfiguration of space such that capital and empire function simultaneous to one another on a seemingly unending circuit; a characteristic shared with modernity itself.

Wagner asserts that 'what is important to remember in this context is that during the nineteenth-century fictionalisations of commercial exchanges between "East" and "West" had considerably less to do with orientalist exoticisation than with critiques of commercial expansion' ('Imperialist Commerce' 5). This was especially true when it related to semicolonial spaces rather than to formal empires. In these sorts of spaces commercial imperialism was all the more likely to work as a metonymy for capitalist aggression at home. 'Since China was never part of a formal foreign empire, it lends itself particularly well to an investigation of commercial driven modernities' (5). The commercial, in its drive, sacrifices novelty for efficiency and duplication. There is no awareness to be gleaned from such an exchange. Rather, what remains residually is a kind of lack of accountability. Indeed, the inherent dullness of enterprise becomes the stuff of a distinctive sort of memory loss, accompanied by a consciousness that is 'semi' in every sense of the word. Men like Arthur therefore carry with them a predilection towards vagueness and insincerity when confronting what is other with any real enthusiasm. It is this aspect of his character that makes Arthur Clennam the hapless object of fraud, both at home and abroad.

Dickens resists infusing *Little Dorrit*'s narrative with exoticism and refrains from providing his readers with specific incidents of colonial violence, which suggests at once that colonial advancement and its attendant aggression were both of banal concern to his reader. Foreign settlement in China necessitated such omissions. Criticism of commercial imperialism was directed away from such examination by the powers-that-be involved in free trade. Those conversant with Britain's hampering bureaucracy were able to transfer it away from London metropolitan business culture and reinstall it piece by piece in exotic locales, to temper the expatriate's work experience abroad through a combination of tedium and detachment. Arthur Clennam never refers to his actual experiences in China during his twenty years abroad, mainly because his time there is a semi-phenomenon; at once oppositional and interdependent with its foreignness, he is neither one nor the other, not Englishman nor Chinaman. Clennam is Irish. Nineteenth-century Ireland is a territory, which shared in common with China a relationship to the Britain of semi-colonialism. The 'semi' of semi-colonalism 'does not denote so much half of something but rather the fractured, informal, and indirect character of colonialism as well as its multilayered-ness' (Wagner, 'Imperialist Commerce' 15, footnote 1). The terms of that multilayeredness play out back in Britain for Arthur when he return to his native land as a 'semi-stranger', after 'semi-goring and semi-boring' his way through the East (Dickens, *Little Dorrit* 525; bk. 2, ch. 8). It is the break with the character of Englishness that plagues Arthur's attempts to reintegrate back into Western society. The way back for Clennam does not come by way of reconnecting with that aristocratic tier of society, but rather through a pedestrian, middle-class business partnership with the itinerant inventor Daniel Doyce.

Clennam is able to assimilate back into British civil society through the routine monotony of bookkeeping. In many ways this would have been a continuation of his work in China alongside his father. He takes on his duties again with enthusiasm. Despite the apparent tedium associated with 'form-filling, corresponding, minuting, memorandum-making, signing, counter-signing, and counter-counter-signing', there is a genius required to doing so that Doyce is aware of (Dickens, *Little Dorrit*

525; bk. 2, ch. 8). Clennam proves himself, at least for now, as adept at manipulating capital's intricate mechanisms. And it is at this point that he cautions Clennam against speculation: "If I have a prejudice connected with money and money figures ... it is against speculating. I don't think I have any other. I dare say I entertain that prejudice, only because I have never given my mind fully to the subject'; and therefore Clennam makes it his business to produce work on the subject on his behalf (525). It is little wonder that Clennam is drawn into the appeal of financial speculation, as it, like all of his other transactions for Doyce, 'exists entirely in the abstract' and functions as he does at a disconnect 'from the realm of hard work and production of actual value' (Kuskey 175). The figures therefore distort the picture of potential earnings Clennam is seeing, and allow him to believe in the possibility of money begotten of money but not the very real danger that one's money could disappear altogether if there were no material functionality behind the investment, or in other words, if there were no Doyce behind Clennam.

Without Doyce, Clennam finds himself back at the mercy of the patricians, 'drawn in by the speculative tendencies of his age', and duped by 'the forces of global capitalism' into 'the idea that all can share in his profits' (A. Anderson 89). The conditions of modern Britain's social and economic reality conspire to make Clennam's detachment, exile and disaffiliation with Britain during his time in China the source of the disabling factor in his judgment, which in turn makes him subject to financial dissimulation. Unlike Little Dorrit, the radical changes in his personal history do not provoke within him a greater awareness of socioeconomic realities. Instead, his lack of provocation becomes the source of his profound limitation in carrying out his various sympathetic duties in Britain throughout the novel. Clennam also falls short in terms of his ability to calculate reality from a potentially profitable position of cultural and historical alterity, and as a result he remains ignorant of the damaging effect of his optimism. Clennam's world-weariness indeed blinds him to the necessary financial wariness he must adopt in dealing with the market, wherein all too often monotony interferes with one's authority over its fluctuations.

The contemporary, cosmopolitan Britain Clennam is returning to is one ruled by self-interest, greed and the pursuit of revenue. The aristocracy, which 'had set itself against the claims and demands of the other classes', was made up of the same individuals who created 'its burgeoning and often corrupt financial empire' (Ackroyd 735). The character of Merdle, the financier, is a master of the City's brand of artful subterfuge in making sure its own needs get met. Almost immediately, Dickens depicts Mr. Merdle as a monstrous product, 'the master spirit of the age', manufactured through the dismemberment and rearticulation of wealth demanded by finance capitalism, which makes of society a beast fiendishly stitched together from the scraps of economic exchange (Dickens, *Little Dorrit* 597; bk. 1, ch. 15). The work of society therefore cannot be separated from capital insofar as its transactions, and the value of an individual's appearance within it, remain constantly in the process of production as if status were something to work at. Nonetheless, the prerequisite for participation in the society implies that any equivalence to work be disavowed at all times, in order to maintain such an abstraction and preserve a perception of equality in origin and rank amongst its members. Dickens describes Merdle as:

immensely rich; a man of prodigious enterprise; a Midas without the ears; who turned all he touched into gold. He was in everything good, from banking to building. He was in Parliament, of course. He was in the City, necessarily ... He was a pleasant man enough: plain; emphatic about public and private confidence, and tenacious of the utmost deference being shown to everyone, in all things, to Society (*Little Dorrit* 246-247; bk. 1, ch. 21).

This passage is telling insofar as Merdle is not *of* Society so much as he is *in* it, as its loyal servant, applying to accumulation a touch that, although certainly uncommon, remains tainted through its association with labour. Nonetheless, this sense allows for him to compensate for the failure of others he might be said to possess. Most convenient of all is his powerful disposition of being deaf to all obligations other than the perpetuation of wealth. What drives him forward is the kernel of confidence provided by those surrounding him, 'which he is always cultivating', and in terms of their investment in him, 'he is always moving it, and always laying out money on it with the greatest liberality' (Dickens, *Little Dorrit* 247; bk. 1, ch. 21). 'Merdle is also, constantly, uncontrollably associated with excrement', which functions as 'a stand in for money', and through its very nature unearths an unpleasant truth: 'in the end everything is valueless' (Jarvie 101). Familiar with that fact as he is with its substantial basis, Merdle, Society's cultivator, nevertheless 'harnesses' himself to 'a watering-cart full of money', and goes about 'saturating Society' every day of his 'life' (Dickens, *Little Dorrit* 396; bk. 1, ch. 33). It is Merdle's duty to saturate Society with abundance, to sacrifice for its wellbeing through the display of excess, whilst concealing all the while the waste material required to speed his powers of cultivation. What covers over the vulgarity of his activity is Mrs. Merdle, whom Mr. Merdle refers to as 'the ornament of Society', complement to himself, 'a benefactor to it' (396). Their marriage is a business arrangement and without such a situation she and he 'would never come together ... you supply the manner, I supply the money' (396). Mrs. Merdle, through her first husband, Colonel Sparkler, and through her son, Mr. Sparkler, a gentleman, has claim to Society. By contrast, Mr. Merdle simply bought into Society through the arrangement of marriage to her, making him forever the subject of slight restiveness in the eyes of Society, whose 'nourishment' he nonetheless furnishes.

In nineteenth-century Britain any manual labour is associated with vulgarity and yet there is no other organ through which its economy may be stimulated. 'As the century wore on, more and more of the attributes of status fell into the category of behavior to be avoided – and things that could be "acquired." One had at all costs to avoid doing manual labor and also one could not be "in trade"' (Pool 47–8). Such rough handling leaves marks, both on the social register as a cipher for social class as well as sexuality. What may be apprehended can just as easily be rejected out of hand. This arrangement between the Merdles sheds light on the failures of another awkward union, which makes up the House of Clennam. In symmetry with Mr. Merdle, Mrs. Clennam benefits from relation to Arthur Clennam, despite the fact that he is not her real son. However, in this circumstance there emerges a deficit, insofar as Arthur's biological mother was a beautiful, yet penniless, young singer with whom his father had entered into an arrangement of sorts, before being pressured by his wealthy uncle to marry the present Mrs. Clennam. Mrs. Clennam agrees to bring up the child as her own, on condition that his mother never reappears in his life. She soon disappears altogether, stricken by grief in entertaining her part of the bargain. The relation between the two did not end in death however, as the wealthy uncle, wounded by remorse, had left a bequest to Arthur's biological mother and to the youngest daughter of her patron, a kindly musician who had taught and befriended her – and who happened to be Amy Dorrit's paternal uncle, Frederick. As Frederick Dorrit had no daughter, the legacy went to the youngest daughter of Frederick's younger brother, who is William Dorrit, Amy's father.

What holds together the complex web of these social relations is the circulating feature of financial indemnity. In *Little Dorrit* that economic machinery includes 'Clennam's private bank spanning from London to China, Meagle's thirty-five-year career as a banking clerk, Merdle's role as "an extraordinary phenomenon in Buying and Banking," and Casby's as banker on "confidential banking business" for Miss Wade, coupled with the informal usury he practices with Pancks, loaning him money at 20%' (Houston, *From Dickens to Dracula* 80). The implication here is that once finance enters into the personal equation, one can never go home again, because to do so is equivalent to languishing in one's duties to the outside world and to produce as it were diminishing returns, should one try ever to get out of it again. The private bank of the home continues to drain sustenance from the 'public' bank or joint-stock bank, as familial sentiment attempts to compete with the invisible powers of multiple, temporary co-joinings characteristic of an age of portable property.

This is why Dickens's novels are unduly populated by male orphans, bachelors and widowers; figures who are ostensibly most attracted to and yet most hesitant to engage in heterosexual intercourse, who nonetheless pursue passionate friendships with males they consider to occupy a space of mutual economic affinity alongside them. Essentially it is these men, whose fortunes are similarly tracked, who have the most to gain through new partnerships born of the new economic and ethical order, which values not so much matrimony but its excessive categorisation into other types of profitable pairing. Moreover, what was formerly generative about the marriage bed faces its ultimate distortion when applied to joint-stock, wherein degeneration in the form of stock devaluation puts its progenitor at risk not of losing progeny, but of losing one's innate domestic worth.

On the other hand one's value could suddenly inflate prodigiously when transported from the homeland of Britain to the larger world of colonial empire. Suddenly those of precarious fortune, when put out to peripheral climes, stood a much greater chance at success simply by virtue of being British, as opposed to the racially and culturally Other colonial subject. There is however an element of hauntology even in this equation, insofar as the working-class British subject harbours within himself a spectre of savagery. Moreover, his person, once of marginal significance, when circulated on the global market has the sudden capacity for worth beyond the labour it can produce directly. 'Dickens reads beneath the superficial prosperity of the City, and implicit in his reading is the fact that the national wealth is based upon, not simply the ornate products of India and China, but far more significantly on an impoverished workforce – in short London is the "capital of capital" precisely because it is the capital of poverty' (Moore 23). If the identity of the nation is constructed around a myth of affluence in danger of collapsing at any time, then the sense of identity will be unstable in the extreme. In some sense this goes as far as to charge the underclass with not being English, in so much as this commercial superiority is based on the fragile fiction of English greatness. 'When British commercial men took over the markets of colonial peoples and places, they were seen as bringing civilization and prosperity to those peoples, as well as to themselves. Thus, rather than the mutual destruction wrought by competition at home, "competition" with peoples abroad brought mutual benefit' (Klaver 104). Such thinking installs within humanity an inherit instability such that competitive violence takes hold as much inside as it does outside, at home and abroad. There is no escape for a culture that has been thus compromised to think not of the body, but rather of its labour, as the true carrier of economic value.

As a man who died from overwork for fear he would become an inadequate provider for his brood, Dickens in life 'regularly expressed his concern about the circulation numbers of his work, he calculates the economic return he can expect as a result, this at the same time he seems to be literally grinding out articles, speeches, and readings, as well as fiction' (Houston, *From Dickens to Dracula* 78). Dickens's freedom of mind is further compromised when his second home, the publishing house, becomes subject to capitalisation, thus taking on the attendant providence of stock offerings. He explicitly refers to feeling imprisoned by the necessity to write, in a letter to Miss Burdett-Coutts on 10 January of 1856, 'I shall try to force myself to write a No. of *Little Dorrit* first and that will hold me prisoner, if I submit, until early next Month' (79–80). Dickens's correspondence with Burdett-Coutts demonstrates the degree to which personal alliances get caught up in financial trappings:

> During the time of writing *Little Dorrit*, he often refers to his bank, the venerable Coutts, requesting for example, appointments to see his account book, or get letters of credit. He expresses disgust too, when his publishers belatedly remit his pay for novel installments because it causes him to be overdrawn at the bank (77).

The fact that he relates these concerns and the condition of his person to Angela Burdett-Coutts, the designated inheritor of the Coutts banking fortune, and at the time the richest heiress in all England, may seem rich indeed until we consider the concomitant rise of socially responsible investment. Burdett-Coutts was part of a newly formed class of philanthrocapitalists, who sought an affinity with the emerging class of professional men like Dickens, borrowing as it were from his literary stock to garner wide social endorsements of their new enterprises amongst the middle class. In terms of social confidence, Dickens was certainly the man to know at this time. Burdett-Coutts and Dickens's newly found public and private association was mutually beneficial in terms of lending their socially minded outputs the appearance of moral righteousness.

In contrast to eighteenth-century mercantilism, which attempted to strengthen the nation with more workers, nineteenth-century capitalism feared more dependent mouths to feed. Canada, Australia and other parts of the empire were to take in those unlikely to prosper in Britain, with the one-way tickets paid for by philanthropists. Burdett-Coutts was a strong advocate for the export of surplus labour, and personally aided Dickens both financially and through social connection to deposit all of his intellectually and commercially forfeit sons abroad to India and Australia as soon as they reached their maturity. Their ideological and entrepreneurial public partnership allowed him to distance himself from their financial failures and mounting proclivities toward debt in a way that was socially laudable. In a greater sense, Burdett-Coutts's genius was to link her bank's public reputation with an enormous range of philanthropic activity, and moreover to allow its ongoing hand in colonial expansion (through Coutts's intimate partnership in the East India Company amongst others) to be associated with 'benevolent' financial schemes such as 'emigration for the poor, the exploration of Africa, the civilisation of native races and the care of the wounded in war. Over her lifetime she is estimated to have given away £3-4 million' (Bishop and Green). It was also said she enjoyed wealth only second to Queen Victoria. She was at least as famous. Today on its website, Coutts Bank speaks of its own imminent legacy:

> During the Victorian era, the Bank had to face new challenges in a fast-changing world. Developing industries were hungry for investment and the new and successful joint stock banks meant fierce competition for the old-established private banking houses. There can be little doubt that the name, reputation and personal fortune of Thomas Coutts inspired confidence in the Bank during his lifetime. It was Angela Burdett-Coutts, as the heir to the name and fortune, who was seen as the public face of the Bank in the Victorian period. In addition the service of younger generations of Marjoribanks and Antrobuses, combined with new names in the partnership

– Coulthurst, Ryder and Malcolm – continued the high level of confidence Coutts enjoyed (Coutts).

Where Coutts would emerge as a winner through its diversification and plurality of partnerships throughout the nineteenth century, Dickens's fictitious House of Clennam demonstrated the catastrophe inherent to the failure to partake in such promiscuous ventures. Those institutions failing to engage in activity beyond the prior limits of pure societal lineage became parasitic to the body politic that now demanded a level of unbridled growth. In the first half of the nineteenth century, with 'the increasing circulation of money, private banking houses, like the House of Clennam, start to lose their clientele and thus their economic force, simply because they cannot diversify their circulation, in the way the newer banks can, as a result they attempt to feed off their novel contemporaries to ruinous end' (Houston, *From Dickens to Dracula* 87). The House of Clennam finds itself out of step with the new financial practices of the times as a private banking house at the time when joint-stock banking is commencing its era of domination. 'One of the most important processes in banking during the nineteenth century was the decline of the private banker and the rise of joint-stock banking (the precursor to modern banks), which with limited liability, increased the amount of money that could be circulated. More importantly, the rise of the joint-stock bank increased the velocity and expansion of circulation' (83).

In addition to capital, there are other fundamental elements missing to conduct a conversion of the House of Clennam into the new types of public currency. Beyond merely the fact of them being off track, Arthur Clennam also considers their other shortcomings:

We have never shown much confidence, or invited much; we have attached no people to us; the track we kept is not the track of the time; and we have been left far behind. I need not dwell on this mother. You know it necessarily (Dickens, *Little Dorrit* 46; bk. 1, ch. 5).

By not keeping up with the twin track of Society, Mrs. Clennam has lost the vital element of confidence that furnishes the crucial juncture between the constituencies of the home and the bank. Arthur's continuing remarks shed light on the fact that the House of Clennam, previously furnished such a 'resort' for interested parties, is in decline:

> 'Even this old house in which we speak', pursued her son, 'is an instance of what I say. In my father's earlier time, and in his uncle's time before him, it was a place of business – really a place of business and business resort. Now, it is a mere anomaly and incongruity here, out of date and out of purpose. All of our consignments have long been made to Rovingham's the commission-merchants; and although, as check upon them, and in the stewardship of my father's resources, your judgment and watchfulness have been actively exerted, still those qualities would have influenced my father's fortunes equally, if you had lived in a private dwelling, would they not?' (Dickens, *Little Dorrit* 46; bk. 1, ch. 5).

Mrs. Clennam, by transferring the resource of temporary resort into permanent abode, has rendered the House of Clennam unusable in the conduct of social equity. She has brought an uncomfortable quality of domesticity into a of space intended for perpetual exchange, and in so doing installed the admissible private element of dwelling into what ought to be a place of public lease. Thus she does not allow for completion, nor return on initial investments. As a result, the House of Clennam has taken on a reputation as a house of infirmity, a dwelling so afflicted in its definition of shelter that it cannot be spoken of on business terms in the present tense. Mrs. Clennam counters Arthur:

> 'Do you consider,' she returned, without answering his question, 'that a house serves no purpose, Arthur, in sheltering your infirm and afflicted – justly infirm and right-eously afflicted – mother?'

To which he replies tellingly:

> 'I was speaking only of business purposes' (Dickens, *Little Dorrit* 46; bk. 1, ch. 5).

Mrs. Clennam continues to wilfully reject Arthur's attempts to put right this past inequity in their business dealings, which forced its conduct to be limited by its tethering to their House. She erroneously equates Arthur's 'journeying and junketing in foreign lands' with 'living a life of vanity and pleasure, 'and equates her own situation as one of imprisonment and bondage to the business. She modulates her anger at her present condition through her servant Flitchwinch: 'but let him look at me, in prison, and in bonds here' (50). She further shackles herself to the failing enterprise by substituting Arthur 'for an old and faithful servant in Jeremiah Flitchwinch', after which she is determined to 'captain' the sinking 'ship', to either 'sink or float with it' (51). She fails in the end to equate perpetual movement with buoyancy, when it comes to her fortunes, and thus threatens to sever the only remaining relation that would allow her to call upon further relations outside her own crumbling domicile. Mrs. Clennam stands in for a kind of historical relic of society in which property guaranteed security. In these new times security can only be borrowed from an economic favour that binds through association and the pooling of wealth. To be left adrift of such currency spells out almost certain demise. During this same era capital experienced its own novel sort of lifespan insofar as 'all commerce is now carried on by the creation, the transfer, and extinction of obligations' (Houston, *From Dickens to Dracula* 80). The collections agent Pancks embodies this new condition in the novel *Little Dorrit*:

> 'Here am I,' said Pancks, pursuing his argument with the weekly tenant. 'What else do you suppose I think I am made for? Nothing. Rattle me out of bed early, set me going, give me as short a time as you like to bolt my meals in, and keep me at it. Keep me always at it, and I'll keep you always at it, you keep somebody else always at it. There you are with the Whole Duty of Man in a commercial country' (Dickens, *Little Dorrit* 160; bk. 1, ch. 13).

One strategy of coping with such intense pressure on the human body to perform value was for individuals to hybridise with the object world around them. 'In crafting his urban characters Dickens gave precedence to the material substratum of their habits and activities, with which the sense of their existence is inextricably bound' (Shin). Hisup Shin observes that 'the human substance of the characters and their material background often become interchangeable' as they meld with 'railways, carriageways, various kinds of vehicles, pieces of furniture and clothing, and other numerous manufactured goods', and that these items 'do not just complement urban dwellers' sense of being; rather they constitute it by becoming their intrinsic parts'. The distinction between Casby and Pancks is one of management to labour. The pressure exerted by Casby upon Pancks transforms him over time into not merely a commercial agent, but more profoundly into a mechanical engine run for the purposes of generating rents. Pancks as 'a little coaly steam-tug will bear down upon it, take it in tow, and bustle off with it' (Dickens, *Little*

Dorrit 160; bk. 2 ch. 13).

During the composition of the novel *Little Dorrit*, Dickens kept a memorandum book in which he made it clear that the mechanical image of Pancks was modeled on the snorting little steam tug on the Thames, towing the unwieldy ship of his commercial master Casby. In order to accomplish such labour, Dickens composes Pancks's entire body from mechanical elements manufactured to endure constant use: 'He was dressed in black and rusty iron grey; had jet black beads of eyes; a scrubby little black chin; wiry black hair striking out from his head in prongs, like forks or hair-pins ... He had dirty hands and dirty broken nails, and looked as if he had been in the coals; he was in a perspiration, and snorted and sniffed and puffed and blew, like a little labouring steam-engine' (Dickens, *Little Dorrit* 160; bk. 2, ch. 13). As items and individuals continue to coalesce through commerce within the space of the novel, 'they tend to adopt characteristics from one another, thus unsettling the notion that the human subject governs the realm of objects', and whilst its characters are 'consistently thrown into a situation beyond the means of their control', their 'claim of authenticity gains its lasting impression not so much through ordered patterns of representation, but by means of evoking a range of disruptive, conflicting tones, clues, gestures, etc.' (Shin, para. 5).

In *Little Dorrit*, the apprehension of experience becomes skewed toward an understanding of the enormous expansion of the global marketplace. Britain's vastly expanded imperial geography of peoples and goods produced a material culture, which was in many ways unprecedented at the start of the new century. This rapid expansion in material wealth had equally unprecedented consequences for Britain's inhabitants. In order to illustrate the displacement caused by the profound changes wrought through the transformation from a system of mercantilism to one of capitalism, Dickens places all the characters of *Little Dorrit* at the periphery of the establishment. In doing so he deploys them as a practicable risk to the smooth functioning of English Society. In this way they are able to pose a subtle challenge to the vast number of social and administrative discourses dedicated at once to promoting capitalism's new commercial ideology whilst maintaining the status quo of patrician power. Despite such impediments, shared among these characters is a sense of unstoppable momentum to bring about social change. Whilst free-market capitalism 'is portrayed as replete with dehumanizing social systems', it can also be observed that Britain's inhabitants continue to offset that potentially debilitating relationship 'with their appetite for life, a will to overcome any obstacle and obtain their objective' (Shin, para. 12).

Little Dorrit, more than any other product of Dickens's imagination, allows parts of the social body to act independently. Characters who achieve self-acting such as the titular character of *Little Dorrit* point the way towards an understanding of 'the body as machine' (Sussman 626). In doing so, 'potentially independent systems' are revealed to the Victorian reader as entirely possible (626). Dickens reveals such a possibility through actions that appear to be repeated, or actions that are undertaken obsessively. Dickens hammers into his readers this type of information, programming them as it were to receive a certain *instruction*. The character and the reader then engage in a type of didactic reciprocity wherein they prefigure a kind of supplemental figure; the prosthetic, posthuman being, who will survive the rise of both industry and capital and emerge as a new class of mobility. They possess a diffuse mode of expression that is not easily captured by liberalism because of its voyeuristic, bureaucratic tendency towards the management of individuals. This new type of subject, by contrast, utilises its parts or subsystems of its body to be able to break free from centralised subjective control. Their organs of labour thus behave autonomously from their egos, allowing such individuals to comport themselves through collective actions. This new social or rather newly socialised body does not need to count individuals amongst itself; rather its agents produce various bodies and dissolve them as needed for operative gain. It becomes substantial, and emerges a subject when it wants or requires something, 'sometimes ... to hilarious effect, as in the intermittent perambulations Mrs. Merdle's bosom throughout *Little Dorrit*' (Sussman and Joseph 622). Sometimes its appearance can be a foreboding one, such as in the tense reoccurrence of Mr. Merdle's complaint, which could never be adequately assessed because it resided

'Where there was a certain point of mental strain beyond which no man could go,' according to his learned physician and yet even he is aware something is taking over an appearance here: 'He has the constitution of a rhinoceros, the digestion of an ostrich, and the concentration of an oyster. I have found nothing the matter with him. He may have some deep-seated recondite complaint. I can't say. I only say, that at present I have not found it' (Dickens, *Little Dorrit* 254; bk. 1, ch. 21).

Like the Physician, who combats Merdle's disease and foreshadows his fraudulent business practice through his observation of his malingering, the social body hangs on and sometimes betrays its paymaster. The shadow of doubt cast by the Physician however is superficial and apparently not catching and yet it does implicate all who surround him by negative example. Dickens writes:

There is no shadow of Mr. Merdle's complaint on Mrs. Merdle's bosom now displaying precious stones in rivalry with many similar superb jewel-stands. There was no shadow of Mr. Merdle's complaint on young Sparkler hovering about the rooms, monomaniacally seeking any sufficiently ineligible young lady with no nonsense about her; there was no shadow of Mr. Merdle's complaint on the Barnacles and Stiltstalkings, of whom whole colonies were present; or on any of the company. Even on himself, its shadow was faint enough as he moved about among the throng, receiving homage (*Little Dorrit* 254; bk. 1, ch. 21).

The shadow for now remains concealed through a combination of cosmetics and accessories. What brought their superficial appearance into wide relief are the traces of labour that surround these multifarious social functions. It is their appearance that 'bring[s] the boundary between the organic structures of the body and the inorganic world of commodities into view' (Novak 32). Within British society, 'the fetishizing logic of the commodity has quietly dissolved the link between the members of the [national] body, making them "accessories," commodities—like two mittens, judged by how well they appear to match' (32). It is clear throughout the novel that the marriages between Mr. and Mrs. Merdle, Mr. and Mrs. Gowan, and Mr. and Mrs. Sparkler do not appear to match well in terms of social status and thus their appearance. In response to these mispairings Mrs. Gowan judges that 'it is in vain ... for people to attempt to get on jumbled against each other in this accidental, matrimonial sort of way; and who cannot look at the untoward circumstance which has shaken them together in the same light. It never does' (Dickens, *Little Dorrit* 254–5; bk. 1, ch. 21).

Their ability to get jumbled together stems from 'the implicit link between economic exchange, currency, and the fragmented body', which makes of these joinings an unhappy union (Novak 39). In each case their forged unity heightens awareness of its differential *composition*, and carries within it the implication of a social order that is decomposing into many rather than just two classes: the rich and the poor. Merdle's complaint, and ultimately his discredit in and amongst all classes in the society, reveals a fiction that subtends all of its produced values, and he must therefore be scapegoated as a fraudster, so as to deflect attention away from the unflattering truth of society's own practice of finance capitalism, which promises wealth for the nation as an organic whole, but in reality offers only piecemeal gains to a limited number of bodies in terms of social mobility.

Merdle's complaint thus stems from his loyalty to a state economy that would rather accept speculation, as opposed to investment, as the villain in finance capitalism than admit that no such distinction exists. Both in the economic discourse and narrative account of the nineteenth-century workings of capitalism, investment stood as the crucial marker for a secure monetary transaction. Its obverse was understood to be financial speculation, which by contrast was the marker of risk. This notion of risk was further underlined by 'speculation's association with gambling', which made it possible to negatively distinguish it from legitimate forms of investment (Wagner, *Financial Speculation* 14). Investment therein came to signify 'the professional, trustworthy, secure, and stable, whereas speculation became linked to the amateurish as well as the risky and ruthless' (14). The two working against one another allowed for a necessary legitimisation of the newly emerging capitalist economy based on the ability of the good of one to overcome the evil of the other. This promise implicated capitalism in a moral vernacular allowing it to participate as it does in the economy of the novel *Little Dorrit* amongst other means of collective faith-keeping.

Despite such adherence, both in the public imagination and throughout the novel there is 'the phobic sense of something repugnant and nihilistic at the core of social life', which is 'fixated on the making and display of money and on the obsessive maintenance of appearances of gentility' (Higbie 201). Such obsession acted to reinforce a dutiful obedience to the market. For its part, society could drive someone to desolation, just 'as Merdle's materialism and consequent inability to believe in anything higher' eventually derive into his mysterious ailment (Higbie 133–4). 'Society and he had so much to do with one another in all things else, that it is hard to imagine his complaint, if he had one, being solely his own affair. Had he that deep-seated recondite complaint, and did any doctor find it out?'(Dickens, *Little Dorrit* 253; bk. 2, ch. 12). It would seem that such a complaint 'has no pre-determined shape of its own, but constantly adjusts itself to the social conditions and systemic logic in which it finds itself. The energy is manifested primarily through incessant gestures and motions of the body, the trajectory of which takes on shifting social as well as physical perspectives' (Shin, para. 12). Mr. Merdle 'clasped himself by the wrists in that constabulary manner of his, pacing up and down the hearth run, or creeping among the rich objects of furniture' in his drawing-room (*Little Dorrit* 558; bk. 2, ch. 12). Such agitation is surely brought on by the inhuman and indeed inhumane qualities of corporeality, which shackle him to the reified world of capital to which Merdle is literally conjoined beyond distinction:

> Mr. Merdle's right hand was filled with the evening paper, and the evening paper was full of Mr. Merdle. His wonderful enterprise, his wonderful wealth, his wonderful Bank, were the fattening food of the evening paper that night ... in the midst of those splendid achievements ... he looked ... like a man in possession of his house under distraint, that a commercial Colossus bestriding his own hearthrug, while the little ships were sailing in to dinner (Dickens, *Little Dorrit* 558–9; bk. 2, ch. 12).

Mr. Merdle's confinement as social fodder is to be short-lived, as his outsized enterprise harbours within it the occasion of a sudden social upheaval. When the day comes to mark his financial gesture, the last of amortised expenditures to boost society, he chooses yet again to borrow another bit of commercial equipment in the form of Mrs. Sparkler's penknife. On that final day, he 'soiled [it] but not with ink' (Dickens, *Little Dorrit* 706; bk. 2, ch. 25). On that occasion, the Physician who attends him observes 'a folded note – half buckled up in [his pocketbook] and half protruding out' (706). This discomfiture foreshadows a reality soon to come: that his complaint has been, simply, 'Forgery and Robbery' (710). That his demise becomes the occasion for the sudden systemic eruption of Society marks him as a man guilty of societal betrayal. Whilst this activity has grave consequence for his many rich patrons, on the other end of the social spectrum Mr. Pancks will carry out his own act of social disobedience, born not of individual grievance, but of communal relief. 'This is precisely the effect created by Pancks's unforeseen renunciation of his servile position in *Little Dorrit*, leading to his final triumph over his stingy employer, when he discloses all the financial and moral shams perpetrated by the latter, to the great delight of tenants who come out to observe the impromptu street tribunal' (Shin para. 12). This act of social defiance bears itself out not through a violent overthrow of the system that inspired it, but rather through its tactical subversion. Pancks's chosen form of action demonstrates how 'the act of challenge becomes effective through the assumption of all the machine-like features remarked upon earlier, thus blurring the line of division between the sign of reification and that of human defiance' (Shin, para. 12).

Quick as lightning, Mr. Pancks, who, for some moments, had had his right hand in his coat pocket, whipped out a pair of shears, swooped upon the Patriarch [Casby] behind, and snipped off the sacred locks that flowed upon his shoulders. In a paroxysm of animosity and rapidity, Mr. Pancks then caught the broad-brimmed hat out of the astounded

Patriarch's hand, cut it down into a mere stewpan, and fixed it on the Patriarch's head. Before the frightful results of this desperate action, Mr. Pancks himself recoiled in consternation ... After staring at this phantom in return, in silent awe, Mr. Pancks threw down his shears, and fled for a place for hiding, where he might lie sheltered from the consequence of his crime. Mr. Pancks deemed it prudent to use all possible dispatch in making off, though he was pursued by nothing but the sound of laughter in Bleeding Heart Yard, rippling through the air and making it ring again (Dickens, *Little Dorrit* 802–3; bk. 2, ch. 32).

Pancks is able to achieve this moment of rebellion as a by-product of his engine-like movement. His act of defiance was carried out with a machine-like precision, spurred by a build-up of corporal momentum within him that finally made him 'attendant not only of himself, but to the whole community of workers in the yard' (Shin para. 12). Banded together in this way, it is possible to witness how they are able to not only survive 'the systemic constraint' of capital, but also 'to transform its negative tendencies into a life-affirming force, if only momentarily' (Shin, para. 12). Pancks's performance 'introduces the intriguing notion that the human body is not a finished form but a kind of structural modality' (Shin para. 12). Such a body can be said to be capable of constantly retooling itself when put under the pressure of outside events. It would also appear that the temporary coalescence of objects and bodies together may find themselves amenable to revolutionary application. The temporary reversal of savagery and civilisation witnessed in the crucial exchange between Pancks and Casby allows for an instant of comparative anatomy and physiology to emerge, and for an eloquent statement of irony about social progress to in turn materialise. Far from appearing to readers as an exact census of a known and knowable world of capital, the labouring classes in the novel appear instead to be expanding the definition of utility profligately in every direction possible.

How this capacity will be housed in the future says everything about the fragility of hierarchy of social and economic value determined by class and gender. London's diligent outcasts toil just below the sight of the wasteful upper classes and the *nouveaux riches*. It is they who are progressively splintering its framework. It is their economic usefulness, which lies just out of sight of 'London's intellectual elite dining inside a dinosaur skeleton at Crystal Palace during the 1851 Great Exhibition' (Sicher 40). It seems obvious that another hothouse would be needed to complement the moral dignity lacking in that one. And yet the common visitor was 'so awestruck ... about the design of the Crystal Palace that they actually began to believe in the transformative power of interior decoration, whereby the arrangement of manufactured objects becomes not only a model for human habitation but also a blueprint for social change ... More than anything else, the Exhibition projected an image of *surplus*' (Richards 28). Alongside its model kitchen was, as the *Edinburgh Review* pointed out, 'its post-office-its branch bank-its telegraph-its miniature railroad-its little army-its police', waking the dreamer up ever-so-subtly to the fact that its model for *Little Britain* was always already foreseen on a monumental public scale (S. Smith 300). This prompted visitors like Horace Greeley 'to imagine the necessity of transferring everything it contain[ed]' beyond 'the already cramped confines of the Victorian home' (Greeley 11). Within the confines of such a reverie, the threat to domestic life was palpable insofar as one was given over to imagining what life would be like once objects necessary to materially circumscribe individual conduct had overtaken the country. *The Economist* purported that the solution to such overcrowding was to at once 'clear the slums and replace them with "the light and elegant, the cheerful and airy, the cheap and wholesome style of building of the Crystal Palace"' and at the same moment expand England as a way to offload the surplus of items, as well as individuals (Economist, 'The Exhibition' 5). The consequence of such a circulation of human capital becomes evident by novel's end when Little Dorrit and Mr. Clennam 'went down' to pass along 'the roaring streets' populated with 'the noisy and the eager, the arrogant and the forward, and the vain, fretted, and chaffed' soon themselves to become attendant to that exercise in offloading (Dickens, *Little Dorrit* 826; bk. 2, ch. 34). For the time being and within the shadow of the collapse of that House, whose chief inhabitant, 'lived and died a statue', 'the storm and dust had cleared away and the summer night was calm again' (Dickens, *Little Dorrit* 794; bk. 2, ch. 31). Without benefit of their former institutional sanctuary, inseparable and blessed, the newlywed Clennams modestly sauntered on towards an as-yet-unnamed future one.

Mrs. Clennam dies only to become a relic not dissimilar to the dinosaur on display at the Great Exhibition, her once imposing house doomed to persist as a barren framework for her successors to contemplate. Nonetheless, there is reciprocity between the newlywed Clennams and their predecessors, insofar as they are driven by a need to strike out on their own, firstly to the space of colonial fantasy and secondly to the place of colonial legacy. What fortunes await them are largely the product of how well they are able to exchange the state's organs of subjective control for a series of autonomous moments that reclaim that spatial imagining and turn what passes for reality into something more. They must continue to do so all their lives not by escaping the gravity of finance capitalism, but by dwelling comfortably within it through belief in a moral velocity that is higher still, and by expressing a novel ambition to make outpacing the market characteristic of their perambulations.

The spaces of confinement and mobility are a matter of degree, and imagination divorced from reality is just so much escapism whose relevance so readily tires when paced against the threat of complacency from without, but also from within. '"Do Not Forget," the phrase inherited from Arthur's father (ironically, appropriately), suggests that whether one is located in the 1780s, the 1820s or the 1850s, in never forgetting the English can never move on. Given the particular economic rise of the United States particularly and Germany shortly thereafter, in the period of publication of *Little Dorrit*, the novel becomes available as all too prescient' (Wolfreys 58–9). In closing it is helpful to consider that Dickens's career ends with a return to a hyper-vigilant nationalism in *The Mystery of Edwin Drood*; a novel that concerns itself not with the inability of Britain to radically transform its political system to stave off competition from the rise of Western imperial powers, but rather with the prevailing political system's inability to account for imperial expansion into the home territory. Toward the end of his life, Dickens feared that Britons, in failing to achieve political reform at home, might radically transform themselves instead and squander their cultural and biological inheritance through a promiscuous (consumer) merger with these foreign contacts or foreign presences that offered temporary respite from the grinding pressure of finance capitalism. Finally he understood that these crowding ghosts that haunted Britain's major industrial cities were the vacated forms once occupied by poor factory workers and imperial subjects. Incarcerated by the system, these workers would never forget nor quite depart from the debt owed to them by their former masters, and would perhaps one day find a way to rally payment.

The Postscript to *Little Dorrit*

In the two intervening centuries since the writing of *Little Dorrit*, it is possible to witness the bank as an institution extending its reach well beyond the domestic sphere to create speculative fortunes, economic and military catastrophes across the globe, which are at once the echo of history and its refrain. In an increasingly multipolar world now almost exclusively governed by neoliberal economics, what might yet emerge may be more extreme than anything we have seen so far in the competition for commercial preeminence. The reason Britain entered into the Crimean War in the mid-nineteenth century was 'to halt Russian imperial expansion, to guarantee ostensible freedom for a weaker nation and most importantly, to protect commercial interests in Asia' (J. Cain 13). The same list could easily apply to the present-day conflict in Ukraine. The Russophobia engendered by 'the real or imagined dangers posed from the threat of oriental autocracy to middle-class economics and democracy', much as it did in the nineteenth century, has shaped the course of superpower politics leading into the present crisis (14). The Crimean War represented for many Britons, including Dickens himself, 'the limitations' of its 'commercial and military power, and of its precarious place in a world of hostile imperial forces' (14). In much the same way, America and Europe are now concerned that such perpetual crisis is being recognised by vast segments of the global population as a structural feature of deregulated and interconnected financial markets.

The elites who control a third of the world's liquid assets, including amongst them the City of London Corporation and EL Rothschild investment firm, have recently come to 'fear the implications of another structural feature of these markets that has come under public scrutiny with the rise of neoliberal free marketisation; the disenfranchisement of the vast majority of the planetary population under decades of capitalist business-as-usual' (Ahmed). The civil unrest generated by this systemised economic inequality has resulted in events that are suddenly overwhelming the western political elite which is hastily preparing itself for further mass unrest, as the implications of its broken economic model must logically and finally visit its societal chaos on their home populations. Today's capitalism,

retooled to service the interests of neoliberal corporatised governance, has made the global situation 'all the more dangerous for
the fact that the elites of the west have not just become powerless
diplomatically, but seen their political legitimacy eroded during
the five years of post-Lehman crisis management' (P. Mason,
'Iraq, Syria, Egypt, Ukraine'). The danger we face perhaps even
more than that jaundiced verdict 'is of an unprecedented
breakdown of the global strategic order in which the exit routes
from economic crisis are getting mixed up in a new, unstable,
diplomatic situation' (P. Mason). That breakdown could easily
lead us into another botched imperial war perpetuating further
economic and societal instability because we are led to believe
that there is simply no alternative to neoliberal governance and
responsibility for such a situation is nobody's fault and
everyone's responsibility to shoulder.

Neoliberalism's retooling of capitalism in the decades since its
inception has resulted in the fall of living standards, the
abandonment of the rule of law, and the flourishing of
government and corporate corruption and collusion. At the same
time it has managed to demonise any other form of economic
arrangement that might promote gainful employment, stablise
costs of living, and guarantee a reliable social safety net.
Neoliberal policy has fractured the sovereignty of the state,
systematically robbing it of its ability to guide its industries and
manage its resources. Top-level government posts, which had
been formerly the domain of the aristocracy in a liberal economy,
have in more recent times come to be the domain of nouveau-
riche oligarchs, corruptly tied to the interests of speculative,
private enterprise. Within such a lurid political atmosphere
multinational corporations have been increasingly able to
establish themselves as mini-states that are in turn able to evade
paying taxes, sock away huge quantities of wealth in offshore
accounts, and park their hot money in prime overseas real estate.
For its part, 'Britain has for years allowed Russian oligarchs to

offload their dirty money in its banks, buy up London mansions, football clubs and newspapers, and send their children to elite British schools and universities' (Figes, 'In Ukraine').

With regard to the contemporary crisis in Ukraine, 'Bob Dudley, BP's chief executive, last month announced it would be business as usual in Russia. BP has a 20% share in Rosneft, the Russian state oil company, whose boss, Igor Sechin, is included in the latest US [financial] sanctions list' imposed against Russia in punishment for its annexation of Crimea and material support of ethnic Russians in Eastern Ukraine (Figes, 'In Ukraine'). Jenkins comments that 'It is beyond hypocrisy for the west to demand sanctions against Moscow when it happily buys Russian gas and sells Russia guns, ships, Knightsbridge flats and places at Eton'. Cameron, for his part, 'has been protecting the City of London by soft-pedalling on financial sanctions' for fear that in pushing harder, 'London would seize up as a conduit for the tax-dodging billions of the Russian oligarchs' with little thought to the consequences for the average Ukrainian or Russian (P. Mason, 'Financial Sanctions on Russia'). It is no coincidence that this trend towards poverty for the many coincides with the decline of Anglo-American predominance in the world. Instead we are entering into a new era where other former great powers such as China and Russia seek to compete with one another to parry their wealth as a currency of geopolitical influence at the expense of their own people's security. The irony for Europe is at a time when its political and economic project faces electoral rejection, former Soviet republics like Ukraine still remain eager to become new member states. What the majority of Europe's citizens are opposed to has been their treatment under the policies of neoliberal governance which have made them poorer and their lives more precarious in the cause of market unification. Even a neoliberal guru like George Soros must concede that the original promise of the EU to pool the financial resources of all its members for the benefit of the greater good has transformed 'into something radically different: a relationship of creditors and debtors in which the creditor countries impose conditions that perpetuate their dominance' (Soros).

Conflicts such as the one in Ukraine have long created financial opportunities for multinational financiers to exploit. Even those powers not directly involved in the conflict stand to benefit from increased military expenditure above the level of revenues for taxation, forcing government parties onto the private bond market. Those who have preeminence in that market stand to benefit the most from such financial arrangements. Such was the case during the Crimean War of 1854–56. At that time it was the Rothschilds who took it upon themselves to underwrite the debt of France, Britain, Austria, and Turkey, which happened in the end to be the winning side. Its rival Barings had the misfortune to be the banker to the losing side, Russia. While the war in general had a major negative impact on international finance, 'the Rothschilds prospered relative to other financiers because of their international partnership structure, which created intra-firm diversification, and their dominance in the bond markets that governments needed to finance military costs' (Ferguson 72). The Rothschilds outcompeted Barings, which lost a significant amount of political capital by issuing Russian government loans. The Rothschilds's ascendancy was the result of their development of a system to finance state debt by state-issued, fixed-interest bearer bonds that were traded on international exchanges but that could also be traded privately. Through their development of the bond market, the Rothschilds played a critical role in the financialisation of the world. Heinrich Heine credited them with bringing down the thousand year reign of feudalism, by destroying 'the predominance of the land, by raising the system of state bonds to supreme power: thereby endowing money with the same privileges as land' (Heine qtd. in Ferguson xxiv). Heine ruefully asserted, 'money is the god of our time, and Rothschild is his profit' (qtd. in Ferguson xxv). This was hardly an overstatement if we consider that by the early part of the nineteenth century, Rothschilds 'had transformed itself into the biggest bank in the world and that by 1825 they had become ten times the size of their nearest rivals, the Baring Brothers' (Ferguson xxv). Equally they played a crucial role in precipitating and resolving the Panic of 1825 to its profitable advantage.

Under Thomas Barings's management, his 'bank was appointed as London financial agents by the Russian government in the mid-1850s, and a string of sterling bond issues followed, confirming the firm's succession to Hopes as the government's most favoured overseas issuing house. However, this was the only significant continental sovereign account which Barings held consistently; elsewhere, especially in central Europe and Iberia, the Rothschilds proved unassailable' (Orbell). The Barings Brothers were tasked 'with the job of evacuating £1 million worth of gold from the Bank of England on the eve of the Crimean War. Little wonder that in London Palmerston labelled Thomas Barings ... the known and avowed ... private agent of the Government of Russia' (Clarke 248). While it was true that the Russian government used Barings to evacuate its gold from London on the eve of the outbreak of the Crimean War, 'during the same war Barings supported Russian credit by marketing sufficient Russian government bonds to cover interest payments due to London bondholders' (Orbell). Consequently, Thomas Barings continued to assert significant influence on Tory politics based on his power to manipulate such events within the realm of international finance.

The Baring Brothers were most certainly viewed as rivals of the Rothschilds; indeed it was this rivalry that made the Barings one of the most powerful financial entities in mid-Victorian Britain. It was the Duc de Richelieu who, in 1817, is reputed to have made the best-known remark about Baring Brothers & Co. when he listed the six great powers in Europe as England, France,

Prussia, Austria, Russia – and Baring Brothers. There was a glaring omission to his list; Rothschild. Vesperoni is not exaggerating by saying that: 'from the Congress of Vienna of 1815 to the Crimean War of 1853, the House of Rothschild had absolute control of high finance, being the largest creditor of most European powers. During the "Rothschild's era" the rivalry between European powers was higher than ever. Their race to world supremacy led to a massive growth of public debt, to fund the making of the modern states as they are known today. The Rothschilds financed each side of this race' (Vesperoni 8). The motive of high finance was financial gain; to obtain and maintain it, 'it was necessary to keep in with governments whose end was power and conquest' (Polanyi 11). How this was won was largely a matter of them moving their battlefronts against one another from the centre of their nations to the peripheral spaces of their imperial outposts. This new geostrategy complemented the aim of the Rothschilds as the wealthy chief financiers of war. In their business dealings, they were impervious to moral consideration; they had no objection to any number of minor, short or localised wars that could send them into further gains. They also understood that 'their business would be impaired if there were a general war between the Great Powers [that] should interfere with the monetary foundations of the system' (11). Hence their interest in the Crimean War was as a colonial event that would allow the Great Powers to flex their economic and political might without coming into direct territorial conflict with one another.

Each of the Great Powers involved entered into the conflict with their own discreet geopolitical agendas: 'the Russia tsar sought to establish a protectorate over the Ottoman Empires' Orthodox subjects, France's prime objective was to restore its international status, following its defeat in 1815. Britain still distrusted France but feared above all that Russia would fill the vacuum created by the collapse of the Ottoman Empire and threaten British India' (Benn 388). As Orlando Figes points out,

'Russophobia was arguably the most important element in Britain's outlook on the world in the years preceding the war' (Benn 388). Of the figures in government Lord Palmerston was the most virulently anti-Russian and it was his conclusion early on that 'the Russian threat could only be countered by the dismemberment of the Russian Empire, including the liberation of Poland from Russian rule' (389). The British, despite their determination to bring Russia to its knees, had done little to establish aims, nor tactics, to actually fight this war. Their awesome failure to plan was soon evident when their commanders equipped their troops with summer uniforms to fight in Crimea's bitter winter conditions. This eventually led to massive illness and death due to frostbite and cholera. Their wounded were sent to Turkey for medical attention and soon discovered that its hospitals lacked the most basic of facilities; there were no toilets, nor bandages. It was a disaster that would end the political career of Lord Aberdeen, with the bellicose Lord Palmerston replacing him in the second year of this hapless war, which Russia eventually lost due to its antiquated weaponry and less formidable war chest.

The physical casualties of this war were large: '25,000 British, 100,000 French and up to a million Russians died', almost all of disease and neglect (Bloy, 'General Comments on the Crimean War'). While the British and French triumphed in their goal to curb the further expansion of the Russian Empire, the war itself was widely condemned due to the incompetence of the government in orchestrating its military campaign and engaging its forces in what was widely perceived as a needless loss of life. In terms of it being a colonial event, it can be said that Russia itself was not really defeated, because the Russian homeland proper was not attacked. So far as Britain was concerned, the end of the Crimean War had a number of results that were little to do with the war itself. What was perceived as a disastrous foreign policy brought down the Earl of Aberdeen's coalition government, making way for Palmerston to emerge as Prime Minister, a post from which he was to dominate English politics for ten years because he brought an honourable end to the war. While the war may have significantly enhanced Palmerston's political reputation, it severely diminished the national coffers to the tune of '£76 million, which had to be met out of increased taxation' (Bloy, 'General Comments on the Crimean War').

Ironically, 'Palmerston had joined Lord Aberdeen's administration in 1852 in the unfamiliar role of Home Secretary, as much because he needed the money as anything else' (Cavendish). When the Aberdeen government dissolved in controversy based on its misconduct of the war, 'the Queen was forced to appoint Palmerston as PM after failing to find anyone who would accept the post' (Bloy, 'Henry John Temple'). Such were the shambles of British government during this era. Perhaps in this way the tale of *Little Dorrit* was a predictive text, insofar as Cameron's neoliberal Conservative coalition government plays out its own affairs in a way reminiscent of the Earl of Aberdeen's liberal Conservative coalition government; the only difference is that his was apparently far more transparent in its aims. Aberdeen explicitly stated that 'the great object of the Queen's present ministers, and the great characteristic of their Government would be the maintenance and prudent extension of Free Trade. That was the mission with which they were peculiarly entrusted' (qtd. in Marx, 'A Superannuated Administration').

Karl Marx, writing from London on Tuesday, January 11, 1853, quotes the Earl of Aberdeen's assurance that there is also no difference between Peelites and Whigs, Conservatives and Liberals. In Aberdeen's opinion: 'The country is tired of distinctions without meaning, and which have no real effect on the conduct or principles of public men. No Government is possible except a Conservative Government, and it is equally true that none is possible except a Liberal Government' (Marx, 'A Superannuated Administration'). Marx concludes: 'the entire

Aristocracy agree, that the Government has to be conducted for the benefit, and according to the interests of the middle-class, but they are determined that the bourgeoisie are not to be themselves the governors of this affair; and for this object all that the old Oligarchy possess of talent, influence and authority are combined, in a last effort, into one Administration, which has for its task [to keep] the bourgeoisie, as long as possible, from the direct enjoyment of governing the nation' (Marx). Here we find ourselves in the orbit once more of the Barnacles and the Silkstalkings and their spurious choreography of Circumlocution. What is transpiring today in Cameron's coalition government is a similar endless shuffle of power amongst the aristocracy and its elite financiers with little if any accountability to the public, who nonetheless remain subject to their whims. On the surface it may well appear that those given bureaucratic supremacy over the masses are a gormless, nepotistic lot, but in reality their apparent antipathy towards anything resembling investments in public health, state education, social infra-structure, and subjective rights has very little to do with enacting reforms to create a system of fairness for the labouring classes prepared to work hard, and much more to do with preserving the idle, skewed well-being of their own ilk. Indeed, if examined closely their policies over what now amounts to hundreds of years have functioned as a kind of socialism –for the rich – wherein the superficial appearance of political folly they project functions nevertheless to ensure their continued profiteering from the manipulation of public finances to suit their private interests.

When Cameron formulated his coalition government comprised of Conservatives and Liberal Democrats in 2010, '23 of the 29 members of the new cabinet were discovered to be worth more than £1m' (Owen). Cameron as Prime Minister was himself valued a £4m. His Deputy Prime Minister Nick Clegg's fortune was officially valued at £1.9m at the time of his appointment.

Like his coalition partner Cameron, Clegg's father made millions in the City. Amongst the most notable fortunes of the other cabinet members was that of Minister of State for the Cabinet Office, Oliver Letwin, valued at £1.6m. Previous to that he was a former Rothschild banker. Even as he was appointed he continued to hold numerous investments from his time in the City. Chief Secretary to the Treasury David Laws, whose fortune is estimated at £1m–2m is said to 'have made so much money in the City that he was able to retire at the age of 28, after betting $1billion of his company's money on the value of the dollar – and guessing the right way' (Owen). Cameron's team of Ministers was almost exclusively drawn from the ranks of the financial elite who obtained their fortunes through speculative City earnings. At the time of the coalition government's formation their total declared wealth combined amounted to a staggering £60m (Owen). This at a time in the nation's history when '80% of civil servants earned less than £30,000 a year' (Barrow). The average median income for a full-time worker in Britain in 2010 stood at £20,801 according the Office of National Statistics, hardly making the case for a shared class-consciousness amongst the nation's leadership with its public.

Cameron's twenty-first century ascension to political power resembles the well-worn path taken by the aristocratic prime ministers of the nineteenth century, following on from 'a long tradition of public-school "toffs" using the party as a vehicle for running the country' (Caldwell). At the time of his election Britain 'was heavily dependent on banking, site of a wild real estate boom and saddled with mind-boggling levels of personal credit-card debt'; an economic shambles 'for which voters blamed Brown'. Even then 'the gap between rich and poor was wider in Britain than it [was] in most advanced economies' (Caldwell). That gap now more accurately resembles a maw, into which a whole generation will be swallowed, in order to appease the greed of their elite financial creditors firmly in charge of the government and likely to win a Conservative victory outright in the next general election in 2015.

We would be wrong to consider the politics of austerity as merely a delusory project on the part of the ultra-rich to bankrupt whole nations. Rather we must add to that an understanding of the role of corporate subsidy on the part of governments to bankroll whole industries including the biotech, computer, aerospace, pharmaceutical and security industries which are lavished with tax giveaways at the cost of creating a veritable 'poverty draft of poor whites, Blacks, Latinos, and Asians looking for a way to earn a living' (Roy 159). If they fail to 'legitimately' do so they are absorbed into the prison system, where their labour can be exploited without the need for anything more than the superficial appearance of payment or promotion. The combination of a precarious labour market for the working classes, and a wide-reaching privatised carceral system brings into sharp relief a society increasingly based on the discipline of its economically weakest subjects, a rationale of military intervention abroad to suit neoimperial corporate interests and the forced transfer of wealth from an expanding class of debtors to an ever-narrowing class of privileged and powerful creditors. Fyodor Dostoevsky once remarked that he measured the quality of a society by the quality of its prisons. The fact that so many have become modern-day debt houses says a great deal about 'criminal enterprise' and how it has come to be reconceived in America and increasingly in Europe as the ultimate profit centre upon which to base other forms of mass exploitation. As we witness more and more disfranchised working-class individuals emerging from failed neoliberal economies, the need to house those engaging in acts of civil disobedience will become paramount with profit once again figuring at the centre of that enterprise.

Cosmopolitan Fortunes: Imperial Labour and Metropolitan Wealth in Dickens's *Great Expectations*

In *Great Expectations*, the spatial history of Britain's relationship to its penal colony, Australia, is mapped by positing Magwitch's imperial labour as both central to the text, and part of a greater spatial history that crucially intersects with the linear biography of Pip's development. This is done in a way that substantially rewrites both Pip's history and the history of modernity more generally to include matters of empire. Taking such a broad view of the events that transpire in the novel reveals within it 'a "domestic" existence thoroughly defined by a world economy and the imperial relations sustaining it' (Lesjak 91). Crucial to the development of this economy is the emergence of a class of capitalistic gentlemen, whose wealth and situation are founded on financial consolidation, speculation and the rise of a global capitalism that brings foreign wealth flooding into Victorian London through licit and illicit means. It is this imperial factor that separates Pip's temporal trajectory from his dead parents and brothers, and allows him to have a second, spatially directed opportunity to be reborn as Magwitch's son, forming part of a new generation: the sons of Empire, whose fortunes are generated solely through imperial wealth. Suvendrini Perera describes 'the processes that construct Australia as an unquiet grave in *Great Expectations*' as the same ones that 'underwrite and complement the establishment of home and place not only in the novel[s] but in the confident English communities achieved' in places like London, Liverpool, Manchester and Bristol where empire is exploited as a constitutive presence in their reification (13).

For this reason Magwitch, as a former convict and forced labourer, figures as a spectre in the narrative of *Great*

Expectations. His appearance represents an unsightly truth underpinning the class of genteel wealth: that its largesse comes as a product of rough labour practices both at home and abroad. It is Magwitch who embodies such a reality, and who must be actively barred and repressed from making an appearance as a self-made man, because his success threatens the bourgeois order that is precariously coming into its own. His appearance must be foreclosed upon in order for this deception about their innate abilities to be forcibly upheld, and the lack thereof upheld as a grievance against their working-class and poor brethren. When held to account for those of working-class origin, 'the novel gives us a sordid tale of endless shame and self-abasement, mediated by acute moments of degradation, fear and the threat of bodily harm' (Lesjak 95). This is the behavioural logic that holds this system of deception in place both at home and abroad, and prevents the nation's inhabitants from questioning the labour system that subtends the production of wealth. It allows the middle class to participate in a culture premised on the invisibility of work and class and its effects upon the body, dissimulating its appearance through a society that revels in frivolity, rather than contemplate the extraordinary evil visited upon the classes that reside below it and furnish its comforts and distractions.

New forms of poverty and debt subtend this sudden rise in financial authority as the nineteenth century dawns, and find their reiteration at mid-century with increasing anxiety around the issue of inheritance. A new Social Darwinism is emerging at the time of Dickens's writing *Great Expectations* in 1860, which lends itself to an atavistic interpretation of those men who fail to achieve the society's 'great expectations' around the accumulation of wealth. The failure to legitimate oneself through financial means becomes increasingly associated with the risk of incarceration. Such a risk beleaguers the prospect of class mobility and functions to delimit the power of the working-class male body through various means – communal displacement, monetary debt, occupational drudgery – which often act in concert to one another to apprehend and burden that body. Dickens responds to this situation through the introduction of the character Magwitch, his labourious body standing in for just so much oppression visited upon the imperial subject in line with the private accumulation of wealth founded on the primitive exploitation of mankind. It is no coincidence that all the major plots in the novel intersect in some way with Magwitch's, nor that the product of his labour is the source of expectations far greater than himself.

Magwitch's appearance makes a particular type of labour visible in a way that unsettlingly reveals a greater truth at the heart of liberal governance: that life itself operates at the behest of the market and as such is continuous with it at every moment. Therefore none of life's activities can be perceived as being unregulated nor free from the constraints of toil. Therefore Magwitch's appearance is never done labouring for a cause, making the superficial British story match up to the deep Australian story, making his fortunes line up with those of Pip and finally making visible by whom and under what arduous conditions great expectations at home are precariously upheld by forces abroad. The anxiety such an appearance would generate in the public's imagination stems from a tacit under-standing and acceptance on their part that all gentlemen are the products of a carefully orchestrated social production, which must meticulously conform to a national ideal.

Together these gentlemen comprise, to use Benedict Anderson's terminology, 'an imagined community' whose charter for belonging relies on the exclusion of undesirable individuals, especially those who are identified as criminal or foreign to its elite composition. 'The ideal of the gentleman therefore must be posed against "countertypes" such as the criminal or the working class man', who must be 'marginalised in order to construct their own superiority' (Golbort v). In the nineteenth century, 'the ideal of the gentleman formed the very basis of the social and political accommodation between the aristocracy and the middle classes' (Gilmour 2). Magwitch's aspiration to make his gentleman born of an act of social evolution fundamentally challenges the belief that gentility is an inherent, natural characteristic of the upper classes, as much as coarseness and criminality is of the lower classes. To pose a direct challenge to the righteousness of this order is akin to performing an act of serious social transgression.

In Dickens's novel he explicitly refers to Magwitch as a monster, with references to Mary Shelley's *Frankenstein* (1818), 'in a way that recalls the word's etymological root in the Latin *monstrare*, to show' (Hutchings 42). *Frankenstein* is written perhaps not coincidentally a couple of years shy of the decade, the 1820s, in which *Great Expectations* is set. In demonstrating such a comparison it becomes possible for readers to fully appreciate the threat inherent in the idea of an Australian convict becoming capable of making a British gentleman, because in the act of elevating Pip's status, Magwitch himself becomes edified in such a way that he threatens to bring down the whole class system. Furthermore, in the shift from mercantilism to capitalism, nationalism to imperialism, that is now taking place across British society, there emerges a very real prospect of the loss of protection for the ancestral class of 'gentleman', whose strict boundaries of inclusion were increasingly permeated by those in possession of financial capital.

Magwitch in this way becomes a doubly unsavoury product himself, and the infernal citizen of not one but two underworlds: the figurative underworld of violent crime in Britain where he has made his illicit reputation, and the literal underworld of Australia where he has made his licit fortune. The fact that Pip as a nascent gentleman can only associate himself with the former, rather than the latter, says a great deal about how the concept of gentleman is effectively plotted within the national imagination, and the price it costs to enact an alteration, which deviates from its strict design. Magwitch's attempt to bewitch the system is cast along the lines of a dark art, which allows Magwitch to possess his creation, acting literally through Pip, inciting him to perform a sophisticated comprehension of gentility to achieve his desired effect: 'admiring the fine books on Pip's shelves, he says "You shall read 'em to me, dear boy! And if they're in foreign languages wot I don't understand, I shall be just as proud as if I did"' (Dickens, *Great Expectations*, 303; ch. 39).

Magwitch's attempts to programme Pip through literature, and foreign literature at that, have vast implications here because the print culture of the nineteenth century is central to the 'imagined communities' of Anderson's argument, as the concept of nationhood becomes formalised across Europe in this new media era of newspapers and novels. Sarah Golbort argues that the category of 'gentleman' functions as a sort of sub-nation in Britain, insofar as the gentlemen themselves operate 'as a unified collective, as sovereign and limited in size, just as a nation does' (11). The introduction of the novel challenges the very basis of this formation, insofar as it serves the dual purpose of educating the reader about both identity and nationality. Moreover, the novel innovatively couples with capitalism to produce original forms of relationality among the classes, which bring their profound interconnectivity with one another into broad relief.

Magwitch describes to Pip the class denigration he endured at the behest of British colonists during his long period of exile in New South Wales as follows: 'the blood horses of them colonists might fling dust over me as I was walking; what do I say? I says to myself, "I am making a better gentleman nor ever *you'll* be!"' (Dickens, *Great Expectations* 678; ch. 39). The social exclusion Magwitch refers to here discerns its logic not in the law, but in nature, the new biological hierarchy of Darwin, which elegantly comingles with the law to explain the emergence of the criminal as a product not merely of social deviation, but of biological regression. By contrast Magwitch's physical reappearance in New South Wales is one that combines a logic of survival with a mutation of the spirit of endurance. It is this spark of ingenuity that he transfers over to create his new breed of gentleman, one that is not animated through pedigree, but through the mongrel materials of livestock, joint-stock and speculation. It is not 'only the older generation that makes the younger out of haphazard materials' (Gallagher and Greenblatt 181). Rather they act in collusion, in manufacturing what can only be born out of the unprecedented enlivening of power and commerce. What fuels such a compact to create has its beginnings at the level of mobility; that is to say 'the mobility of society itself', which in turn creates the ground that eventually elevates men like Pip 'to the developmental stages of civilisation' (Tamai 4).

The summons that Pip anticipates receiving from his past does not come in the form of a ghostly ancestral visitation, but rather in a much more sinister type of calling: a familial relation to come not born of affiliation, but rather accident, or indeed happenstance. Or worse still, imposed exile by the state of one's lawful biological antecedents. Pip's parentage comes at once from the already reanimated dead, making it easy for him to recognise that condition residing in other persons such as Magwitch and Miss Havisham, who somehow come to resemble them in the ambulatory world, 'corresponding to the odd idea that [his father] was a square, stout, dark man, with curly black hair ... and that [his] mother was freckled and sickly' (Dickens, *Great Expectations* 373; ch.1). These are the novel's undead characters who return to Pip as possessive parents. Other figures as well seem to have the capacity to unnaturally persist despite the attempted murder of them, including Mrs. Gargery, Compeyson and Magwitch. These characters come to death and to life by degrees. Pip's interest in suspending animation backwards and forwards was in no way unique, as he was the fictional product of a real age preoccupation that attempted to straddle the increasing divide between theological and epistemological knowing. The fact that doubt and guilt were twin agents pursuing Pip from a very young age suggests that he is a product of a certain crisis in understanding in the origins of life itself.

In the nineteenth century, life was observed to dwell beyond the flesh, through various media including electricity, magnetism and ether. All form the basis for an understanding of life as something transferrable and capable of transit. Being able to summon the spark of life beyond the boundary of a discreet physical body became the key pre-occupation of mesmerists, who believed that there is a shared medium of vitality that can be tapped to bring into concert beings either very close or very far away, and that instances of apparent death allow the spark of life to travel while the body itself is dormant. Dickens himself became an avid mesmerist. He, as well as his dear friend and fellow mesmeric devotee Chauncey Hare Townshend (to whom he dedicated the novel *Great Expectations*), believed that 'people might sometimes "send emanations" of themselves across distances through the ether, so that their bodies could be located in one place, and their selves viewable in a subtle form, in another' (Gallagher and Greenblatt 194). The more the seemingly inanimate characters of Magwitch, Miss Havisham and Mr. Jaggers come alive, the more the ordinary living characters of Pip, Estella and Molly seem subordinated to their very particular expectations. These extraordinary characters appear to busy themselves organising social categories in which to ultimately place these subordinated individuals. They operate through devout belief that the individuals whom they produce for this purpose will supersede their makers, when they are released into the social marketplace as perfected models. Their mystique, once placed there, derives not from 'their successful impersonation of reality, but from the energy invested in them' (204).

The currency of the age was supported not just by wealth, but also through a strict biological hierarchy, which is why Estella is able to overcome her poor background by becoming the ersatz daughter of Miss Havisham, who literally reprogrammes her to pass into society undetected despite her degenerate beginnings. Her development figures into the narrative as an act of societal revenge on the part of Miss Havisham. It is cruelly enacted through a number of scenes, which suggest Estella's emotional abandonment and virtual imprisonment within Satis House for the whole of her upbringing. Her situation says a great deal about the inequality of such a bargain struck between the two parties of Mr. Jaggers and Miss Havisham. Equally these parties themselves are the products of a highly differentiated national body where economic, ethnic and gender inequalities were produced on 'strongly biologized terms' (Zwierlein 338).

Along those same lines, we must consider that the manufacture of Estella as a gentlewoman is no less radical a project than Magwitch's determination to fashion Pip into a gentlemen. The crucial difference is the stage of development at which such interference into nature is attempted. It may be argued that for an adolescent Pip, the experiment in transformation comes too late to be convincing, whereas in the case of Estella, such manipulation takes place at the formative age of infancy, wherein a far greater influence might prevail. Nonetheless the risks to the individual in terms of success are great, and Estella's profound lack of emotionality is invoked by Dickens as evidence to the reader that she has turned out wrong as a result of Miss Havisham's most unnatural form of child-rearing. Her presence in society represents a serious breach to ideas about the physiological formation of individuals in nineteenth-century culture at large, which helped 'to construct a culture of separate corporeal realities where the bodies of men and women, the poor, the aristocracy, and the middle class were not only treated differently but were thought to have radically different needs and desires coming out of different bodily configurations' (Michie 409).

Estella's appearance challenges the norms of representation in the nineteenth-century novel, insofar as she, unlike Pip, appears superficially to bear none of the undesirable physical character-istics that would relate any aspect of her appearance to her lower-class origins. This at a time when the lower classes conven-tionally appeared in Victorian novels as differentially embodied. Dickens does not entirely part ways with this convention however. The marginal characters who torment Pip on the road to bettering his class status by-and-large inhabit either grotesque bodies such as Orlick's, or outwardly exhibit repulsive character traits such as Mrs. Joe's angriness and aggression. The socially deviant nature of these working-class characters underlines, by way of contrast, what is perceived as the physical and psychical normality of Herbert Pocket and John Wemmick, as the novel's middle-class protagonists. Anne-Julia Zwierlein discerns that Dickens's writing 'frequently combines the idea of a hierarchical social order with a metaphorical "biological ladder"' (342). It is this order of appearance that makes it impossible for someone like Magwitch, whose moral ambiguity cannot be overcome, to be capable of even superficial reform, let alone innate reform, as the novel's criminal subject. Pip reluctantly observes that:

> Whatever he put on, became him less (it dismally seemed to me) than what he had worn before. To my thinking, there was something in him that made it hopeless to attempt to disguise him. The more I dressed him and the better I dressed him, the more he looked like the slouching fugitive on the marshes ... I believe too that he dragged one of his legs as if there were still a weight of iron on it, and that from head to foot there was Convict in the very grain of the man. The influences of his solitary hut-life were upon him besides and gave him a savage air that no dress could tame (Dickens, *Great Expectations* 321; ch. 40).

Magwitch's body therefore stands in for both a criminality and a biological atavism that cannot avoid capture when observed by those who occupy a superior social standing. Whilst these are portrayed as innate realities bearing upon his form, it is also apparently the case that 'experiences and habits have become inscribed on his organism; un-conscious movements and modes of behavior' thus advertising the fact that in his attempt to pass for a gentleman he is not only 'betraying his social position', but more importantly his biological one (Zwierlein 342). 'In all his ways of sitting and standing, and eating and drinking ... in these ways and a thousand other small nameless instances arising every minute in the day, there was Prisoner, Felon, Bondsman, plain as plain could be' (Dickens, *Great Expectations* 321; ch. 40).

How one status had become the other is revealed when we as readers are made aware that in the past the gentleman Compeyson and the criminal Magwitch were involved together in 'swindling, handwriting forging, stolen bank-note passing and such like' (Dickens, *Great Expectations* 705; ch. 42). Together they are 'acting as agents in the "black economy", the presumed converse of legitimate commercial activity (Watson 494). The results of this are their conviction and transportation for such crimes, which were 'comparable to the status of treason only a century before', and as such 'held a special horror for the capitalist society' Dickens's readers had begun to formally inhabit as the new century dawned (Watson 494–5). To appreciate the significance of their threat to society we must come to understand what forgery meant operationally for this society in the midst of its epoch-making transformation. The forgery of a signature or the counterfeiting of banknotes, in their striking likeness to the legitimate article, disrupt the confidence crucial to the maintenance of capital as a trustworthy form of exchange. This is because signatures and banknotes, despite their association with authenticity, have no intrinsic value. Therefore their role as the genuine article, whose presence is nothing more than a vacant signifier, is nonetheless made to bear the weight of the whole symbolic system of capital. Value is accrued through an acceptance of constant deferment and an act of good faith, exemplified by the promise to pay the bearer of the note at a later date that makes up the very act of exchange. Genuine forms of currency therefore are only able to secure their legitimacy in comparison to their illegitimate counterparts; it is only through such comparison that their validity can take be retained and given preferred status within capitalism, and by extension lend capitalism elevated status within the hierarchy of monetary systems.

The paradox legitimate currency faces within this process of identification, as legitimate class tender becomes the stuff of scientific precision as the nineteenth century progresses, begins to be filtered through a language of societal discipline when addressing matters of class. As the century wore on class hierarchy was increasingly represented as a question for scientific analysis. Within this schema class had become racialised with gentility acting as whiteness does in colonial discourse. It occupies the position of the invisible norm, disavowing its place in the structures of difference and claiming for itself the position of the ideal, universal man, as a self-identical and self-producing unit. The gentleman is never seen in these illicit transactions, because his is by nature a product of the order that claims its status by being at the very centre of society, where his idealised innocence forms the very basis from which another's guilt can be drawn. The presumed moral integrity of the centre simply excludes the possibility of the admittance of criminality within its ranks and therefore by definition must dissociate from it, rather than be seen to be associated with it on any other level barring its surveillance and apprehension. The criminal Magwitch, for his part, must be literally transported away from this sphere to New South Wales for the remainder of his life, so as to reify a construction of otherness that is always already geographical in logic. The need to repress it creates a hegemonic paradigm wherein gentility must alienate him if its coercive power is to be maintained.

To the degree that whiteness became synonymous with an exulted natural invisibility, blackness had to be made synonymous with an abject unnatural visibility. Enlivened in the public's imagination through its representation in popular culture, criminality took on particular race and class connotations. Those who made up the criminal class were understood to be both racially and geographically abject. One common archetype of this form was found in the morally debased Irish convict, whose chosen territories were the grim rookeries of London. Dickens played his part in generating this phenomenon, by publishing articles in which he depicted the criminal type as an individual who was constitutionally savage. Kirsty Reid argues that 'imperial as well as metropolitan events informed his attitudes on race', making it possible for him to intellectually and indeed creatively connect the actions of 'demonised convicts' with those of colonial savages 'by accusing them of sodomy, rape and cannibalism, among a range of other unnatural acts' that separated them from the category of humanity (59). According to Reid's analysis, 'Magwitch would have been read by some as a symbolic reaffirmation of the horrors unleashed when the monstrous convict came "home" from the places where his innate savagery had presumably gone unchecked' (59).

The prospect of their reappearance reified Britain's justice system and inaugurated a scientific formalisation when it came to the apprehension of criminals who were now carefully measured and classified, and their sentencing categorised and calibrated to complement the demands of a hardening penitentiary system. This hardening extended itself outward to interpolate and discursively capture its desired subjects. Magwitch explains to Pip and Herbert that through the act of being incarcerated, he 'got the name of being hardened'. The prison guards in turn, further apprehended him to so-called 'prison wisitors' by 'picking' him out and explaining to them, 'this is a terrible hardened one' (*Great Expectations*, 703; ch. 42). In the case of the latter, their process of selection was informed by the new science of phrenology, 'the study of the head and brain to interpret character traits, intelligence, and intellectual capability [that] was an important scientific tool in determining racial capabilities in the nineteenth century' (Ghosh 28). Magwitch goes on to explicitly describe his examination by the 'prison wisitors', who turn out to be a group of phrenologists. 'Then they looked at me, and I looked at them, and they measured my head, some on 'em ... and others on 'em giv me tracts what I couldn't read, and made me speeches what I couldn't understand' (*Great Expectations* 703; ch. 42). Through these methodical exchanges, these phrenologists are able to literally compose the discourse of science, producing a preset account of the prisoner as biologically inferior to the standard of physiognomy requisite to a reliable gentleman. Phrenology was crucial to the formulation of the dominant political discourse of the time supportive of racial hierarchy. Widely accepted as an objective science, it 'aided an imperialistic "worlding of the world"' to maintain 'established racial hegemonies' (31–2).

Magwitch appears to buy into this scientific discourse when he informs Pip that he would not be able to develop beyond his current class status because of his lack of proper cerebral acumen, presumably because he is an Irishman. Anthony S. Wohl explains that 'in much of the pseudo-scientific literature of the day the Irish were held to be inferior, an example of a lower evolutionary form, closer to the apes than their racial "superiors" the Anglo-Saxons' (Wohl). Phrenology acted as a scientific framework wherein 'the structure of the skull, especially the jaw formation and facial angles', could be utilised to determine 'the position of various races on the evolutionary scale' (Wohl). Phrenological evidence formed a crucial aspect of the Victorian debate about the genesis of mankind, as a singular (monogenism) or manifold (polygenism) happening. Phrenology argued for the latter. The Irish race was believed to be the product of a lower evolutionary order, their faces displaying 'bestial, ape-like or demonic features and invariably given a long or prognathous jaw', thus bearing the biological characteristics of degeneracy (Wohl). By contrast, the eminent phrenologist, John Beddoe, wrote in his book *Races of Britain* (1862) 'that all men of genius were orthognathous', having less prominent jaw bones than their Irish or Welsh racial counterparts who were prognathous (Wohl). Beddoe believed that 'the Celt was closely related to Cromagnon man, who in turn was linked, according to Beddoe, to the "Africanoid". The position of the Celt in Beddoe's "Index of Nigrescence" was very different from that of the Anglo-Saxon' (Wohl). Such views were widely accepted amongst the scientific community at the time and made their way into the public's imagination. Whilst they were not wholeheartedly embraced by the mainstream of British scientists, a significant minority of them were convinced of the efficacy of such beliefs, and amongst them 'it was even hinted that the Irish might be the elusive missing link' between apes and humans (Wohl).

In this way, phrenology gave rise to the notion that the Irish were the blacks of Europe, allowing not only for the malevolent cliché of the ape-like Celt to become a cornerstone of Victorian racism, but also for the Irish to be perceived in much the same way as their Africanoid brethren in terms of being fit to perform brute labour rather than highly reasoned tasks. In a way eerily similar to black Africans and Caribbeans, 'it was broadly argued that the Celt was poetic, light-hearted and imaginative, highly emotional, playful, passionate, and sentimental ... thus the Irish were "immature" and in need of guidance by others, more highly developed than themselves' (Wohl). These same arguments that conveniently supported British rule in Ireland were universally applied to all non-white peoples subject to British imperial rule, and by association presumed that the Irish themselves were of a far lesser biological derivation of whiteness than their Anglo-Saxon contemporaries. Moreover, it created a racial differentiation between the Irish working class and the British working class that would allow for a presumption of racial superiority on the part of the British to prevent any sort of class-based solidarity forming between the two. This racial logic functioned much the same way as it did in their understanding of other groups such as blacks and Asians as being fundamentally inferior in their labour capacity, based on the fact of their racial differentiation.

Pip as an Anglo-Saxon, in contrast to Magwitch as an Irishmen, will be able to educate himself beyond the means of brute force to foster his elevated situation in life. 'I lived rough', Magwitch exclaims, in a passage that might be read as a wider commentary upon relations between labour and capital, colony and metropolis, 'that you should live smooth; I worked hard, that you should be above work' (Dickens, *Great Expectations* 302; ch. 39). The distinctions that Magwitch makes between himself and Pip bear the balance set between imperial and imperialised populations, because empire relied upon the maintenance of rigid divisions and fixed hierarchies between them, which at base fundamentally sustain the idleness of the Victorian-British social elite. It also barred the return of convicts to Britain to preserve the geographical and cultural boundaries that legitimated the distinction between metropolis and colony, and gave privilege to the former over the latter. Such was the power of the imperial state, that it was able to control and filter communication from the penal colonies it had founded. Part of the terror built up around transportation involved blocking correspondence between the convict and his loved ones, thereby rendering 'the condition of the convict horrifyingly unknowable' (Reid 63). The character of Magwitch is made to assent to that bargain, insofar as the story of his time as a sheep-farmer in Australia remains a lacuna within the narrative's sequence of events. Only what happened in London to necessitate his transportation is revealed to the reader over the course of the latter chapters. This period of exile remains peripheral and obscure, and yet is evocative insofar as it allows Magwitch to create a redemptive alibi for his sentencing, and to rechristen himself as Provis, thus lending temporary providence to Pip's otherwise harsh trajectory.

Magwitch, like most members of his colonised race, internalised the logic of the British social classificatory system and throughout his exile continued to aspire to the class of gentleman. While he can never claim to have blood relation to that class, Magwitch adopts a stance of bourgeois consumerism, in his attempt to manufacture such a lineage for his purchased 'son' Pip. It is only when he tries to float his currency beyond the confines of his colonial geography that real trouble begins again for him. Applying his force of person once again within the metropolitan core, Magwitch challenges its authority in such a way that it must place him in an ever more incriminating position, thus further reifying his criminal identity. This time around Magwitch's crime is not one of capitalistic offense, but rather of imperial implication. His transgression of class norms through the flaunting of his extravagant, excessive colonial wealth threatens the supremacy of the nationally, socially recognised currency. It displays the colonial manipulation at the heart of such wealth and exposes moreover the myth that only gentlemen are entitled to its possession. It is Pip, rather, who internalises the City's message: that while wealth can be acquired, class cannot be bought at any price. The moral panic this creates within him forces Pip to 'aggressively render his [previous ersatz father] Joe "Other" through his disparaging scrutiny of the blacksmith's behaviour and clothing, maintaining his privileged genteel status through the formation of a supplementary dialectic that discriminates forge from metropolis' (Watson 499). Nonetheless he remains a product of the forge unable to achieve the satisfaction of truly possessing gentility within his adopted home of London. Moreover, he is the product not of Miss Havisham's largess as he has hoped against hope to be, but rather is shamefully the class rehabilitation project of the convict Magwitch, who can never quite dismiss his fraudulent beginnings, any more than Pip can fit comfortably within the mould of 'gentleman' based on this same position. Because of this Pip finds he can never go home, because home is the purview of those who innately possess social propriety. Such propriety can never be assigned to colonially generated spaces.

Once his inheritance reaches British shores its value must be cleansed from within through the quasi-legal channel of Jagger's office. Despite Jagger's best efforts to preserve its authenticity and stability as a legitimate asset through retaining the secrecy of its origins, he is aware that it remains subject to political seizure should its true origins ever be revealed. It is for this reason that Wemmick advises Pip to quickly launder it, breaking it down into its transmissible value as portable property. What destroys this enterprise is Magwitch's insatiable desire to inspect his manufactured gentlemen. It is this financial calculation that brings Pip up against a formidable bourgeois interiority, which must sustain its authority through the vacation of not only Magwitch's wealth, but also his very person. It is he who initiated his criminality through financial transactions, which betrayed the security of the Crown, and now it is time for the Crown to enact a re-absorption of its loss, through the seizure of his colonised body back into its imperial form as prisoner. The nation in this way is able to profoundly devalue him, in the same instant that it re-establishes the separation of deviant black and dominant white economies. Here Magwitch is restored as political tender on one level and biological tender on another, making him once again available to apprehension on the level of life in its essential form. There is another conduit of working-class criminality still to be explored through Dickens's novel. His creation of a working-class Irish character in Molly, as

Magwitch's former wife and mother to Estella, enlivens an associative structure that will interpolate all three in bonds of both race and homicide.

We are told that Molly murdered a woman twice her size by strangling her with her bare hands and she, unlike her husband, was not punished for her crimes. Due to the shrewd defence mounted by Mr. Jaggers, the jury becomes falsely convinced that she was too weak to have strangled the woman. There is something larger at stake here in the inclusion of her back-story in the novel than merely the outstanding guilt of her crime. Peter Capuano's reading of *Great Expectations* hones in on Dickens's conspicuous emphasis on Molly's Irishness throughout the text. According to Capuano's argument, Dickens does so most obviously, through her name, which is 'a lower-class Irish nickname for Mary, and Wemmick's assertion that she has "some gypsy blood in her"' which for Capuano, 'only confirms Terry Eagleton's observation that Gypsy blood in the nineteenth-century novel was "simply an English way of saying that [the character] is quite possibly Irish"' (193). Ireland and Australia were historically identified as Britain's white colonies. The convergence of Molly's nationality, class status and violent nature in the novel construes her criminal behaviour within the context of her overarching animality. This presumption is borne out ironically, through a sudden act of violence on the part of Jaggers, who is compelled to entertain his company by forcibly pinning Molly's hands to the table for vicarious inspection by Pip and his other rarified young clients:

'There's power here,' said Mr. Jaggers, coolly tracing out the sinews [of Molly's hand] with his forefinger. 'Very few men have the power of wrist that this woman has. It's remarkable what force of grip there is in these hands. I have had occasion to notice many hands; but I never saw anything stronger in that respect, man's or woman's, than these' (Dickens, *Great*

Expectations 204; ch. 26).

Through her hands Jaggers is able to map onto her larger body a social deviancy that is both natural and figurative, insofar as it 'serves to collapse the disavowed discourses of gender, labor, and criminality into a single bodily organ. The "remarkable force of grip" in Molly's hands alludes to her previous crime but, as we have seen, the method she uses in the performance of this criminal act reflects contemporary anxiety regarding the fragility of the barrier between the human and the animal' (Capuano 193).

Another barrier is crossed when we discover that Molly is Estella's biological mother, but curiously in the opposite direction. 'The improbability of their biological association ... rests on the putative difference between what their respective hands mean in the text's symbolic economy: if Molly's hands connote animality, violence, and labor, then Estella's signify refinement, beauty, and leisure' (Capuano 199). It is not through symbolic appearance, but rather subtle attraction, that we see how the formation of her nature, 'or what we might call [her] personality, is antedated by Estella's biological kinship with Molly and Magwitch. Beneath her genteel aloofness and apparent refinement there are important parts of Estella's identity that link her disposition, as well as her hand movements, to Molly's "wild" nature' (201). It is interesting to note that the incidents of violence we are aware of in her youth with regard to her interactions with her working-class counterpart Pip are enacted outside of Satis House and beyond the confined purview of the aristocratic Miss Havisham.

We see Estella first exhibit the violent capacity of her mother's hands when she slaps Pip's face with great force. In a second incident she appears attracted to the atmosphere of physical aggression itself, as she watches Herbert and Pip fistfight and becomes physically aroused enough to allow Pip a kiss as his reward for bloodying the hopelessly middle-class Herbert's nose.

Estella shows her attraction to Pip not when he learns to act like a 'gentleman', but after he cuts his hands on Herbert's teeth and confesses to feeling like a 'species of young wolf, or other wild beast' (Dickens, *Great Expectations* 461; ch. 11). The attraction of Estella to physical violence, apparent in her subsequent marriage to physically abusive Bentley Drummle, suggests the emergence of a long-buried barbarism, one that helps to reveal her biological relationship to Molly.

Estella's long-buried barbarism is a trait shared by Jaggers, who is desperate throughout the novel to conceal his own violent actions from the purview of society. Dickens nonetheless gives us inordinate clues about his lesser origins through his repeated emphasis on Jaggers's 'dark complexion, his deep-set eyes, his bushy black eyebrows … his strong black dots of beard and whisker, and even the smell of scented soap on his great hand[s]' as markers of his mysterious origin as well as his compulsion to outwardly and hastily groom himself away from these inborn characteristics (Dickens, *Great Expectations* 336; ch. 18). When brought into relation with Molly's subtly comprised appearance in his home, these characteristics coalesce to reveal a deeper more sinister union between them than master and servant, one born of the bargained suppression of their common (biological) propensity to express violence. The menacing qualities of class origins are never far from view and from his habit of biting his hands and throwing his '"great forefinger" [which] frightens clients and magistrates alike in nearly every professional scene the reader witnesses' (Capuano 195). It is not Molly alone who requires 'taming', it is Jaggers himself who recognises through her intimate presence within his home the ever-present possibility of eruption of the ferocity that resides with them both. Jaggers, however, feels tht Molly is a far greater threat than he is, and therefore he is convinced her 'old violent nature' must be 'kept down whenever he saw an inkling of its breaking out by asserting his power over her in the old way' (Dickens, *Great*

Expectations 185; ch. 11). Put within this context the 'taming' sessions at the dinner table with Molly allow Jaggers to temporarily subvert the expectations of the middle-class Victorian men who surround him, and reveal to them in a thrilling though controlled way their proximity to manual labour and racial degeneracy. This spectacle presents them with a kind of class tourism for the evening, the sting of which is keenly felt by Pip, connecting his recently acquired veneer of refinement back to its primitive components. Although he will not at this moment link Molly's story to her husband's, nor for that matter to her daughter Estella's, Molly's wild display will linger as a threat in Pip's mind to the careful social signification he has enacted through his own contrived persona.

Having gone to London to learn its elevated norms, Pip keeps on finding himself lodged near to the precincts of criminal law, and therein he learns something far different about how society constitutes itself primarily and primally through the expulsion of its transgressors. Pip, in a way typical of the nineteenth-century subject, 'is haunted by crime, its signs and stories, the shapes of its institutions designed for its regulation' (Gallagher and Greenblatt 205). Once in London, Pip finds yet again that he is consumed by thoughts about how strange it is that even here he should remain encompassed by all this taint of prison and crime, as he had once been out on the 'lonely marshes on a winter evening'. (Dickens, *Great Expectations* 624; ch. 32). It was there that he first encountered this underworld, only to have it reappear in London through the shadowy, obscure reappearance of his illicit benefactor 'starting out like a stain that was faded but not gone; that, it should in this new way pervade my fortune and advancement' (624).

Great Expectations is based on the misapprehension of debts owed to others. Pip's fate appears to coincide with the sudden appearance of a 'foreign guest', who will soon emerge from the depths as a domestic product: a prisoner marked for transport to the colonies. Derrida notes that 'Britain's "great unifying projects", all come down to the apprehension of this shadowy figure, a figure who unites the centre with the periphery of the Enlightenment project, and links the concentration of wealth with the concentration of individuality' (*Spectres of Marx* 4). Equally this shadowy figure belies the fact that our freedom spring forth from others' confinement. As Britons we all emerge as 'ghosts chained to ghosts', racked with the guilt of our collectivity, mounting up, over the course of history, as unpaid existential debt to the others who made our lines of credit worthy (4–5). Dickens recognises this 'ghost' as 'the violence of domination, an oppression of the weak by the strong, in the name of any form of hierarchical superiority', including but not limited to cheap labour, indentured servitude, or slavery, which in quick succession could be made to translate into 'the abstract value of money or capital' under the terms of that very same unifying project (Klaver 104). Indeed, the political economy of British imperialism boils down to 'the totalizing system of monetary value' (107). The reality of this fact is small comfort to anyone who, thanks to the cold gales of global capital, finds themselves poor or disenfranchised. Those who were the labouring classes, i.e. the vast majority of Britons, 'were evaluated by society according to their body's capacity for work, giving sexual pleasure, or for taking punishment. All three activities, were tightly controlled by rigid institutions and their representatives – factory owners, the police, the lawyers, prison guards, and landlords, who had license to detain, injure, trade or sell any person, anybody lacking the means to defend themselves' (Logan 4).

The attempt to distance these activities from one another is founded with the concept of transportation, where literally masses of people for whom Britain had no further need (due to the rise of industrialisation) could be sent out of view to work jobs no free settler would do. It was perhaps too easy for the Peel government to criminalise this segment of the British population. The workers could not overcome the challenges of mass unemployment, a saturated labour market, falling wages and rising prices created in the wake of mass industrialisation. When conditions of desperation naturally set in, the government in turn endeavoured to apprehend and punish them severely when they resorted to thievery to maintain their survival. The trick of it was to institute poverty through the rapid expansion of capitalism and then to appear to resolve its appearance by shipping an entire class of people elsewhere as criminal charges, this as the new cost of doing government business.

What subtends both the wealth and civilisation of Britain is a matter of far greater moral ambiguity than many Britons were prepared to fully realise as the eighteenth century drew to its close. If colonial exile was something imagined as a solution for the country to do away with unwanted classes, few appreciated the true conditions of these exiles as on par with the brutal conditions of slavery. What makes the picture all the more puzzling is that critics of transportation condemned it for its financial 'extravagance', and argued that 'for less cost per man and woman the convicts could be clothed in velvet and fed on beef and claret in London's strand'. Nonetheless 'the Prime Minister, William Pitt, assured the house of commons in 1791 that "no cheaper mode of disposing of convicts could be found"' (Judd 29). It stands to reason, then, that the costs were offset by some other means. Unremunerated labour could be garnered from these convicts to develop Britain's new colonial holding at Botany Bay at virtually no cost to the state during the typical seven years of their sentencing. Essentially what Britain was doing was making a slave class from their convict class, which in every way mirrored the African and Caribbean slave trade that had made their former American colonies so prosperous. In Australia they were merely duplicating the methods of slavery to produce a novel unwaged labour population elsewhere capable of repeating such financial gains.

The eight-month voyage to Australia was in some cases literally a terminal one for the human cargo on-board who bleakly accepted that their exile there was to be a permanent one. In the event of their survival, and disembarkation, they faced a future that held 'nothing but hard labour and vile rations' where 'the cat of nine tails, the chain gang and the unrestrained sexual demands of their overseers, and their stronger, more dominating fellow prisoners', made any distinction from their counterparts in the new world colonies virtually meaningless (Judd 29–30). This was taking place at the same time as a settler community was forming; the Australian colonies began to receive hundreds of thousands of free immigrants from Europe, hoping to stake their fortunes through gold or wool. It was through this dual economy of population that a system of social apartheid was established, not between blacks and whites as had been the case with other colonised societies, but between free whites and convict whites, creating an intra-racially divided territory, wherein even those who eventually gained their freedom through a combination of hard work and good behaviour could not overcome the stigma of their former status. Financial standing played no part in this economy of exclusion. It was this damning economy that begot another one, in the form of genocidal hatred directed toward Australia's Aboriginal tribes. As Judd writes, 'the vehemence with which they were condemned and ridiculed probably owed a great deal to the need of the transportees to find human beings worse off and lowlier than themselves' (31). This hierarchy held great resonance with the biologism at home that justified such class brutality across a wide spectrum of society.

During this same era, back home in Britain the poor were established as an enemy cohort in the minds of a nascent bourgeoisie. In their moral indignation they would care little for the fate of such deviant individuals, and were only too happy for the issue of conspicuous poverty to be forcibly shipped abroad and out of societal view. The denigration of these individuals effectively stripped them of their rights to maintain their place in British society. It also removed their identity as British subjects because they were legally barred from returning to the shores of their birth, or having communication with their loved ones, who would continue to reside there. As the privileges of national belonging were torn away from their bodies, their remaining purpose shifted to one task alone: to provide 'slave labor for colonial development ... undergoing such mutations towards respectability as whips and chains might induce' (Lesjak 99). What mattered most was that such events were happening far away and out of sight, with few Britons realising what bargains had been struck between the colonial seizure of foreign territory and the slave labour coerced from any number of dominated peoples (including these former Britons themselves) to create and maintain Britain's illustrious empire.

The making of a gentleman relies on a disavowal of such exploitation, and at the same time remains hopelessly tethered to it, by capitalistic design. There is no place elsewhere for that situation to reside and yet those who aspire to become gentlemen remain wilfully blind to its inherent destructive qualities. This was the case for both Pip and Herbert Pocket, who literally end up buying into this economy of wealth and success, only to find themselves becoming the commercial servants of empire, rather than its masters. In the end they become capitalism's imperial distributors, engaging not coincidentally in a trading company that specialises in the insurance of ships and their cargo, including those vessels that transport slaves and convicts, as well as free settlers and the goods consumed and manufactured by such labourers.

This course of events is determined thematically, when Pip is given the opportunity to re-encounter Herbert as a result of 'coming into his good fortune' (Dickens, *Great Expectations* 167; ch. 22). This development, in turn, furnishes a financially strapped Herbert with a position as Pip's class mentor. Once the two are re-established on felicitous ground, Pip plucks up the courage to ask what exactly Herbert 'was' (174). That the question is framed ontologically rather than empirically, in terms of qualifying a professional attribute, says a great deal about how identities are formulated in this nascent era of capitalism. Herbert replied, 'A capitalist – an Insurer of Ships' (174). Pip initially misinterprets Herbert's occupation as domestic in nature, where again Pip is at a loss to classify his position, in a manner that prompts Herbert to correct him: 'I suppose he saw me glancing about the room in search of some tokens of Shipping, or capital, for he added, "In the City"' (174).

Despite Herbert's spatial qualifier, Pip remains fixed to a notion of *being* rather than *doing*, and reasserts a biological value to these proceedings. This scenario leads to Pip's silent admission that 'I had grand ideas of the wealth and importance of Insurers of Ships in the City, and I began to think with awe, of having laid a young Insurer on his back, blackened his enterprising eye, and cut his responsible head open' (Dickens, *Great Expectations* 174; ch. 22). The sequence of allusion follows on from Pip's pattern of thought to include profit, notoriety, domination, violent competition and cannibalism. These terms point the way towards a darker underside that subtends capitalist grandeur. Investigation of this aspect of capital enthrals a naïve Pip, enticing him to imagine his own position within the larger world of commercial enterprise that resides far beyond their immediate domestic surroundings. Such ambition however is quickly halted when Pip is called back from such reveries: 'there came upon me, for my relief, that odd impression that Herbert Pocket would never be very successful or rich' (174). Herbert then is ejected from Pip's internal thoughts, only to be transported into his own, which are decidedly external in their mode of projection:

'I shall not rest satisfied with merely employing my capital in insuring ships. I shall buy up some good Life Assurance shares, and cut into the Direction. I shall also do a little in the mining way. None of these things will interfere with my chartering a few thousand tons on my own account. I think I shall trade,' said he, leaning back in his chair, 'to the East Indies, for silks, shawls, spices, dyes, drugs, and precious woods. It's an interesting trade' (174–5).

Pip is rattled by the scope of Herbert's ambitions to profit from imperialism, causing him to 'waver again' in his appraisal of Herbert, as Pip begins to think Herbert's prospects for profit in the East are 'greater expectations than [his] own', which he presumes are limited to his inheritance of Miss Havisham's ancestral wealth at this stage of the narrative. Herbert's ambitions go so far as to touch on methods of trade that intersect directly with slavery and brutality against nature: '"I think I shall trade, also," said he, putting his thumbs in his waistcoat pockets, "to the West Indies, for sugar, tobacco, and rum. Also to Ceylon, specially for elephants' tusks"' (175). Herbert next affirms an understanding of the military aspects involved in the maintenance of imperial trade; when Pip enquires tentatively, 'You will want a good many ships', Herbert replies, 'A perfect fleet' (175).

Pip's mind is 'quite overpowered by the magnificence of these transactions', until he realises that the wealth Herbert has alluded to thus far is merely conjectural, and that furthermore his situation in life as a lowly clerk employed in a counting-house is very unlikely to put him in a position to accumulate actual and direct profit from these imperial ventures (Dickens, *Great Expectations* 175; ch. 22). Herbert's futile strategy to 'look about' himself in the hopes of attracting capital seems to resonate in Pip's mind with his boyhood encounter with a younger Herbert, who even at that time bore his condition of poverty with a manner of gentlemanly grace. For Pip, 'it was evident that he had nothing around him but the simplest necessaries, for everything that I remarked upon turned out to have been sent in on my account from the coffee-house or somewhere else' (175). The less he senses that Herbert holds some economic advantage over him, the more Pip realises that despite his own prospects of coming into great capital, he remains in a position of subordination with regard to Herbert's innate class status: 'having already made his fortune in his own mind, he was so unassuming with it that I felt quite grateful to him for not being puffed up' (175). What elevates Herbert over Pip is his healthy reverence for capital as a saving grace, given over even to gentlemen who find themselves, temporarily, in less than adequate circumstances.

Herbert's ability to project success by 'looking about' garners a solution to Pip's dilemma, when Herbert uses his connections in shipping to foster both passage for Magwitch out of London, and a situation for him and Pip in Clarriker's firm's new enterprise in Egypt. While Herbert savours this prospect fully, Pip is far more reluctant to embrace this hasty solution to their problems. Still for Pip 'there was recompense in the joy with which Herbert would come home of a night and tell me of these changes, little imagining that he told me no news, and would sketch airy pictures of himself conducting Clara Barley to the land of the Arabian Nights, and of me going out to join them (with a caravan of camels, I believe), and of our all going up the Nile and seeing wonders' (Dickens, *Great Expectations* 395; ch. 52). Grace Moore observes that 'the East for him is a place of employment, where he can live frugally and pay off his debts. He has no imaginative relationship to the location, and we learn almost nothing of his life there, beyond his visions of the forge' (181). The vision of the East as a place of enterprise is one that remains solely within Herbert's class purview. From Pip's working-class perspective his situation there is no better than that of a criminal exile or indentured servant. It is for this reason that 'Pip's treatment of Egypt is perfunctory', and that despite his surroundings he contents himself by expressing an 'endless nostalgia for the Kent marshes', whose loss he equates in his mind with 'the home he cannot regain and [with] Estella, the woman he cannot have' (181). Moore contends that Pip's 'time in Egypt is almost akin to Magwitch's banishment to the Antipodes' (181). This temporal affinity has everything to do with a goal they share in common; an economic determination to make good of themselves in exile despite their past failures at home. Thus Dickens needs only to register the growing presence of the Empire in everyday life at the level of its domestic interference.

Meanwhile, Pip and Herbert will go up the Nile and be supported by a caravan of camels for their trouble, but never be commissioned with any arduous type of work, which conspicuously differentiates them from their less fortunate British counterparts who might reside there under less cheerful circumstances as imperial workers. It is never explicitly acknowledged that the initial premise for Herbert's commission to enter into Clarriker's firm is furnished to him through the employment of Pip's commercial fortune, which is the product of Magwitch's post-convict imperial labour. When Pip goes to Clarriker with his offer to secure Herbert's future, Clarriker tells Pip that he's planning to open a new office in the East which he hopes Herbert will run. It is here that it is possible to see how peripheral spaces and populations become central to Britain's development, and how imperial labour reasserts itself time and again as a source of domestic wealth. Capital is the force that insinuates itself in this arrangement and implicates all that form and occupy the means of its circulation. The novel *Great Expectations* therefore can only resolve itself through Pip's return from the periphery to the centre of its operation. Once there, the resumption of his love affair with Estella is made possible through his new appreciation of her class ascendency as something that perfectly exemplifies the trappings of the imperial system. In that, there is much to be admired. Pip by novel's end has enacted the process of acculturation in the imperial age, and in so doing Dickens has introduced the reader to the pleasures of modern industrial life, which require us to admire our own discipline. For that Estella becomes the ultimate mistress at Satis House, appropriating the currency of the age to suit the purposes of a manufactured good.

In the end, Dickens must remind us that *Great Expectations* is a portrait of an English gentleman and not an Irish convict. Therefore the thematic resonance of colonial solutions to metropolitan problems must be tempered along class lines that justify the preservation of that title for Pip, despite his material losses. Thus it is crucial that the reader appreciate that Magwitch's experience in Botany Bay is, in an obvious sense, socially and economically asymmetrical with Pip's in Cairo. If Pip chooses to work in Egypt, Magwitch is transported against his will to New South Wales. If work as a trader in Egypt is worthy employment for a middle-class English gentleman, imprisonment as a convict in Australia represents the antithesis of 'normal' bourgeois respectability. And if economic initiative in the East is seen as a healthful overflow of the forces of Victorian improvement from the imperial centre to the periphery, then maintenance of the Australian convict colony is regarded as a necessary diversion and draining-away of dangerous social energies that threaten middle-class progress.

Edward Said contends that Pip, by virtue of his free status, can trade in his idle appearance as a London gentleman and reconstitute his social position as a working trader from the East. Indeed, he can even return to London with gainful prospects, all without the repercussions that would face Magwitch as a fact of geography: 'Australia [is] a penal colony designed for the rehabilitation but not the repatriation of transported English criminals' (14). In contrast to this, Egypt was set up 'in discourses of imperial free trade' as one of the places 'of unlimited opportunities for commercial advancement abroad' (14). It is possible to say that British interests in Australia were equally founded on 'the pursuit of profit, the building of empire and what Hughes calls social apartheid', which separated out those who were free to organise themselves, from those who remain subject to that freedom, as determined by their own circumstantial limitations of race, class or gender (14). One privileged social class authorises their lesser Others in a hierarchy of colonially inhabited spaces, constructed to reflect the values of their British metropolitan origin. In the colonial context whites confronted non-white immigrant populations and sought to capture them within a framework that reflected their desire to keep the inferior subordinate, both in reality and in representation through the naturalisation of the institutions of both capitalism and class. Dickens is himself a product of such a colonial enterprise and historically informed as much by events in Britain as he is by events in Egypt or Australia, which complement a worldview of British cultural superiority and exclusivity that extends itself even within the context of these foreign lands.

At the same time the barbarism that was regularly practiced in Australia had to be viewed as fundamentally different from the conditions at home for the working classes. In the words of Marx, 'the veiled slavery of wage-workers in Europe needed, for its pedestal, slavery pure and simple in the new world' (Marx, *Das Kapital* 235). One is forced to ask whether the abolition of transportation in 1840 and the end of convictism in 1867 were in fact steps towards class hegemony in the British metropole at a time when its colonial empire was reaching its period of greatest historical consequence. The question is nascent in Marx's comment above, for it is telling that the middle class's concern for the work and living conditions of the penal settlements did not also extend to those of working-class Britons caught in the thrall of wage slavery. It is interesting to note that the emancipation of West Indian slaves in 1833 took place in a similar era to the abolition of transportation. Both are viewed by contemporary historians as acts motivated not by a concern for the wellbeing of oppressed peoples, for indeed attitudes towards penal reform were if anything hardening, as were beliefs about racial superiority at this time. Rather, the abolition of these policies must be viewed instead as 'a function solely of class interest, whether understood consciously or unconsciously' (O'Quinn 270). It simply was no longer profitable to spend large sums of money to send groups of felons to perform essential labour, when increasing numbers of would-be settlers were coming to work of their own accord as free labourers. The potential fortunes to be made in wool and gold created an unprecedented commercial viability for the struggling New World colony and 'from the 1830s large-scale investments of private British capital began to be made in the Australian economy. The City of London also waxed enthusiastic giving strong financial support to various emigration and land developments schemes fostered by private companies and government agencies. British banks sprang up in Australia and for a time threatened to eliminate their local colonial competitors' (Judd 36).

Something similar was happening with regard to the abolition of slavery in the West Indies during a comparable period. Initially, slavery increased the amount of labour introduced into the economy, and introduced a new economic machinery. At the same time, it invented a new way of securing wealth insofar as slave labour could be held as a capital asset in the portfolio of the investor. Slavery brought this productive factor into the category of capital, because slave labour, in contrast to free labour, could be purchased outright as opposed to being rented. Barbara S. Solow contends that to fully appreciate the importance of the institution of slavery in unoccupied or underpopulated places like the Atlantic Islands and the New World, we must put it into this economic equation, wherein slavery becomes a newly invented 'productive asset ... in which capital can be immediately invested' ('Capitalism and Slavery' 56). Through the adoption of slavery as an asset class, British colonies could be built up quickly without waiting for a population to voluntarily immigrate or capital to be generated. Not only can the productivity of these holdings be generated at once, the returns of the European investor can be multiplied through the subsequent export of colonial products.

Foremost to this line of colonial products was sugar. It became essential to the cause of international trade. Its production via the institution of slavery became the source of numerous flows in what would become a complex network of 'labor, capital, manufactures, sugar, raw materials, shipping, banking and insurance'. The rise of this network 'did not cause the Industrial Revolution, but played an active role in its pattern and timing' as the nineteenth century dawned (Solow, 'Capitalism and Slavery' 71–2). Slave labour was understood at this time to be more productive than free white labour, which meant that the return on investment would be even greater than anticipated, making investment in slavery more productive and fuelling increased output. Slave output became so great from an economic perspective that over time it generated a glut in international trade, based on the overproduction of sugar. As a knock-on effect of this overproduction, London warehouses soon found they were full of unsalable sugar. 'This sugar could not be sold on the world market because the West Indians were high-cost producers. Their economy was protected by the mercantilist commercial policy of the old colonial system, which had ceased to function as it had in the past' (Solow, 'The British & the Slave Trade'). To the capitalists in charge of this trade, this situation was to prove intolerable. 'Overproduction in 1807 demanded abolition; overproduction in 1833 demanded emancipation' (Williams 153). Eric Williams explains that 'whereas before, in the eighteenth century, every important vested interest in England was lined up on the side of monopoly and the colonial system; after 1783, one by one, every one of those interests came out against monopoly and the West India slave system' (154).

Whilst the slave plantations played a major role in creating the economic basis for capitalism, they were not compatible with it once it developed beyond mercantilism to embrace global free trade. Slavery was used almost exclusively to cultivate crops in a way that relied on manpower, as opposed to mechanisation. Based on the brutal physical nature of the type of work that required slavery, it was necessary to resort to coercive means and indeed the threat of brute force to compel individuals to labour. This system provided absolutely no incentive for slaves to wish to work harder or master more complicated techniques, because there was no means of individual progression or recognition. A consequence of this fatalistic enterprise was a lack of productivity on the part of the slaves, which meant that in comparison to wage labour, their labour was recognised as being less profitable over time. When it came to sugar production it was soon understood that West Indian sugar could simply not compete with East Indian sugar, as British trade interests in the Indian sub-continent swelled, and with it the promise of the full development of British trade in sugar all over the world once the colonial system's protections on West Indian sugar were finally lifted. This would take place formally in 1846, when sugar duties were equalised with the repeal of the Corn Laws.

With that came a vogue for free workers to aid the rapid rise of industrialisation. Would-be Industrialists themselves were not sold on the idea that greater profits could be made by the proliferation of this class of labourer, who unlike his enslaved predecessor could be motivated to work through the incentive of wages; although more often than not their pay was pitiful and they were subject to gross exploitation by their employers. Nonetheless, in the minds of the British ruling class, the era of protectionism as represented by its interests in the Caribbean was a thing of the past, and a more lucrative source of wealth was on the horizon. The free Indian labourer would take the place of the enslaved African. According to Williams, 'the real significance, however, of the abolitionist support of East India ... is that the issues involved were not only the inhumanity of West Indian slavery, but the unprofitableness of West Indian monopoly' (Williams 188). Conversely, without the monopoly on West Indian sugar, British slave-trading became substantially less profitable.

Crucial to all this was the American colonies' independence from Britain, which suddenly uncoupled Britain from its financial dependence on slavery for economic prosperity, thus inaugurating a new colonial era in which it could become renowned as a global distributor of goods. The sudden loss of the American colonies also motivated the founding of the Botany Bay colony in Australia in 1788, because their independence meant 'the colonies of the deep south were no longer available as the receptacles for Britain's transportees' (Judd 29). It can then be argued that this colony became itself an experimental space for the blending of the economic techniques of mercantilism with the emerging realm of free-market capitalism. The consequences of this have everything to do with the rise of a concurrent, sophisticated paradigm of race.

Williams asserts that 'slavery was not born of racism: rather racism was the consequence of slavery. Unfree labor in the New World was brown, white, black and yellow; Catholic, Protestant, and pagan' (7). It was the poor white moreover, who preceded the African black into servitude in the New World. Some were indentured servants, while others were convicts, like Magwitch, cast out by the deliberate policy of the home government, to serve their sentence for a specified period. Williams argues that 'this emigration was in tune with mercantilist theories of the day which strongly advocated putting the poor to industrious and useful labor and favored emigration, voluntary or involuntary, as relieving the poor rates and finding more profitable occupations abroad for idlers and vagrants at home' (9–10). A great deal of indentured servitude was not only involuntary, but also criminally coercive in its own right. Transportation became tied up with commercial speculation, which over time generated a trade in kidnapping which itself became a regular business in towns such as London and Bristol that would later emerge as crucial hubs for the African slave trade. Both adults and children were enticed by food and drink into the hands of kidnappers who would then sell them onto a ship that would sail to the West Indies. The captains of the ship themselves would make visits to houses of correction in order to 'ply with drink the girls who had been imprisoned there as disorderly, and "invite" them to go to the West Indies. The temptations held out to the unwary and the credulous were so attractive that, as the mayor of Bristol complained, husbands were induced to forsake their wives, wives their husbands, and apprentices their masters, while wanted criminals found on the transport ships a refuge from the arms of the law' (11). Convicts provided another viable source of white labour and could be transported for even the most minor forms of crime. 'In 1745 transportation was the penalty for the theft of a silver spoon and a gold watch' (12). White (criminal) labour remained a desired commodity for decades to come: 'One year after the emancipation of the Negro slaves, transportation was the penalty for trade union activity' (12). Such penalties are perhaps further evidence of the close relationship between the edict of the law and the control of labour. Williams concedes, 'It is difficult to resist the conclusion that there was some connection between the law and the labor needs of the plantations, and the marvel is that so few people ended up in the colonies overseas' (12).

Without the transportation of white convicts the early development of the Australian colonies in the nineteenth century would have been impossible. It is for this reason that even the most serious crimes, including murder, were overlooked to swell the ranks of those who could be sent over. Similarly the West Indies were prepared to accept all and sundry, in the hopes that hard labour and harsher punishment by their masters would curb the excesses of these individuals. What separated out the lot of the convict versus the slave was that their loss of liberty was of limited duration whereas the Negro remained un-free for life. Over time the supply of convict labour was diminishing and the need of the plantations outstripped the number of English convictions. This led to an increase in the use of black slave labour to fill that need, which was procured using similar methods to those used on white convicts, including kidnapping. Cities like Bristol that had once been centres of the servant trade, became centres of the slave trade. It was simply a matter of retro-fitting the 'capital accumulated from the one to finance the other. White servitude was the historical basis upon which Negro slavery was constructed. The felon-drivers in the plantations became without effort slave-drivers' (Williams 19).

The substitution of Negroes for Whites was not of racial significance, but rather founded on one basic economic principle: black slaves gave a greater return on investment than their indentured white counterparts. Not only was one able to purchase their labour outright and in total for the duration of their lifetime, but also that of their offspring as the children of Negro women were enslaved in perpetuity. Slaves could be bought and sold at will and could not only be used to produce crops, but equally to perpetuate themselves as a stock of labour. A black slave thus constituted a tightly closed economic loop, out of which emerged free-standing profits, more capital and more slaves. The moral ambiguity of this scheme was later justified along racial lines, but in reality the business of slavery came down to pure economics. So long as the system was profitable, it was rationalised, defended and praised. Over time, its economic continuity became the source of its own ideology and its own legitimacy. The business of slavery was so integral to the British economy 'that there were few men and institutions of wealth who did not want to invest in it, from the royal family and the

Church of England downwards. Slavers could count on the Archbishop of Canterbury to defend them before God, and on politicians, like the young William Gladstone, himself the son of a plantation-owner, to plead their case in Parliament' (Economist, 'Breaking the Chains').

Slave ownership was one of the most lucrative investments, and in the eighteenth century whole industries sprang up to support it. Even the currency bore the impression of African slavery, in the form of the guinea. Slaves for sale were plainly advertised in shop windows and in newspapers. They were purchased openly at auctions taking place in metropolitan centres around Britain. Contrary to popular understanding, black slavery was not a feature of society found strictly outside of Britain. Rather, it penetrated into the heart of domestic and commercial life, particularly amongst those with means. 'Negro servants were commonplace and little black boys were put to use as the appendages of slave captains, fashionable ladies or women of easy virtue' (Williams 44). They were considered valuable merchandise, fashionable accessories and even adorable pets. Those who owned and traded slaves were lauded members of society, and were often gentleman who held positions of great authority in trade and government. 'Many held seats in parliament and the House of Lords in particular was populated by a number of men whose seats in the Upper House were owed to them based in their involvement in the slave trade' (48). Their vast political capital and economic influence meant 'that when the time came to abolish slavery in the British Caribbean, Mauritius and the Cape in 1833, the planters and the West India interest in Britain were able to drive a hard bargain. British taxpayers paid £20 million in compensation to the owners' (C. Hall 148).

This figure represented a staggering 40 per cent of the Treasury's annual spending budget and, in today's terms, calculated as wage values, equates to around £16.5bn (Manning). This extraordinary level of compensation 'confirmed the slave owners' view that the law and the state had legitimately sanctioned their ownership of the enslaved as they had always claimed: they deserved recompense, money for requisitioned property. They were not a stain, there was no need for guilt, they were part of the nation' (C. Hall 152). This legislation made provision for staggering levels of compensation for slave-owners, but gave the former slaves not a penny in reparation. Meanwhile, slave-traders were not offered any form of compensation. In contrast to the vast numbers of slaves, it was only 'some 3,000 families that owned slaves at the time slavery was abolished in Britain's colonies in 1833' who directly benefited from this compensation for their lost property (Manning). The British government acquired '£20 million (over £1bn today), to be dispersed to this end. The sum was so vast it had to obtained as a loan from the Rothschild banking family' (Sherwood).

Dr. Nick Draper from University College London, who has studied the compensation papers, says as many as one-fifth of wealthy Victorian Britons derived all or part of their fortunes from the slave economy. 'As a result, there are now wealthy families all around the UK still indirectly enjoying the proceeds of slavery where it has been passed on to them. Dr Draper said: "There was a feeding frenzy around the compensation"' (Manning). A John Austin, for instance, owned 415 slaves, and got compensation of £20,511, a sum worth nearly £17m today. And there were many who received far more. Those who received compensation after the abolition of slavery contributed disproportionately in their number to the formation of modern British society. 'Some families used the money to invest in the railways and other aspects of the industrial revolution; others bought or maintained their country houses, and some used the money for philanthropy' (Manning). Prime Minister David Cameron had slave owners in his family background on his father's side. 'The compensation records show that General Sir

James Duff, an army officer and MP for Banffshire in Scotland during the late 1700s, was Mr Cameron's first cousin six times removed. Sir James, who was the son of one of Mr Cameron's great-grand-uncle's, the second Earl of Fife, was awarded £4,101, equal to more than £3m today, to compensate him for the 202 slaves he forfeited on the Grange Sugar Estate in Jamaica' (Manning). Similar to her husband, 'who is fifth cousin, twice removed, of the Queen', David Cameron's wife Samantha Cameron descends from aristocracy on both sides of her family. The Prime Minister's wife can trace her roots back to businessman William Jolliffe, who 'received £3.25million in compensation for a sugar plantation in St Lucia which had 164 slaves' (S. Miller). Today 'the Camerons' combined wealth is estimated in excess of £30m' (S. Miller).

The rise of their predecessors to the ranks of the new capitalist classes born of slave wealth in the eighteenth century meant that privileged families like the Camerons were destined to be ruling classes in the West in the centuries that followed. Their ancestral wealth 'was in no small part due to the outlet the slave trade opened up for the investment of the cash surpluses accrued by merchants, as well as monarchs, aristocrats, guilds and clergy' (McFarlane). The profits from slavery 'tripled between 1770 and the end of the century, precisely the span of years in which it is generally agreed that the industrial revolution began. In 1770 profits from the plantations contributed between 20 and 50 percent of the funds of fixed capital formation in the metropolis, depending on the estimates' (McFarlane). From this data alone it is possible to ascertain that slavery was the major contributor to the primitive accumulation of capital, which would later solidify the economic fortunes of these families well into the future.

Such capital harnessed the resources of colonised lands to promote the development of Britain's capital cities, creating in effect an interdependent First and Third World that continues to thrive to this day as a contemporary outcome of globalisation.

The colonial city, both in its metropolitan and peripheral guises, persists in today's era of global capitalism, and bears within its design the elements of imperialism. The most unmistakable elements that persist include that of racial hierarchy and spatial segregation, but also, perhaps more subtly, a nostalgia for empire, which bears itself out through 'the self-conscious elaboration of tradition ... in the preservation of historic buildings, [and] through the emergence of new industries of consumption which build on the past, the primitive, Nature' (Jacobs 4). Whilst these elements remain a dynamic part of today's postmodern urban landscapes, they are by no means stable entities.

In the early 1960s sizeable numbers of individuals from Britain's commonwealth countries emigrated to Britain's metropolitan centres. While they had been involved for centuries in the production of Britain's wealth from their peripheral colonial vantage points, the wealth they produced largely flowed out from their nations and back to the Motherland. Over time this created economic conditions in these nations that virtually guaranteed economic hardship for the great majority of their citizens. Those who were financially able to travel followed the flow of wealth from their countries back to Britain to partake of the economic opportunities disproportionately assigned to it as a singular nation through the mechanism of colonisation. The pattern of migration of these citizens of the British Commonwealth to Britain corresponded not coincidentally to those cities formerly involved in the slave trade.

As a consequence of that former lucrative trade, these cities had become prominent financial and industrial centres over the course of centuries. The appearance of these individuals born of empire in the British metropole stressed the postcolonial system and created within it lacunae of colonial memory and form, which could not be easily reconciled with mainstream conceptions of British national identity. Even today Britain continues to tacitly promote a racially homogenous understanding of national belonging, which must necessarily exclude blacks from recognition as fellow citizens, both in an historical and present sense.

It remains up to these post-imperial subjects themselves to activate this social geometry and fashion the equations necessary for their survival in what are now the staging grounds of neo-imperial enterprise in these same metropoles, which over the course of recent decades have loosened themselves from the strictures of territory and binary opposition between domestic and foreign, only to open the expanse of struggle even further to include any variety of economically motivated migratory peoples who may be potentially affected by the opening of 'free' labour markets dating back to the early 1960s. Because of widely accessible advances in technology and travel, it is possible for a variety of economically motivated migratory subjects to lead lives that are both here and there, in a material sense. Therefore, it is possible for a variety of individuals to relate to both Self and Other simultaneously and dwell in both past and present as a matter of everyday course. This further fragmentation of the subject has grown up around terminology such as the transnational and has become conversant therein with habitation on a very complex level.

As a result, the experience of British imperialism is able to interpolate individuals from a dizzying array of locales around the globe, and moreover is able to make those individuals, ostensibly the product of its metropole, become deeply comparative in their outlook to homelands elsewhere in terms of the construction of their identities. 'London ... as a First World City, precariously classified as "global," is also a disaporic city which contains a Third World within its boundaries' (Jacobs 5). In this new postmodern invocation of the former colonial city, it becomes quickly evident that power and privilege share intimate association with disenfranchisement and poverty, in any one of its neighbourhoods that seek on one level to promote a hyper-locality, whilst at the same time reminding the inhabitant that Britain as a nation has become synonymous with London as its capital.

This becomes more evident when we look at the pattern of recession in Britain over the past several years, wherein London stands in stark contrast to its old metropolitan and indeed colonial contemporaries such as Leeds and Liverpool in terms of economic impact. This is a fact scarcely recognised by both parliamentary politicians and international investors, but readily felt on the ground by the majority of Britain's urban dwellers. It remains unacknowledged that this exceptionalism largely has its founding in London's enduring affective relation to its colonial territories which continue to favour it unduly, in terms of the flow of human capital that continues unabated and indeed is fuelled by ongoing economic crisis in Northern cities, Europe and the Middle East. London's enduring advantage comes to it by way of the geographical practices of imperialism, which had the effect of creating a single vantage point from which Britain could continue to maintain its imminently localising authority both at home and abroad. It can be argued that this purview was temporarily disrupted by the loss of empire and the economic upheaval that ensued as a result, but it must also be recalled that Britain remained powerful enough in its dealings with its former colonial territories to persuade them into the acceptance of a common interest that endures to this day. The reason for this is because colonial occupation utterly transformed the cultural outlook of these occupied populations. Moreover, the instal- lation of Britons themselves into the colonial spaces to create the necessary bureaucracies of rule profoundly altered the racial geography and spatial hierarchy of these places. England became the ideological Motherland for those who would live and die perhaps never to set foot on her shores; yet nonetheless remained unquestioningly loyal to her despite the numerous examples one can raise of the incompleteness of her imperial project to dominate them locally. In so doing histories were generated that overlapped and intertwined their fates as nations, and created a legacy of adaptation that persists today and in some ways makes for Britain's continued economic success, despite the obvious economic challenges of becoming a postcolonial nation in its own right.

Much of this activity took place in a skewed temporal dimension. Michael McMillan observes that 'In his book *Home Cooking in the Global Village: Caribbean Food from Buccaneers to Ecotourists,* Richard Wilk sees respectability as a merging of time, space, and culture in terms of what he calls "colonial time," meaning that the past is merged with the spatial concept of isolation and the cultural dimension of tradition and custom. The three are aspects of the same phenomena, as time, distance, and culture become interchangeable ways to talk about how people, spaces, and places are different' (139). The effect of 'colonial time' can be a culturally negating one insofar as it 'makes all kinds of cultural difference appear as natural aspects of isolation, backwardness, and being stuck in the past. In the colonial system, colonial time served many important purposes, such as producing consumer goods and furniture like settees and pianos, which became emblems of progress' (139). The absurdity and circumlocution involved in achieving such progress amongst those West Indians who laid claim to the identity of the colonial elite, is made evident in the fact that they would often import British-made furniture, made from tropical woods such as mahogany that were originally exported from the Caribbean. Using these sorts of refined productions, Wilk explains, 'was not a symbol of civilisation, it was itself civilised behaviour. The objects really did transform your body and make you civilised' (qtd. in McMillan 139). Practicality was not the object here. Colonial material culture was essential on a different level to that of use. It was crucial to maintain the 'now' of colonial time within the colonial world. Those who occupied that domain had to acquire a taste for such things, to relish in their appearance as a mark of status and privilege, and see their possession as a special honour permitting them to take their own part in the spoils of empire.

Following that same ethos, the West Indian front room of the early 1960s becomes a similarly resonant 'contact zone' with the Victorian-British parlour of the 1860s. 'Mary Louise Pratt uses the term "contact zone" to refer to social spaces where cultures meet, clash, and grapple with each other, often in contexts of highly asymmetrical relations of power, such as colonialism, slavery, or their aftermaths as they are lived out in many parts of the world today' (McMillan 139). Through such contact, 'the notion of respectability inscribed in the colonial parlor resonated with an emergent aspirant black middle class in the West Indies and working class in Britain in creating their front rooms', allowing them to register these diasporic front rooms in line with 'a trope of etiquette of decorum, protocol, polite manners, and proper behavior performed as rituals of respectability, dignity, and self-reserve associated with the Victorian parlor' (139). McMillan richly describes the aesthetic quality of these front rooms, which emulated the archetypal Victorian parlour insofar as they,

> included floral-patterned rugs, wallpaper, fabric curtains, and upholstered chairs and sofas with 'antimacassars' lace dollies (Victorian gentleman used Macassar hair oil) on the backs to prevent soiling. Prized ornaments and ephemera were displayed in a wooden cabinet or on a mantelpiece, ornate-framed black-and-white photographs stood on a lace-covered wooden sidetable or hung from a picture rail running along the top of the four walls … the room was lit from the ceiling or from the wall by baroque-styled light textures (138).

For the colonial elite of the Caribbean this romantic restaging of the English Victorian parlour served as a mark of status within their social milieu and reinforced their elite position as imperial superiors residing respectably within a 'tropical' climate. To fully comprehend this phenomenon we must recognise that 'these immigrants, coming from the colonies, saw themselves as British citizens, and through education sometimes knew more about English culture than the English themselves' (138). As part of their project of aesthetic authenticity, they retroactively adopted a puritanical Victorian ethos, which captured them and froze them in colonial time, their surroundings composed in artificial, staged environments that were reminiscent of neither homeland in a contemporary sense. These front rooms reveal a great deal about how the immigrants imagined themselves: as idealised reconstructions. These persons, made out of the subjects who went abroad, were meant to document their present experiences to send back home, to family and to real and desired spouses. Part of this idealised reconstruction 'took the form of photos and letters that often omitted telling them about signs in windows reading No Irish, No Dogs, No Coloureds, seen while searching for accommodation,' i.e. the material aspect of their belonging (141). Their unenviable task was to structure a presence out of these recurrent absences, or exclusions, and at the same time to allow the unsaid or unsayable to penetrate in some way against what is subtly represented to others; the erased and invisible narratives of these individuals brutally subsumed into an undesirable class upon their arrival to Britain. 'Though they had to daily negotiate the covert and overt vagaries of racism, their ever-positive faces say so much about what is in the frame, but also about what is beyond the frame' (McMillan 141). These private dramas were destined to play out 'among the legacy of a racial hierarchy based on a "pigmentocracy" instituted in plantation societies', which found its way home to the British mainland as an effect of slavery and perhaps still remains (142).

This racialised framework was just as important as what it

represented. The front room of the 1960s provided a stage for the display of certain types of reconstructed and reimagined memory that had its antecedents in Victorian colonialism, and it is for this reason that such a profound censure remains evident in the black appropriation of its composition of domestic propriety. Whether ancestral or contemporary in its constituent parts, the front room is deeply inscribed into the representation of the black experience in Britain. Behind it was a race relations agenda about assimilation. The front room, as an emblematic motif, was there to signify the West Indian community as conservative, upstanding and god-fearing citizens who strove to become more English than the English themselves. The older 1960s generation not only 'spoke or attempted to use the "Queen's English" better than the Queen, they also accented to the analogy, "When in Rome, do as the Romans do"' (McMillan 143–4). Such an analogy can now take on a double meaning in our discussion of how intergenerational identifications are signified in the representation of the front room, because they speak to an aspiration of societal triumph that tragically was never realised. Despite their dogged determination to hold onto the values of the Victorian past, their dreams of dwelling in a better tomorrow where they are counted as local have yet to be achieved.

There can be no doubt that those of West Indian origin have transculturally absorbed a British identity and an English culture into their everyday lives in the decades onwards from the early 1960s, nor that their children have disavowed their parents' colonial domestic aesthetics in favour of highly cultured and politicised reconstructions of their contemporary domestic spaces. It is in part within those spaces that their contested cultural identities play out within the context of a complex race politics of multiculturalism that began to arise in the Britain of the early 1980s, corresponding with the age of their first generation children's maturity as native-born Britons. The front rooms of their youth emerged within a colonial context, wherein the realities of diasporic migration, independence, postcolonialism and globalisation informed both their aesthetic and practical values. For them the Caribbean has become synonymous with a contested ancestral past, further occluded by the limitations of memory, which nonetheless persists as a crucial basis for the constant process of refashioning their contemporary British identities. By exploring how certain types of memory are created and embodied by the material culture of the front room, we might be able to address the profound neocolonial potential still available within it, some element of which remains ambivalent and disruptive to the process of assimilation even to this day. This phenomenon creates an evocative interior line within the discursive field of present-day multiculturalism.

Outside of these sheltered domestic spaces, the first generation of British-born Afro-Caribbean youth struggled to escape the kind of poorly paid manual labour their immigrant parents had undertaken as a highly exploited migratory class. Paul Gilroy explains that 'their battle to be free from "shit work" was buoyed up by an ill-defined but nonetheless alternative conception of social life, affirmed in the unruly, dissident (sub)culture that they improvised from the residues of insurgent Ethiopianism, Black Power, and democratic, anti-racist sentiment' ('1981 and 2011' 552). The racial tensions that emerged as a result of the dissolution of the British Empire contributed to a powerful sense of commiseration with the ethno-national conflict in Northern Ireland and the struggle against apartheid in South Africa amongst Afro-Caribbean youth in Britain. These conflicts also weighed heavily on 'the minds of those in charge of the police and the army', because they 'feared the possibility that a similar breakdown of law and order might appear in Britain's noisy pockets of minority settlement, which would then become "no-go areas"' (552). Added to this was the ongoing fear of an imminent race war, a concept that had gained political currency since the infamous 'rivers of blood' speech made by the racist Conservative politician Enoch Powell in 1968, which sparked fear in the minds of whites. The most extreme of these fears would distort the political discourse around race and further aggravate racial tensions culminating in the lead-up to the 1979 election that brought Margaret Thatcher's government to power. The turn of the decade would mark the start of neoliberal economic policy in Britain, which quickly brought about recession, mass unemployment and social discontent. These, as much as racial tensions, figured as the major factors in widespread rioting across Britain during 1981. They captured the public imagination because they underlined a general feeling amongst the population that England was entering into a period of protracted societal crisis, as a result and response to the rapid deindustrialization of its cities and towns.

In 1981 a discourse began to take shape across the government, state and media arguing that black communities suffered from a potentially insurmountable combination of familial pathology and related intergenerational conflict. It was claimed that the Afro-Caribbean rioters' determination to cause public disturbance was based upon a fundamental cultural difference between them and their white, British, working-class generational counterparts. This divergence in values was purportedly visible along generational lines: 'primarily between the Victorian attitudes of immigrant parents and the more modern outlook of their disobedient, locally born children whose vulnerability was compounded by their psychological and cultural disorientation' (Gilroy, '1981 and 2011' 554). By the summer of 2011, the official statistics on unemployment, police stops and searches, and school exclusions bore out this narrative about the bleak prospects of black youth rooted in their communal dysfunction in a way that was eerily similar to 1981. It appears that little had changed in the intervening thirty years, in which a new generation of poor and socially disenfranchised youth came into their adulthood. Gilroy's account of these latest riots produced a counter-narrative to the one being touted by contemporary politicians and media outlets, which pointed to the 'institutionalization of racialized inequality, prejudice, and discrimination' and 'a neoliberal revolution' which strategically generated norms of 'individuation and privatization' in order to reframe the discourse around black youth, so that race could be decoupled from violence and the talk of crime (555). In this way, the issue of race and racism could be rhetorically sidestepped through the introduction of ostensibly neutral civil orders to confront and deter 'antisocial behavior'. These new measures were meant to counteract the rise of an ungovernable gang culture populated with youths whose primary crime was their inherent fecklessness, which prevented them from being able to 'buy in' to the consumer culture in the normal manner like their middle-class brethren.

There is much to be learned from following along the logical path of the neoliberal catechism, repeated as a gospel of wealth in inner-city academies and mentorship programs by the adult staff, that the preconditions for personal (read monetary) success are now in place regardless of growing inequality. This echoes their Victorian liberal forbearers' message of uplift to those facing a lifetime of grinding poverty that subtends the wealth of the elite. The 'deserving poor' are those who seize upon the opportunity to work, in whatever condition such labour presents itself and for whatever precious little reward. Young people are told that 'failure is a matter of one's own personal responsibility' (Gilroy, '1981 and 2011' 556). Gilroy argues that amongst a certain class of gentleman 'selfishness' will always be perceived 'as an innate virtue', something that is commonly practiced amongst an elite class that includes within its ranks corrupt bankers, expenses-fiddling politicians and others seeking the addictive thrill of acquiring 'something for nothing' (556). By contrast, for those at the bottom rung of society to possess such characteristics is a sure sign of social deviancy and impracticable greed. It was only during those warm summer days of 2011, when 'money-free shopping' briefly entered into the pageant of this social disorder, that the collusion between these value systems was brought into sharp relief for all who cared to look. Regrettably, few were prepared to address this reality and the riots were met with predictable public contempt and systematic disavowal. Along with the loud condemnation of the crass actions of Britain's contemporary poor youths, came another silent feature of disapproval: the lack of respect for Britain's imperial greatness, and appreciation of a time when Britain was still considered Great. For many it was a country that still could be that way, had it been 'less burdened by the [imperial] past and less anxious in the face of alterity' (557).

Mayor Boris Johnson told BBC Radio 4's Today programme on 6 August 2012 that the London 2012 Olympics were 'playing a role' in the solution to 'deep social problems' by 'sending a clear message about effort and achievement, and what it takes to connect the two' (qtd. in BBC News, 'Riot problems still an issue'). What it takes to connect the two appears to be the application of sizeable financial resource, the fact of which was made evident when 'the mayor said £70m had been pumped into inner city areas of London to try to avoid a repeat of the violence and looting'. Johnson observes that the superficial utility of this cash injection into poorer communities will alone do little to address the problems they are aimed at solving. Those take place at a deeper level, which we must examine 'by looking at what happens in the lives of young people, their role models, their ideals, what they want to achieve'. Johnson believes that 'sport and the Olympics play a role' in building 'self-esteem, character, confidence and the ability to understand how to lose – all those vital things'.

Johnson implies here that their role models, their ideals, what they want to achieve, had been drawn from a field of moral alterity, which promoted a youth sub-culture 'of easy gratification and entitlement' in the years before the global economic recession. Little is made of the fact that this was equally the ambition of the rich as well as the poor, and indeed would continue to feature as an attribute of both classes' immoral behaviour following the economic crisis. Johnson asserts that the 'clear message' that the Olympics were sending in 2012 to the previous year's rioters was not that they could participate as confident equals, nor project an image of themselves as talented potential victors, but rather that they needed to make the 'difficult psychological adjustment to a new world without easy credit, where life is considerably tougher than it was before the crunch'. Essentially what they needed to appreciate instead was how to lose and how to adjust to their sudden discredit in a dignified manner. Moreover, Johnson contends that this same 'clear message' that the Olympics were sending 'could not come at a better time for a country' where a new generation of young working-class people needed to ready itself to compete for the 67,000 additional apprenticeships generously laid on by the government and private-sector employers, many of these positions unpaid and few leading to long-term gainful employment. This initiative functioned as another spurious solution to solve the 'crisis in values' brought about through coping with yet another era of poorly paid work.

Victory, for its part, would be obliged to make its appearance elsewhere, as it had done when Britain had hosted the World Cup. When football 'came home' in 1966, it then suffered a dramatic decline. The same could be said perhaps for its colonial project. 'With the age of television, there was a fall in numbers at the turnstile, which eventually led to bigger clubs and a more commercial, rather than community-based, game' (University of York, 'Lessons from the past'). The goal of winning the World Cup was never really one of local community coherence, but rather the promotion of an image of postcolonial relevance for a postwar Britain that would mitigate the reality of its long economic decline dating back as far as July 1947, when sterling progressively ceased to be the world's standard currency in favour of the US dollar. In the mid-1960s, 'the Labour Government of Harold Wilson clearly saw the World Cup as an opportunity to put a modernising Britain in the world's shop window, while boosting national morale. As well as financing ground improvements, Foreign Office files in The National Archives suggest that the occasion was seen as an important political and diplomatic event game'.

It is worth remembering that the World Cup of 1966 was held during at era when Britain's troubled economy provoked international speculation, wreaking havoc on the pound. At that time central bankers from 11 nations came together to offer an IMF bailout loan to balance sterling against further speculation. In 1966, British national sentiment was at a low point as various youth movements were sweeping across Eastern Europe enlivening fears about the looming threat of communism spreading to the West. There were also the deaths of John F. Kennedy and Winston Churchill, each marking an end of an era of hopefulness for each country respectively. The independence of South Africa and Rhodesia played its part to bruise the national ego. Finally, the involvement of the US in the Vietnam war signalled a new threat to Britain's interests and investments in South Asia should communism in that region of the world prove triumphant.

Upon entering into the competition, England had never held the World Cup. The reality of actually winning the tournament within this geopolitical context was of enormous significance. Nonetheless to this day there remains much controversy surrounding the win itself, especially in light of the fact that it has never come close to being repeated. Thus it seems plausible that there may have been some collusion on the part of England and West Germany to rig the matches and competition in order for a Western European team to claim victory, rather than a team from Latin America (Tuohy). Some speculate that the desire to win was great enough to compel Prime Minister Harold Wilson to agree to such an arrangement. It would crucially boost public morale at a time when Britain was entering into what would amount to a decade-long period of economic crisis. 'Wilson had only returned from the United States shortly before the kick-off of the World Cup final, where he had been negotiating a large loan from the International Monetary Fund' (T. Mason 90). During the start of that rather difficult period, football provided a much-needed source of self-esteem for Britain to continue to present itself favourably both at home and on the international stage. In Boris Johnson's 2012 address, 'the prime minister's insistence that the 2012 Olympics would be "like 1966" in the national psyche' resonated with a similar need to express triumph amidst another long era of economic decline and redrafting of Britain's postwar national identity (Gilroy, '1981 and 2011' 557).

In popular culture this melancholic duty finds its fulfilment in the refrain of 'two world wars and one World Cup', a chant evoked by British fans at international sporting events. Its odd fusion of class and masculinity betrays a deeper historical amnesia. 'All the latent violence, all the embittered machismo, all the introjected class warfare articulated by defeated victors (mostly men and boys who were baffled and bewildered by a new postwar world that refused to recognize their historic manly qualities) is coded here in a dynamic and still explosive form' (Gilroy, *Postcolonial Melancholia* 107). For Paul Gilroy, the explicit linkage of war to football provides a rare vantage point 'from which all the remorseful processes of Britain's vanquished imperial status can be observed. In this light, the phrase "two world wars and one World Cup" becomes a means with which to consider the bewildering effects of Britain's postcolonial melancholia – even where they are intermittently offset by the compensations of the country's rare but nonetheless significant sporting successes' (107). In contemporary postcolonial Britain, sport has taken on a synonymous value to war, and allows the country to believe that the long-established place of Britain as one of the world's leading powers remains essentially intact, despite Britain's persistent failure to competitively modernise its institutions to offset its path towards downward mobility for much of the latter half of the twentieth century. During the 1960s, a small, newly arrived, multicultural, postcolonial audience would have been loyal to such a belief even as Empire was progressively being diluted into Common Wealth. By 2012, their grandchildren were made to dwell within another Britain, where 'manifold neocolonial, biopolitical, and environmental dangers await them on the perilous pathway to Britain's mismanaged decline' and 'where once again incarceration, social containment and transportation become the founding institutions of expedient governance, as they had been previously in a nineteenth century Britain', in the cause of reinforcing a post-imperial nationalism (Gilroy, '1981 and 2011' 557).

Such arrangements in the Victorian era made possible the divorce of capitalism and imperialism in the public's imagination, allowing nonetheless for market rule to govern both home and imperial populations. In more recent decades, Jane M. Jacobs argues there have been critical counter-flows to what in the past was 'a spatial imaginary of British imperialism based on the forceful flow of power from what came to be understood as the "core," to what was relationally designated as the "periphery"', which in a contemporary situation must be revised to accommodate the definition of a global city' (5). This global city 'must be competitive on a new playing field comprised from new global and regional alignments that emerged with the reformation of the world in an era of at least ostensible postcolonialism' (5). That said, empire is never very far from the culture and imagination that continues to shape London as one of the world's great cities. Even today most Londoners continue to adopt 'an internalised view of the city', which imagines itself as the purveyor 'of hospitality', towards 'those who come to "us", who remain as "strangers"' despite their being tolerated 'within the gate' (Massey, 'London Inside-Out' 64). Jacques Derrida elaborates on the concept of '"open cities" (villes-franches) or "refuge cities" (villes refuge)', when he asks us to think of the cosmopolitan city as a space of meeting, reflecting and sheltering otherness, where the city itself becomes an open refuge, where migrants may seek sanctuary (Derrida, On Cosmopolitanism and Forgiveness viii).

Doreen Massey reflects on Derrida's concept of the open city with the caveat in mind that 'the geographies of places aren't only about what lies within them', and that 'a richer geography of place acknowledges also the connections that spread out from the metropole: the trade-routes, investments, political and cultural influences; power-relations of all sorts run out from here around the globe and link the fate of other places to what is done in London' ('London Inside-Out' 64). Given this perspective, for Massey 'this tendency towards inwardlookingness' belies a truth at the heart 'of the characterisation of London as a multicultural future city of the world': that alongside its multiculturalism sits 'a vast and intricate cultural and economic infrastructure' that is crucial to the functioning of both 'neoliberalism and globalisation' (65). The project of the city of London therefore is disproportionately responsible for managing not only the flow of the world's global foreign wealth, but equally its poverty. This situation relates both to Britain's colonial past and to its neoliberal future, which relies on a burgeoning population in London drawn out of the confused movement and violent turmoil of neoliberal globalisation that has left millions of individuals economically destabilised in its wake.

The actions of London as a centre of neoliberal power bear responsibility, in part, as the cause of their hardship if we view it as a city with a much larger impact than we might imagine. The wider geographies of place it has occupied historically continue to hold significant resonance in this present era of globalisation. Given this situation it is possible to conceive that a superficial agenda of multiculturalism and a politics of anti-racism exist on some profound level to distract attention away from the morally unsavoury activities of London's financial sector and multinational corporations, which can be said to routinely and ruthlessly exploit the wealth of economically weaker nations. It is this, rather than the distinctive character of multiculturalism, that defines the basis of London as a global city and to which it is dependent to guarantee its future success. The majority of Londoners remain oblivious to this reality and therefore ignorance prevails when they attempt to grasp the true dimensions of this state of affairs.

The central tenet of being a global city rests upon the premise of its unremitting expansion as a global financial power. An over-reliance on the financial sector in the formulation of London's success as a global city has led to gross inequalities, on both a spatial and a social level, which take place as a direct result of the skewed prioritisation of capital over individuals that occurs routinely within the metropolitan area itself. Massey argues that while it is important to recognise that 'London is the most unequal place in the UK', it is also crucial to grasp that its 'internal inequality is intimately linked to its economic structure and its global role' ('London Inside-Out' 67). One aspect of this inequality is the fact that London is profoundly dependent on labour from abroad, including from the global South, to sustain its urban living standards. Workers who have been raised and educated abroad flood into London to secure relatively well-paid employment and in the course of doing so deny their countries of origin the benefit of their labour and contribution of their skills to enhance the status of their native economies. In effect this means that places like 'India, Sri Lanka, Ghana, South Africa are subsidising the reproduction of London' (69). This 'perverse subsidy, flowing to the rich from the poor', echoes earlier patterns of colonial domination and 'yet in its postmodern guise is tolerated because this mechanism is able to drape itself in the philosophy of transterritorial labour markets' (69). Criticism of such practices is deflected by the spectre of racism through the denial of immigration rights to these black and Asian postcolonial nations. Little if anything is ever said about the losses suffered by these same nations when it comes to their workforce, nor how it relates back to the economic legacy of slavery that continues to impact them economically, through these modern-day schemes of labour-plundering by the West. Such practices deny these countries the full benefit of their prior investment in cultivating their native human capital, without a thought given to any form of restitution which might make up for the perversity of this profoundly asymmetrical financial arrangement which slants wealth in the opposite direction of need. It is for this reason that we have to reconsider the expansion of multiculturalism through a prism of economic necessity as opposed to a more banal understanding of London's diversity, which fails to take into account the potential neocolonial ramifications of its largely diasporic workforce.

This contemporary reality brings us back to *Great Expectations*, and its emphasis on the barring of former colonial (British) citizens from returning to their 'mother country'. The British Home Office announced in mid-2013 that it is going ahead with a plan 'to force some visitors from India, Nigeria, Kenya, Sri Lanka, Pakistan and Bangladesh to pay a £3,000 bond for a visitor visa allowing them to stay in the UK for up to six months' (Sparrow). The initiative is coupled with the introduction of other measures of racial intimidation, which include the 'Go Home' van campaign, which echoes the National Front graffiti slogans of the 1970s and features the message: 'In the UK illegally? Go home or face arrest'. This campaign is targeted at poor, racially mixed urban areas, as are 'the immigration raids on tube stations ...

which according to Doreen Lawrence and eyewitness accounts, have involved racial profiling' (Sparrow). In addition to this, the Home Office wants to charge non-EU migrants for healthcare and to require private landlords to check the immigration status of prospective tenants, opening the door to further incidents of racialised discrimination and public abuse. These initiatives, combined with their inflammatory promotion through recent political discourse on the part of the Conservatives and UKIP, represent an increasing politicisation of Home Office policy. Fears about immigration are now routinely exploited for desired electoral gain, while inciting a local atmosphere of intimidation for migrants and people of colour. The Home Office's hostility towards migrants takes on a distinctive racial and economic bias when we consider the government's enthusiasm for appointing mainly white immigrants from the Common Wealth to senior appointments within Britain with little controversy or alarm. Today in Britain a white Canadian is governor of the Bank of England, a white New Zealander (who failed his accountancy exams) is head of the publicly owned RBS, a white Australian lobbyist is head of Tory electoral strategy and he has a white American as his deputy (Sparrow).

The Home Office's tacit establishment of such racial and class hierarchies in determining the 'right' sorts of economic migrant, does a great deal to enliven the climate of fear and discrimination against what is perceived as the 'wrong' sort. Today London's migration trend echoes postwar Britain in the early 1960s, insofar as 'the free flow of capital is followed inevitably by the flow of labour, as people move from areas of forced economic decline to wherever there is a prospect of work. Employers benefit from cheaper labour but the migrants are blamed for displacing unskilled workers and competing for scarce resources in housing and health' (Philo, 'Capital's role in the economic crisis'). This trend continues because of a concentration of wealth at the top; wherein 'the £4.5 trillion owned by the top 10%', which could 'easily pay off the national debt four times or finance re-skilling, infrastructure, green technology and much else', remains taxably unaccounted for by an equally elite class of politicians and media who require no accountability as regards the source of these earnings (Harris, 'The Tories Are Creating a Hostile Environment'). Instead they opt to fervently condemn the migrants, refugees and other victims of the system as the parties responsible for Britain's contemporary social and economic crisis. UKIP tells us explicitly that this surplus population has to be in some way shipped out voluntarily or by 'enforced return'.

It is here finally that we turn back to the figure of Magwitch and how his character might be projected onto an understanding of the present debate around migration. James Rhodes argues that contemporary British society would wish to identify itself as postracial. Much evidence to the contrary suggests that whiteness remains the universal guideline for the construction of societal norms, and moreover that they persist in reifying white privilege, even if a certain class of whiteness must be disadvantaged 'to diminish the significance of racial stratification, obscuring the disproportionate rates of white poverty in comparison to that of black and minority ethnic groups' (Rhodes 64). This common feature of poverty allows the emphasis to shift from race to class, as an explanation for 'social, cultural and economic marginalisation', which allows for the invocation of marginalised white identities to be 'paradoxically used as evidence of a raceless society, or at least a society where the significance of race is declining' (64). The advancement of multiculturalism goes hand in hand with the advancement of global capitalism, though few in British society are prepared to admit overtly that the recent financial crisis is also a racial crisis, wherein both financial and racial privileges are being compromised in what appears to be an epoch-defining shift towards larger inequalities across the full spectrum of society. Because of the general unwillingness to address these forms of inequality at their material level, immigration and multicultural policy debates are made to stand in for that vital discussion, with the consequence being that certain whites are now being justified in their exclusion from their former position of privilege. We are told by prominent politicians and mainstream media commentators that this white underclass, which was formerly described as the 'working class', can no longer be defined as such because it is effectively sustained by the welfare state and through such dependence has devolved into a uncultivated underclass stereotypically associated with a criminalised form of 'blackness'. Such a racialised logic accords perfectly with a neoliberal discourse that utterly disavows the relationship between increased global competition and scant local resources as the real culprit in their progressive marginalisation.

The coverage of the riots of August 2011 frequently referenced the 'whiteness' of many of the individuals involved, while making no mention of the fact that they started roughly one year on from the Coalition government's first large-scale welfare spending cuts. Writing in *The Independent*, Michael McCarthy concluded that, the riots were 'a multiracial phenomenon. There were plenty of black rioters; there were plenty of white rioters, too. But what united them was the abandonment of all restraint and the cultural norms which had once been so powerful in British society were irrelevant to them' (qtd. in Rhodes 49). On 12 August 2011, the historian David Starkey stated his belief that the events demonstrated how some sections of the white population 'have become black', as 'a particular sort of violent, destructive, nihilistic gangster culture has become the fashion, and black and white, boy and girl, operate in this language together, this language which is whole false, it's this Jamaican patois which has been intruded in England and this is why so many of us have this sense of literally a foreign country [sic]' (BBC News, 'England riots'). This group of working-class whites was thusly stigmatised for failing to adhere to the dominant 'white' norms and practices, associated by the English middle-class with respectability. Much of the media fanfare around this class has been preoccupied by themes of interracial contamination and racial degeneracy, which today, three years after the riots, remain central to such representations of the white underclass.

Through such rhetoric, it is possible to justify a system of discrimination that is no longer explicitly hinged on a biological racism, but instead on a cultural racism, wherein whites might be accused of separating themselves from their racial assignment by voluntarily adopting the values, needs and motivations stereotypically assigned to 'black' culture. Moreover, 'such discursive constructions of whiteness seek to displace racism and enduring attachments to nativist forms of racial identity from the centre to peripheries of whiteness. In doing so modern forms of whiteness are presented as modern, multicultural, and even "postracial"' (Rhodes 65). Those who remain white but are peripheral to white privilege are then invoked as a threatened class requiring protection, so not as to be pitted against a tide of (black) migrants in the competition for the limited state resources directed at them as a disadvantaged class within the spectrum of 'whiteness'. The belief that the social position of minority/migrant groups should never exceed those of poor whites 'is based on a premise "of some sort of priority citizenship," in which it is assumed that groups such as the white working class "should be doing better"' (66). In this neoliberal schema, those who fail to maintain their position of racial entitlement are confined to a zone of economic illegitimacy through their own actions, and as such their lives of intense hardship and poverty should not warrant care or valuation. The government's feinted moral outrage at their existence allows them to more easily dehumanise those who suffer most under their draconian budgetary reforms.

If Magwitch were a contemporary character, Dickens would have surely given him the attributes of a 'chav', framing him as a member of the white working class 'cast as endemically racist, backward and lacking in a form of "multicultural" literacy' (Rhodes 51). We have been here before in the reckoning that takes place in *Great Expectations*, through the imaginary correspondence sent by Jagger's, as a representative of the law, to a socially exiled Magwitch: your money's welcome here, so long as you're prepared to acquiesce to the fact that you will never again be a rightful denizen of London. Despite such forfeiture, he is drawn back to the great metropolis to witness his creation in the shape of another man who may be able to regenerate the currency of a lost white privilege. That Pip fails to do so says a great deal about how the odds are stacked against him and the generations of white working-class Britons who will succeed him, as the capital similarly risks everything to maintain its identity and character based on the concealment of the sources of its illicit wealth, wherein we are finally reminded by Dickens that society itself is built upon a legacy of a criminal enterprise fuelled by plunder and debt. Witnessed at this level it is possible to read Great Britain as the ultimate punitive settlement upon which these others are based.

Age and Ills: Dickens's Response to the Indian Mutiny of 1857 within the Present Context of Neoliberal Empire

The rise of Dickens is like the rising of a vast mob. This is not only because his tales are indeed as crowded and populous as towns: for truly it was not so much that Dickens appeared as that a hundred Dickens characters appeared. It is also because he was the sort of man who has the impersonal impetus of a mob.
– G. K. Chesterton, *The Victorian Age*

Dickens's writings dealt with a set of persistent anxieties and uncertainties that plagued the maturation of the British Empire within his lifetime. The concomitant rise of finance capitalism with the rapid expansion of commercial imperialism provided Dickens with a literary strategy with which to both incorporate and interrogate the social implications of these formations both at home and abroad. Every category of individual touched by these twin formations makes its way into Dickens's novels. What unites this cast of characters is their existence as British subjects captured within the newly emerging structures of economy, law, governance and policing that emerge in the wake of the British Empire's intensification in the latter half of the nineteenth century; a period which not coincidentally coincides with the pinnacle of Dickens's career as an author and commentator.

One way to view the continuing relevance of Dickens's writing is through the dissolution of that empire and the social narratives of the late twentieth century and early twenty-first century which 'exhibit a need to recover and recover from the atrocities of empire in the past' on one end of the political spectrum, and on the other, a need to deprecate such activities for failing to recognise the triumphs, both moral and economic, the empire achieved (Ho 11). What is at stake from the postmillennial standpoint is the delineation of neo-imperial and neo-colonial arrangements, which promote a nostalgic, sanitised image of Britain's former empire in order to sanctify the continued expression of imperial aims in the present. As it had done during the Victorian era, the new imperialising vision extends such a perspective both inward and outward to embrace empire as a positive value.

Such a value arguably has a greater currency in today's era of free-trade agreements and nation-building than it did in the nineteenth century, simply because there are more competitors in the race for neo-colonial ascendency; including the United States, China and Russia, as well as the European Union. While these parties may no longer wish to participate in the official governmental colonisation of their desired territories, they most certainly wish to partake in the unofficial commercial colonisation of the world's lesser economies. With the trend of the past thirty years towards privatisation and the mass selling off of state-owned enterprises to private entities, both at home and abroad, this new generation of empire-building governments have become less like sovereign states and more like enterprise zones, pouring billions of state funds into fuelling speculative private industrial expansion. In the process of doing so they explicitly link economic interests to state governance, in a way that perhaps is greater than at any time since the latter half of the nineteenth century.

One of the more privileged activities of these governmental enterprise zones is the engineering of 'greater freedoms' for those populations 'trapped' in conflict areas around the globe. Today such interference by the world's leading nations quickly becomes synonymous with the (forced) installation of free markets. The paternalistic relationship to these developing nations, which appear to require the more powerful nations' international intervention, does little to promote a greater cosmopolitanism amongst their domestic populations, but rather functions to reinforce presumptions of national superiority in the opening up of these countries and regions 'to our way of life'. The political rhetoric about 'our way of life' shares a very conspicuous confluence with Dickens's time and the Victorians' self-confidence in their destined mission as beneficent rulers of other races. 'At that time they too believed they were replacing barbarism with the *Pax Britannica* and spreading enlightened civilisation to grateful coloured peoples around the globe' (Kohlke & Gutleben 370). Little is said of the economic component of civilisation and indeed most Britons at this time would remain unaware of the profound economic interdependency that was developing between Britain and her colonies, in particular India. Dickens himself was a great believer in Britain's civilising mission around the globe and as such he and his countrymen were very badly shaken by the Indian Mutiny of 1857, which challenged assumptions of a grateful people benevolently handing over its wealth, population and physical resources in exchange for access to a superior culture. The transformation in awareness was complete when the limits of the colonial project involved in subordinating colonial peoples were communicated to their apprehensive racial betters by way of a baffling ingratitude and an unwavering appetite for independence in the decades to follow.

The Indian Mutiny struck at the heart of Victorian liberalism and its laissez-faire approach to colonial governance through commercial fiat. Following the Mutiny, it became apparent to the British government that its vast commercial domination of India, heretofore managed exclusively and monopolistically by the East India Company, would now have to be augmented with a 'vast, thriving military-industrial machinery', under direct control of the Crown (Kohlke & Gutleben 371.) The Mutiny served as a catalyst to two major events that would make explicit for the first time the contour of Britain's formal empire: the Government of India Act of 1858 and the subsequent proclamation of Queen Victoria as Empress of India in 1876. Both the act and proclamation signalled to Britain's political and commercial rivals their exclusive right to formally administer this territory and, by right of such authority, possess ownership over its projected wealth. It is for this reason that 'more than any of the other bloody conflicts during Queen Victoria's reign, the Mutiny threw into doubt not only the temporal limits of Britannia's power, but also her people's very identity as the chosen race and nation, the standard-bearers of civilisation' (370). The potential loss of the 'Jewel in the Crown' threatened to leave Britain irrevocably weakened as the world's colonial authority. Moreover, at home the British cultural imaginary of heroic nationhood was by now inextricably entwined with her colonial 'Other', and therein a Britain without India was almost inconceivable.

Empire was increasingly a source of pride for Britons and the achievements of British rules seldom questioned. Even the most dispossessed inhabitants of Victorian Britain, 'could luxuriate in an unaccustomed feeling of superiority and virtue when regaled with tales of 'the conquest, control and reordering of indigenous societies in India and elsewhere' (Judd 67). It was for this reason that disgust at the rebel's delinquency was able to penetrate down to even those at the bottom rungs of domestic society and enlivened within them a racialised hatred against such individuals. The British government for its part had rapidly devised a campaign of retribution for the uprising in India of both macabre and legendary proportion. Their so-called 'civilised' British troops descended with a bloody desire to avenge both their nation and their people. The list of atrocities to follow that order included: the stitching up of Muslims in pigskins prior to their hanging as a way to degrade their bodies before Allah, the violently enforced clean-up of the bloodstains of women and children from their massacre at Kanpur by Indian prisoners at lash end (with those refusing to be forced to clean the area with their tongues), and the blowing up of mutineer's bodies into fragments when shot from the mouths of British cannons (Judd 73).

Despite heinous atrocities occurring on the part of the British as well as the native Indian population, and the widening gulf of racialised hatred between the two cultures, the Raj remained a source of great pride on the part of Britons and most accepted on some level that the wealth wrought from India outweighed its burden. British rule of India held enormous financial and tactile advantages crucial for the maintenance of the whole of the Empire. As a territory, 'India was an enormously profitable, self-financing enterprise, approximating very closely the Victorian capitalist and imperial ideal' (Judd 77). It provided the British Empire with a vast source of population, with Indians making up 'approximately 80 per cent of all subjects' living within the British Empire at its height (78). Equally the Empire relied on its Indian subjects to swell the ranks of its military personnel making up the majority of soldiers and allowing it not only to become a formi-dable world power with the ability to fight against its imperial rivals, but equally to forcefully control and maintain its other colonial territories. It is for this reason that Indian Viceroy Curzon's remark made in 1901 still resonates in the British cultural imagination in the postcolonial era: 'As long as we rule India, we are the greatest power in the world. If we lose we shall drop straightway to a third rate power' (qtd. in Judd 78). The prescience of this remark reveals the precarious nature of British colonial power, which in reality was backed neither by numbers in the civil service nor in military rank. The total number of Britons in the sub-continent at the end of Victoria's reign was no more than 20,000 individuals. Rather it was the longstanding caste divisions within Indian society that allowed British authority to be maintained for nearly two centuries.

For most Britons, including Queen Victoria herself (who never bothered to visit India despite crowning herself its Empress), the impression of imperial control was largely a product of the imaginary. The inability for Britain to imagine itself nationally without India and its colonies elsewhere, and yet at the same time disavow utterly its coercive interdependency with them, has led to what Paul Gilroy terms 'postcolonial melancholia': a situation wherein post-imperial Britain is unwilling and unable to face the loss of national greatness and prestige. Elizabeth Ho comments that 'Faced with a racially diverse population from the post-colonies as a daily reminder of the hidden, shameful story of imperial horrors and exacerbated by an unsettled economic and political climate, (white) Britain has refused to work through its feelings of guilt and shame and has instead turned to active forgetfulness and silence punctuated by racial violence and debilitating nostalgia for a prior cohesion based on racial homogeneity' (17).

This racial violence reflects back a clash of cultures inside multicultural Britain, where the individuals mass-migrating from the Middle East and Asian subcontinent are viewed with suspicion as cultural outsiders. This view actively disavows the colonial legacy of British commercial and government presence in their home territories spanning centuries. Britain as a nation 'started to yield melancholia as soon as the natives and savages began to appear and make demands for recognition in the empire's metropolitan core', which led to Britain's first identity crisis in the sixteenth century when Queen Elizabeth I complained about the numbers of 'blackamoores' suddenly appearing in her 'fair' nation, bringing into sharp relief the core understanding of empire as something deeply rooted in the strict maintenance of a racial hierarchy (Gilroy, *Postcolonial Melancholia* 92). In 1596, Queen Elizabeth I issued an 'open letter' to the Lord Mayor of London, announcing that 'there are of late divers black-moores brought into this realme, of which kinde of people there are allready here to manie' (qtd. in Bartels 305) She ordered them to be deported from the country, expressing her 'good pleasure to have those kinde of people sent out of the lande' to transport them into 'Spaine and Portugall' (305). In 1601, she complained again about the 'great numbers of Negars and Blackamoors which [as she is informed] are crept into this realm'; defaming them as 'infidels, having no understanding of Christ or his Gospel', she reauthorised their further deportation (305).

What Queen Elizabeth I disavows in the course of calling for the mass deportation of blacks is the fact that their initial appearance in London came as direct result of either commercial privateering ventures or wartime bodily seizure. Such activities took place during a period in which England was locked in a bitter commercial and military competition with Spain. Despite this situation, Elizabeth I was still able to make the case to her Lord Mayor that 'the infiltration of "blacks"' stood 'as a threat both to England's economy and to its national unity and "natural" identity' based on their fundamental racial and religious difference from her kind of people (Bartels 322). Her assertion of their cultural deviancy as non-Christians allowed her to classify the black migrant as inferior to his white British counterpart. Such logic became crucial to the maintenance of a racial and national hierarchy that as centuries wore on proved essential to the crafting of the British national identity as synonymous with whiteness, Christianity and commercial ascendency.

In the early twenty-first century British nationalism remains founded on those same discourses of cultural essentialism, which cast blacks as permanent outsiders. The rise of the heritage industry in the 1980s 'represented an effort to create secure borders for a British identity perceived as being under siege by a multicultural other and under threat from European integration' (Dworkin 12). For the past sixty years much of this had to do with the romanticising of World War II, which goes hand in hand with a nostalgic longing for a society secure in its ethnic and racial homogeneity. In the past thirty years this narrative has been coupled with an upsurge in interest in the Victorian period, a time when global capitalism purports to grant social mobility across race and class divides, but in reality relegates more and more of the world's people, including Britons themselves, to the condition of servitude.

Contemporary neoliberal political rhetoric suggests that the chaos and alienation of a globalised economy can be repaired through the recovery and preservation of a privileged 'whiteness', which in the past managed to produce an exhilarating triumph over its global competitors, and can do so again through the imposition of an economic scarcity model, wherein the funnelling of money upwards to society's elite will guarantee their continued relevance in the emerging new world order. Despite the considerable spoils still obtained by its perceived 'whiteness' as a nation around the globe, the general population of Britain seem to remain gripped by a dismal discourse of decline characterised by their 'obsession with decay, the resignation to second-rate status, the endless rounds of self-recrimination and finger pointing' that characterise a postwar Britain (Dworkin 2). All the while they are tacitly informed by the Cameron government, in a plethora of ways, that in order 'to make Britain great again' the government must be allowed to restore 'an ethnic symmetry to a world distorted by imperial adventure and migration' (8).

On the other side of the equation, the distance of these postcolonial subjects from the legacy of British colonial rule has been of short duration; their decades of independence brief as compared to the centuries of their domination. This situation reveals its enduring might when we consider that the ruling classes of these newly independent nations were very often cast in the image of their British predecessors, thus allowing them to retain 'a catalog of hypocrisy, misogyny, violence, poverty and prurience often excised from' official versions of Britain's colonial past (Ho 29). The documents related to Britain's colonial atrocities we now know have been destroyed in their thousands and their disappearance coincides with another catastrophic error in judgement on the part of the British that is less easily disposed of: 'the error of judgement of imagining that postcolonial people are only unwanted alien intruders without any substantive historical, political, or cultural connections to the collective life of their fellow subjects' (Gilroy, *Postcolonial Melancholia* 90).

The error was also to believe that those who were expropriated, empressed and abjected would carry no sadness of their own, no story to tell of what befell them, and that somehow those narratives could be simply disposed of in the act of military and governmental divestment. The British Empire progressively decomposed itself through the founding of other national orders of dubious distinction. Its final official actions included laying 'the foundation for South Africa's apartheid state, the establishment of the state of Israel in Palestine as a novel historical experience in both nation building and colonization as reparation, ... the Partition of India', and the christening of the birth of Pakistan in bloodshed (Gilroy, *Postcolonial Melancholia* 15).

All of these closing acts of twentieth-century British imperialism have in common a racially separatist logic, which could no longer be actively ascribed in the wake of the Nazi's final solution to the question of how best to deal with racial differentiation. Britain wanted very badly for race to be forgotten, to usher in a second half of the century where it could be colour-blind; this of course was impossible given the colonial population's investiture in the fighting itself and the necessity of their labour as postwar Britain attempted to rebuild itself physically and financially after the war when it found itself facing a shortage of young able-bodied white working-class men. The tide of immigrants of colour who came to postwar Britain to fill their vacancies faced relentless antipathy, based on the widely held perception that heterogeneity would mark a point of irreversible departure from the homogeneity of whiteness that many believed provided them with the ethnic unity as Britons who won them the war. This same assumption had held when the Indian soldiers rebelled and suspended for a time the social classificatory system, in favour of an 'unchanging, pure form of Britishness' that 'cohered them into a nation, a people re-interpolated with common identities, values, aspirations and culture, notwithstanding differences in class, origin, regions and backgrounds' (Mohanram 32). This conspicuous homogeneity amongst whites had to be achieved, so that it was also possible to homogenise blacks and control them, based on the rationale that they could not demonstrate an equally laudable coherence as a race and thus required the rule of superior whites to guide their nations for them.

Pamela K. Gilbert maintains that in his later writing, Dickens worked hard 'to break down the geographic concept of otherness within London in favour of a potentially equal homogenous, equally civilized and malleable modern urban space' (141). He did so despite the fact that London had been functioning as the metropole for the whole of the Empire and as such it both defined and was defined by its commercial dynamics throughout the eighteenth century. As the nineteenth century dawned and metropolitan capitalism became more sophisticated in drawing resources from its imperial holdings, it became necessary to create an economic dualism wherein the underdevelopment of the colonial site corresponded to the hyper-development of the metropole. Creating this deviation in terms of developmental trajectories allowed London to position itself 'as a modern, at least potentially utopian space' against 'a colonial landscape' that 'was increasingly defined through the first two-thirds of the century as permanently dark, diseased, and barbaric' (P. Gilbert xix). Such preoccupations took on national significance in the decade following 1857, when India increasingly became the Other against which Britain would define itself, despite the continued assumption that the two nations were linked intimately in their territorial destinies.

In this new post-Mutiny configuration, Britain's rise must be converse to India's fall. Modern conceptions of metropolitan civilisation and health were often vividly contrasted with the unhealthy and barbaric colony in the sociological rhetoric of the day. Such a narrative obscured the reality that epidemic diseases, especially cholera, were actually increased by Britain's imperial presence in India. This occurred through 'the combination of new economic conditions with the mobility they sponsored and, paradoxically, the extensive water transport systems the British constructed', which 'were responsible for much of the appalling rise in Indian death rates in the mid-to-late nineteenth century' (P. Gilbert 145). This was not the only innovation that would prove fatal to the local population, 'the canals built to modernise India were often built without drainage systems; moreover they changed the ecosystem and caused contamination of drinking water sources' (145). These economic and ecological changes also sometimes contributed to famine, which could triple the death rate of cholera epidemics.

Not only did Victorian-British sanitation practices foster pestilence and demise; they also ushered into being an era of devastating climate change for the Indian sub-continent. Through a programme of mass deforestation and irrigation, Britain 'literally made parts of the environment more tropical in the negative sense of the term acquired by Europeans, which then justified domination of the Indians, who were believed to be the racially degenerate products of such an environment' (P. Gilbert 146). The perception of India as substandard in its physical condition bolstered Britain's rationale of natural superiority and right to rule. 'Bengal came to represent the Indian landscape for many Britons, and Bengal, a low-lying, moist, warm delta, was envisioned by the midcentury as the very type of diseased geography, insusceptible to remediation' (147–8).

The widely held belief that diseases such as cholera were able to transcend the limits of space and race to infect the urban working and under classes 'at home in Britain, speaks to a symbolic geography connecting empire and metropole wherein the ills related to barbarism become synonymous with a problematic geography' (P. Gilbert xix). The threat of barbarism however is interpreted differently in an imperial context versus a metropolitan one. In the Indian context there was a preoccupation with population, whereas in Britain the threat of disease was portrayed as bearing down on one singular, vulnerable individual. In Dickens's novels the savages he wrote about were simply identified through their unchanging locality, whereas even the poorest of his British characters were portrayed through a name and a circumstance that defined the contour of their regrettable, individual condition. In narrowing his sympathies thusly, Dickens failed to recognise the coterminous nature of the economic body of capitalism set against the social body of the native, as indirectly producing such conditions. As a consequence, he routinely failed to resolve the plight of those figures in any reassuring way beyond the notion of an obscure (and more often than not colonially derived) fortune that would fortuitously free them of their dire poverty.

The problem of population however was not limited to the scope of colonial enterprise alone, and took on particular contours when formally enacted back home in Britain. The liberalism of the Victorian-British state operated by quantitative register, its statistical imagination becoming the cornerstone by which its people were conceptually and characteristically settled as numerical charges. Dickens's writing assented to this practice of governing by numbers, when he returned time and again in his own political rhetoric to the principle of security. As a consequence Dickens's fiction confronted the central ideological problem of biopower at the very moment in which he endeavoured to preserve Britain's national stability. It is here that the Dickensian project appears most to intersect with the Victorian state. Its operational grid-work was overlaid by the functions of the police, and subtended by the function of a variety of institutions that acted upon the object of population, working over its politicised body with scalpel-like precision in an attempt to standardise it into a predictable entity. However, in their diligent surveillance they found that they routinely encountered 'the aggregate of humanity as something other than this: a surplus of ungovernable life that exceed[ed] and threaten[ed] the survival of the social body' (Steinlight 246). It was the tracking of that surplus population that became the stuff of Dickens's local beat. He tasked himself with enlivening such aberrations and trained his readers to become aware of these extraordinary figures within their ordinary midst. The Victorian imagination, thus shaped, thrust itself forward and progressed in erecting a sociological discourse to surround this incongruity and to name it. In order to aggregate it from the mass, it required the invention of a new class of individual for whom difference must conform reliably to its outward appearance.

Such an apparatus cannot be prefigured in economic terms, which are far too changeable in nature, given the erratic proclivities of the market, but rather in biological terms that cannot be in any way altered over a single lifetime. Here we find ourselves looking, as Michel Foucault suggests, not for a degenerate subclass, but for 'a degenerate "subrace" that is ceaselessly infiltrating the social body," and deviating it from its routine advancement' (Steinlight 246). Emily Steinlight argues that despite Dickens's outward hostility towards liberalism, by continually probing its founding 'hermeneutic, without seeking to contain its projected threat', he 'not only allows such a process of infiltration to take place' in the space of his great works, 'but also collapses the qualitative distinctions that ground all attempts to naturalize bourgeois normativity, to domesticate and sanitize the "dangerous classes," and to police the abject' (246). The novels themselves may be viewed as literary experiments in population management, which go horribly wrong when they attempt to confront the contradiction they necessarily defer, and thus not only introduce the contradiction of the supernumerary into their narratives, but also allow such social practices to embed themselves further into the foundation of British society.

According to liberal principle, the totality of the population will always emerge in excess of itself, and effectively require certain members of the human species to appear at odds with society. Thus the problem of social deviancy becomes the condition of possibility for society to exist. 'Much as institutions and governments require that which exceeds their administrative capacities and violates their law in order to exist, so too does the novel find in the unmanageable mass of supernumeraries its own peculiar reason of state' (Steinlight 246). In producing the longing for an ending it does not offer, 'the Dickensian novel stakes the future of the social on the solution to a problem that the institutions of capitalism, modern states, and biopolitical apparatuses of security are structured to leave unsolved' if not, indeed, to perpetuate (247).

Dickens's prodigious output is not founded upon the desire to remedy society and solve the problems it creates, but rather to relentlessly reproduce such problems, exposing the perverse logic by which liberal governmentality sustains itself not despite but precisely through its administrative failures and contradictions. The continued interest in Dickens's writing throughout the world in the twenty-first century is the product of a similar collusion of aims insofar as today's dominant culture of empire, the United States, 'romanticizes, naturalizes, and authorizes narratives and structures of empire' proper to its imperial predecessor, the United Kingdom (Ho 11). Despite its global preeminence the United States still struggles to come to terms with a global order which universally registers the continued resonance of Britain's imperial past in judgment of America's present imperial function. The colonial scene of the 1880s, with its attendant racial profiling and military-style policing of peripheral zones, has the rebellions of the 1850s bleeding into the enterprise culture of the 1980s and beyond. The subsequent wars of the twentieth century, which made it the most murderous century in recorded mankind, are far from inexplicable or mysterious, or indeed part of some 'explosion of extrinsic' evil, but rather a logical step in the process 'of patriarchal roles, values, needs and the rule of force' that have their beginnings in a chronological sequence that matches well to the prints of Dickens's own lifetime (Ho 11). Britain's imperial height and demise are equally traceable when we consider that the confluence of the attributes of military power and the authority of the state were forced to cohere simultaneously to the embodiment of empire as a universal mother determined to fulfil the demands of a yearning domesticity whatever the cost.

Today Dickens's compatriots have devised a no more lasting or indeed probable solution to the question of alleviating poverty. As a result private philanthropy and charity have increasingly taken over responsibilities from the state in addressing this perennial concern, whilst maintaining complicity with the very system that guarantees its perpetuation. Indeed, the economic disparities associated with the rise of globalisation in the last forty years in Britain are seldom understood because it would require the admission that 'metropolitan capitalism requires poverty, both local and peripheral, as a resource' (P. Gilbert 195). As poverty levels continue to rise so too do the vice and disease that are produced alongside them. The government tells us that the poor are draining away vital state resources through their gaming of the benefits system and refusal to engage with the legitimate workforce, whilst at the same time selling off public-housing stock and neglecting to build more low-income housing to shelter this class, nor install a living-wage system in London that would truly make work pay and allow for a dignified labour existence that could reasonably live apart from state subsidy.

As a result large parts of the city are subject to racial and spatial tensions, which have progressively sought to price the poor and working classes out of the centre of London, and into the urban periphery where their decay can largely go unnoticed by the elite of the city. The contemporary rhetoric that generates an image of the poor as unruly, unreliable and unprincipled to stoke racial and spatial anxieties has its origins in Victorian rhetoric around the barbarism of the periphery entering and conquering the metropole. Like Victorians who could not see 'cholera marching north or east – only west – what we perceive is shaped by our expectations, racial and spatial' (P. Gilbert 204). The racialised geography that enabled the governance of empire would be brought back to Britain to reformulate the boundaries of British culture at home. This new configuration of national belonging went well beyond class hierarchy to encompass a new national identity in which immigration and war played equal parts in creating a new defensive nationalism founded upon the necessity for racial differentiation.

We can see a marked change in Dickens's writing after the 1857 Mutiny towards this singular set of concerns. His fear at the end of his life, as evidenced in his unfinished novel *The Mystery of Edwin Drood*, was that Britain itself would soon be on the receiving end of its own liberal doctrine of imperial power, with its attendant commercial and military aggression, against the interests of its own population. Today Britain retains an alternating fear of itself becoming a colonial dependency of the United States. 'This apprehension was expressed most vividly by Peter Kilfoyle, M.P. during the summer of 2003 when the disastrous character of the invasion of Iraq was becoming apparent. He pointed out that we are to be to the US armed forces what the sepoys were to the British Indian Army' (Gilroy, *Postcolonial Melancholia* 92). The British forces' resistance to imperial command by the Americans makes strange political bedfellows of them with their former military charges, acknowledging on some level a long overdue culpability for the part colonial mismanagement played in sparking the Mutiny. There is another resonance possible to pick up on here as well, and that is the principle of cultural affinity versus antipathy, that guides the (predominantly white) coalition partners, in a campaign against what amounts to an insurgency against white cultural hegemony.

With that in mind, 'the Mutiny's excessive violence and conjunction of racial, religious, and nationalist causes could be read as eerily presaging today's "clash of cultures" and the age of global terror, exacerbated by Western nations' neo-imperialist engagements in the Middle East and Asian subcontinent' (Kohlke & Gutleben 370). This subject warrants further consideration because, like 9/11, the Mutiny was framed in the public's imagination as an act of religious fundamentalism and revolt against Western modernity. It was widely accepted that the Sepoys rose in revolt because of a rumour that the carriages of their new Enfield rifles were greased with beef or pork fat. 'Beef was taboo for the Hindu solider and pork for the Muslim, and the insistence of the British officers that they unwrap the cartridges by ripping them open with their teeth' was perceived as yet another British affront towards their respective sacred traditions (Mohanram 6). In this instance, the Sepoys' resistance to religious subversion is underwritten by the popular belief on the part of the British that all Hindus and Muslims were superstitious, religious fanatics. Rather than participate in the reasoned exercise of efficiently and economically greasing their carriages to comply with the rational nature of the British armed forces, the Indians were portrayed as not only bereft of Enlightenment, but of the Christian obedience that would equip them with faith in the benevolent actions of their superiors. Even in contemporary readings of the Mutiny, the greased-cartridges explanation prevails, lending itself to a legacy of colonial historiography that refuses to admit any other possible explanation for these events. This despite the existence of a wealth of Indian historiography proper to that era that asserts other probable causes, including the fact that Indians could not progress beyond the rank of soldier in the British imperial military structure. Its absence from the contemporary historical record speaks to a time when Britain had almost 'total control' of India through 'military collusion' with 'its native rulers' (6). The native rulers were significantly diminished in their authority, however, by changes to the rule of succession by the British, which meant that these native rulers lost control of their lands if they could not prove they had natural heirs in place to succeed them. Moreover, if they were deemed to misrule their territory it could be annexed by the British outright, and thus quickly incorporated into the expanding territory of British occupation.

The seizure of power in India did not just come by way of the military, but also through the control of commerce. 'The growing influence of the East India Company meant monopolies were established that disadvantaged their Indian competitors. The company's political-military power resulted in goods not being subject to local tariffs or taxes. The British could undersell their goods at local markets', thereby making it possible for 'the company man' to amass 'great fortunes at the expense of Indians' (Mohanram 8). A great deal of these products were agricultural in nature, and the British were determined not only to control the price of goods for these products, but also to obtain the lands on which they were cultivated by driving landowners into default, resulting in foreclosures that transferred the ownership of these lands to British ownership. They changed administrative systems and practices and failed to inform the Indians properly of these changes, so that all classes of Indians, not just the peasant class, would be caught out through these land-grab strategies on the part of the British. They also gave unrestricted access to missionaries to flood into India in a campaign to rapidly Christianise it, to create religious division inside the country, and therefore create a lack of solidarity when it came to resisting these new modernising measures.

Whilst most of these forms of control were centred on the main civilian population, another area of unrest elsewhere was brewing amongst the Indian soldiering class, the Sepoys, who were becoming increasingly disaffected by the swelling numbers of British men infiltrating their ranks and outstripping them in terms of racial and financial status. Radhika Mohanram argues that 'there were periodic uprisings based on the increasing recognition that an Indian soldier had little to no actual authority within his own military dating back nearly one hundred years (the first being 1764), before the Mutiny of 1857 transpired, so the idea that the British were caught totally unawares has a more than specious quality to it' (8). If we want to truly appreciate the notion that such discontent was spontaneously generated on the part of a subset of Indians, we have to take seriously the British assumption that they were bringing the rational working of law, of education, Christian morality and free trade to India, as an act of unfettered benevolence.

After the Mutiny, British public opinion shifted to conclude that whilst the Indians could mimic any number of British institutional characteristics, on a deeper level their loyalties would always remain with their own race. What 'progress' was achieved out of their adoption of the tastes, morals, opinions and intellect of the British only ever partially offset the presumption of their inherent racial inferiority. This racial difference could not be overcome no matter how closely the two countries intertwined with one another, because to do so would profoundly compromise the hierarchical premise in which all society was based in Britain: the social classificatory system. The Indian shared a common status with the working classes in Britain, insofar as his character could only be verified in his relation to his social superiors. His presence, in a way similar to theirs, was a cause for concern because his substance could only be lent to him with respect to the figure of the British gentleman. The Indian's presence took on an added burden by virtue of his racialised appearance. As an Indian under British colonial rule, his very form was charged with a suspicion of cultural duplicity. The innate hybridity of his condition naturally demanded suppression, governance and Christianisation at the most basic level in this configuration of his subordinate status. The campaign to bring literacy and civilisation to India coincided with the adoption of English as the official state language, which in turn created a further layer of ambiguity in the British interpolation of the Indian subject.

Through the colonial education system Indians were taught two incompatible truths about liberal democracy: firstly that the British were intrinsically superior to them, and secondly that all men are created equal before God and country. The paradox of this framework did not go unnoticed by India's colonial population, and would eventually lead to the undoing of the colonial framework the British so carefully put in place to subordinate these 'lesser' subjects. At the same time as Indian subjects were being systematically diminished abroad, British subjects were being systematically promoted at home. With high literacy rates amongst all classes of Briton, it was easy to contrast them favourably with their colonial counterparts. It was also easy therefore to make their assumed racial superiority something that was discursively universalised to the point where the only bodies that required material apprehension in the popular British mind-set were black. This complemented a liberal ideology, which equated invisibility to the principle of universality, and therefore what could be made visible naturally required social, cultural and juridical injunction to be captured. What is compelling about this is that in order for the discourses of capitalism, colonialism and liberalism to be reified, 'the dissensions between classes, regionalisms, and sexualities' must disappear, and 'whites, regardless of their individual circumstances, must cohere as a group to homogenize blacks and rule them' (Mohanram 24). This whiteness, moreover had to be fortified in a way that exceeded the ideological reach of capitalism, colonialism and liberalism, and therein militarism had to join this cadre of imperialism as its implicit complement.

At home the military tactics learnt abroad could be applied to the English population through the aggressive policing of slum areas, identified as 'internal colonies' (Poon 112). Dickens, in the wake of the alleged atrocities carried out during the Mutiny, called for 'the complete and absolute evisceration of otherness', and literally spoke of wiping out the Indian race as fair punishment for the rebellion (112). Whilst some of Dickens's profound horror can be explained by the fact that his son Walter was a cadet in the East India Company at the time of the Mutiny, his writings before and after these events in works such as 'The Noble Savage' and 'The Perils of Certain English Prisoners' also display a defensive nationalism and therefore this quality can be construed as characteristic of his political ideology and completely concomitant with his concerns for the promotion of the British (white) working classes. What threatens their status in British society, but also reveals itself as an opportunity to challenge the prevailing classificatory system, is the figure of the mixed-race colonial male, whose loyalty unlike his wholly white counterpart is always the source of suspicion and eventual betrayal. Whilst he may mimic being English, on a fundamental level he can never be so. His appearance thusly carries with it a dangerous external racial threat, which when contrasted with his white working-class counterpart serves to elevate his racial status and as such takes on the superior caste of Englishness. This privilege, formerly only assigned to his societal betters, is now one they are willing to countersign in order to verify his racial authority abroad. This allowed for some degree of social mobility for the working classes willing to go and fight to defend colonial holdings on behalf of ruling-class interests.

The fact that Dickens's last novel is centred on a missing body points to the increasingly puzzling disappearance of the normative English body once it enters onto the colonial world stage. Once there, its contact with Otherness causes it to break down, as foreign elements breach its core on a sensual level through the consummation of interracial sex and the constitution of interracial commerce. *The Mystery of Edwin Drood* is set in an English cathedral town purposefully in an attempt to re-orientate the character to a moral and geographical economy that has been all but surrendered in Dickens's writing, and the English nation space itself polluted irrevocably by the influence of foreign customs and consumptions. The fact that *Drood* is often classified as one of the first British detective novels points to Dickens's insistence on the need for policing and surveillance around the English national body, which is set up in every direction by foreign interests keen to rob it of its rational mooring. The forces that threaten to disappear the English national body are themselves dispossessed; having once populated great empires, they ceded to corruption and decay and now wish to bring those same elements of decline to Britain's shores, making the country over in their image: abject, servile and dependent. It is for this reason that Dickens's writing conveys a deep ambivalence, bordering on antipathy at times, for empire, which at best is intrusive and at worst invasive for England. All that is troubling for England comes to it from the distant, disquieting elements of empire that threaten the safety of its venerable institutions at home.

One of those venerable British institutions was the corporation, and one in particular the East Indian Company, which 'straddled the globe' and 'at its height ruled over one-fifth of the world's population' (Robins 79). Its power easily outstripped that of the British government, through its capacity to generate 'a revenue greater than the whole of Britain and to command a private army a quarter of a million strong' (79). It was the East India Company, and not the Crown, that conquered India. The corporation itself stood for 250 years, longer than any ruler or monarchical power could sustain influence. As Nick Robins asserts, 'For many Indians the Mutiny was preceded by a long campaign by the corporation to plunder their wealth by de-industrializing their country and then to use those proceeds to finance Britain's industrial revolution' (79). This belief would tie Dickens's agrarian workforce to India's, which was likewise forced to rapidly convert its labour from the countryside to the urban factory, only to find greater poverty and misery in this new situation. The British workers' plight came to eventually mirror that of their Indian counterparts insofar as the East India Company found India rich and left it poor for the majority of its subjects. In so doing it authored the blueprint for the British worker's lifestyle of diminishing returns, based on the Company's new formulation of alienated labour later exported from Indian to British shores. Indeed, the company was so powerful that it was able to 'reverse the ancient flow of wealth from West to East and then put into place new systems of exchange and exploitation that were unprecedented in world history' (80).

The East India Company was able to seize assets in the wake of the decline of the Mughal Empire. The Company was able to start to acquire territory in India, and from there, to tax those lands heavily. It was able to manipulate the terms of trade locally, and through war to halt the export of bullion internationally to India, and instead use the East's own resources to pay for exports back to Europe. It effectively siphoned off huge amounts of wealth from India, which was wholly dependent on London to obtain bullion through indirect routes of a global scope. This stratagem to deny bullion to the East created a link between the East and the expanding slave trade of the Atlantic. It created an extraordinary web of commercial relations, wherein 'African slaves were being purchased in part with Indian cotton goods, then being sold in the Americas for new-mined gold and silver, which in turn found its way via London to India where it produced more textiles' (Robins 80–81).

When China emerged as a competitor to India's textile trade with its profitable export of tea, the Company's strategy was to flood the Chinese market with Indian opium, a highly addictive substance. Through this strategy the Company made China a dependent nation of Britain. It was not considered essential to rule China directly, so long as it remained possible to balance out the cost of Britain's purchase of tea with China's purchase of opium. War was used as a means of securing the Company's foothold in these markets, through the waging of not one, but two opium wars to coerce the perpetuation of this semi-colonial arrangement. War was not the only morally corrupt instrument the company employed to further its commercial interests. Equally, monopoly formed the cornerstone of the Company's commercial strategy from its beginnings in the seventeenth century. Its 'royal charter gave it exclusive control over trade with the East. This enabled the company to manipulate the prices paid by British consumers for its goods' (81). If others wished to enter into trade with the East, the Company would simply bribe members of the Court and the Parliament to maintain its singular ascendency. The Company did not limit its efforts to colonial enterprise. It also flooded massive amounts of cheap, high-quality Indian textiles and tea into the British marketplace, forcing the government to bring in trade protections so as to not crush its native textile industry.

When such protections were introduced the East India Company turned its sights to Britain's American colonies, which became another massive market for textile and tea consumption. The Boston Tea Party, the infamous revolt of the American colonies in response to a modified tax on tea, had its origins in a government bailout of the East India Company, which at the time was on the brink of financial collapse (Klein). The British government at the time decided the East India Company was 'too big to fail' and thus it was compelled to pass bailout legislation to salvage the commercial enterprise that had become profoundly linked to Britain's national fortunes from the seventeenth century onwards (Klein). It was Queen Elizabeth who originally chartered the Company in 1600 to conduct trade with Asia. The Tea Act passed by Parliament on 10 May 1773 greatly lowered the tax the Company would have to pay on tea to the British government. This started a trade war with American tea merchants, who were suddenly priced out of the market by the cheap tea the East India Company was now flooding into the colonies. Rather than appreciate the cheaper tea as a bargain commodity, many colonists viewed the act as yet another example of British commercial protectionism, precisely because it left an earlier duty on tea entering the colonies in place, whilst removing the duty on tea entering England. Anti-British sentiment soon gathered steam until a revolt was formally staged in the form of the Boston Tea Party. During that event they swiped the East India Company flag from the masthead of the company's largest ship, the Darmouth, and used it to mark out America's independent territory when it triumphed in the war of independence.

If tax reform ultimately created independence for America, on the other side of the globe, in India, it became the source of its demise. The Company installed a system of tax collection by supplanting the British system of land tenure wholesale onto India, inventing a new class of landlords that impoverished millions through land taxation and denied their hereditary rights to lands that had heretofore been in their possession for generations. The tax reform literally resulted in some '10 million people dying of an ordinary condition of drought', simply because they could not pay for grain based on a combination of scarcity and inflation, which added burden to the already cash-strapped Indian's ability to purchase the basics of sustenance (Robins 84). The Company promoted famine as well as inflation during this horrendous time, by seizing grain by force 'from peasants' and selling it 'at inflated prices in the cities' (84). This famine was accompanied by other natural disasters, wrought by the Company's avarice. When the British navy experienced a shortage of oak timber for their ships, the Company's solution was to create a monopoly on timber, locking out local Indian traders and totally denuding local teak forests. In the textile trade a similar monopoly was imposed and those who would not participate willingly 'had their thumbs cut off to prevent them ever working again' (85). Peasant workers were taxed at two thirds of their incomes and priced out of essentials such as salt, leaving them prey to many diseases. 'The Company forced salt consumption well below the minimum prescribed for prisoners in English jails, the effect was to treat people as sub-human, a class below the criminal' (86). During this time most English citizens would be told that their presence in India was a civilising force. They could not be more mistaken.

Ironically it was the loss of commercial monopoly in the 1830s that ushered in the Company's greatest cultural atrocities upon India. Prior to that the Company leadership was merely content with financially extorting the country. In what would be the Company's last period of explicit colonial control, the mood turned to a new project: the total refashioning of not only India's cultural legacy, but also her person. Through a sinister combination of technological, economic and educational intervention, India's subjects would be utterly transformed into docile bodies at the service of Empire. Racial and religious separatism became part of the Company's operational protocol, which directly led to the Mutiny. Fury with the Indian population became synonymous with fury against the Company charged with their control. The company's legacy was then literally and forcibly erased by Queen and Parliament, when the iconic India House was demolished in 1861. Nick Robins cannily observes that 'in a country like Britain that is so drenched in the culture of heritage, the public invisibility of the East India Company is suspicious' in itself but also points to the spectre of a much larger series of cultural omissions that help to obscure certain geopolitical realities to this day (87). Therein, 'the East India Company's escape from reckoning' as a key institutional player in the creation of Britain as a global power, takes on a further contemporary significance through its expurgation from the cultural imaginary, which in turn 'enables the people of Britain to pass over the source of much of their current affluence and allows India's continuing poverty to be viewed as a product of its culture and climate rather than as something manufactured in pursuit of external profit' (87).

Dickens's immediate response to the Mutiny was to call for the extermination of the Indian race, as punishment for their uprising and massacre of British people. What he failed to recognise was that that course had already been undertaken, through the systemised violence perpetrated by the East India Company on India's people in the form of commercial and military warfare against them, which starved, sickened, disenfranchised and indeed murdered them in their millions. At home Dickens castigated the Company for their inefficiency, without grasping fully that in the age of globalisation these same tactics could and would be used on Western peoples in a way similar to that of the Indian population: through exploitation of their capacity to produce the objects of wealth, thereby transferring the productivity of many into the hands of the few for the sake of unimaginable profit. Today as the nation state withers in its capacity to rule and is steadily being replaced by a transnational plutocracy similar in character to the Company, it is worth remembering this much: what defined the company for 250 years was a relentless aim toward profiteering through manipulation of the institutions of trade, taxation and war to secure its interests. The dispossession of land and the disenfranchisement of labour form the touchstones of the Company's legacy of success, which finds resonance everywhere in today's laissez-faire global economic situation.

Today India is in the midst of its first Gilded Age; its success, like that of the Company that once ruled, it is based on a relationship of illicit wealth between those with power and those with money. Similarly, its corporate wealth is based on a collusion between the government and private industry to allow the elite to purchase expensive contracts and establish monopolistic control of mining rights, the key infrastructure rights allowing the society's richest members to be involved in rent-seeking and profiteering from the plunder of these former public assets. Far from inheriting the best of Britain's lauded societal values, these new Indian oligarchs 'broke the balance of a level playing field' (Freeland 202). As a consequence it allowed those with access to power through education, access to capital, and the opportunity 'to court corruption' and 'to effectively game the system' (202) Perhaps not surprisingly this game was most effectively played by those who were already winning it. 'In the words of a young, up and coming businessman who prefers to remain anonymous, "You could be a billionaire if you moved to India too ... All you need is the luck to meet the right government official and a willingness to risk going to jail"' (202). The institutional corruption wrought by empire remains largely intact for a modern India modelled on its British-Victorian counterpart. The author Salman Rushdie recalls reading Dickens before he ever came to the West: 'these cities that Dickens describes, this great rotting metropolis ... felt like the city outside my window ... If you grow up in a city like ... Bombay or Delhi it feels exactly like Dickensian London. It has exactly that characteristic ... of corruption and filth'.

David Harvey observes that, despite its inherent risk of white-collar criminal culpability, 'neoliberalism has been a huge success from the standpoint of the upper classes. It has either restored class power to ruling elites (as in the US and Britain) or created conditions for capitalist class formation (as in China,

India, Russia and elsewhere)' ('Neoliberalism' 152). The current era of neoliberalism can be said to have much in common with its Victorian liberal predecessor, insofar as it 'was from the very beginning a project to achieve the restoration of class power to the richest strata in the population' proper to a new capitalistic age (148). When Britain's aristocracy in the nineteenth century could no longer generate its wealth strictly through land ownership, it devised a strategy of rapid financialisation of the British economy through the industrial revolution on one hand, and colonial enterprise on the other. These twinned formations worked in tandem to institute London as the epicentre of global finance and thus legitimated the role Britain's imperial power took in manipulating global financial flows to fuel the unprecedented growth of its wealth as a nation. In the twenty-first century, the United States followed a similar route to both power and influence as it worked tirelessly to facilitate 'the Americanization of global finance and helped embed the imperial role of the United States into global financial flows. In particular, the deepening and the global expansion of financial markets made it possible for global savings to flow to the United States at an unprecedented scale' (Tayyab 475–6).

The rapid financialisation of Britain in the nineteenth century affected every class in society; however it was the lower classes that bore the brunt of this systematic revolution in capital. Its subsequent, widespread deterioration was said to hinge on this particular class's inability 'to enhance their own human capital' to attract buyers on the open labour market. Often this was characterised as a personal failing, a lack of competitive strength that allowed only the fittest to survive, as dictated by the new Social Darwinism over political and societal discourse at this time. Accumulation at the top required further and further dispossession at the bottom rungs of society. Those who ran the nation's factories deliberately created unemployment to produce a pool of low-wage surplus labour convenient for further accumulation.

This expanded pool of unemployed labour quickly ushered in a change in public welfare, which separated the deserving poor – those who could not be reasonably asked to conduct manual labour – from the undeserving poor who were classified as work resistant at best and criminally deviant at worst. Many were forced to care for themselves during periods of economic scarcity, and were often obliged to amass private debts, in order to stave off the forced labour of the workhouse or orphanage. Today the bottom-rung of the labour markets in free-market economies face a similar bargain, as 'public welfare is replaced by self-care, and working classes are obliged to fund their private welfare through private debt while calibrating their conduct with the demands of precarious labor markets' (Tayyab 469).

This new reserve class of labour, 'made possible by new information technologies, [expands] the scope of immaterial labor, helping blur the boundary between work and nonwork' (Tayyab 479). As a consequence, a rationale of factory-like, constant output 'spreads throughout the whole of society', which is no longer limited to activities within a discreet workplace (Tayyab 480). For such neoliberal rationality to succeed over the long term it must alter subjectivity in such a way that the market's goal is internalised as a rationale for being itself, and that it embody that cause by becoming 'a *homo economicus*' (482). In order to stabilise that body it must be instilled with a further gravity of debt, to counter the force of its inherent instability when it comes to the task of earning and retaining its own private accumulation of wealth. This Sisyphean bargain fetters the free-market subject to 'a dependent subjectivity, a subjectivity conforming to capital, and in which the rationality of *homo economicus*, of human capital, replaces the idea of social rights and common goods', in such a totalising manner that the subject's self-discipline is positively insured against political resistance (Vercellone 107). This is why we are mistaken in our assumption that 'young people are supposed to be left-leaning idealists, [when] polls tell us that today's under-34s don't believe in handouts and high taxes – and they're voting for David Cameron' (Harris, 'Generation Y').

The Conservative government's Work Programme encourages such young people to engage diligently in the search for 'hidden jobs' in the economically depressed urban centres outside of London, where not coincidentally the long recession has hit the working population, already in precarious low-waged labour, far harder than their southern counterparts. Towns like Warrington and Peterborough carry with them 'the sense of somehow being modern Britain incarnate' (Harris, 'Generation Y'). Here the Work Programme, which ostensibly aims to get people who are suffering long-term unemployment back into work, does so by convincing them that their unemployment is usually the result of character failings rather than the failure of state to distribute wealth through the economy. 'There it was again: the up-by-the-bootstraps Conservatism of Norman Tebbit and Margaret Thatcher, largely unchallenged during the New Labour years', reasserting itself now by a New Conservative government, determined to build into the minds of 'millions of young lives' the idea that the cause of their economic instability is none other than themselves (Harris, 'Generation Y').

Britain's modern workfare schemes were closely aligned to those of the United States, which during the mid-1990s began a campaign to abolish welfare and institute workfare with the pretext of setting the indigent on the road to 'independence', by making their deskilled wage labour their sole means of self-support. Not only were these poor and poorly skilled individuals turned onto the open labour market, without any social safety net; they were at the same time surreptitiously turned out of their houses. One example of this was Thatcher's programme for the privatisation of social housing in Britain. At first it appeared to be beneficial to the lower classes, allowing them to 'convert from rental to ownership at a relatively low cost, gain control over a valuable asset and augment their wealth':

> But once the transfer was accomplished, housing speculation took over, particularly in prime central locations, eventually bribing or forcing low-income populations out to the periphery in cities such as London, and turning erstwhile working-class housing into centres of intense gentrification. The loss of affordable housing in central areas produced homelessness for many and extraordinarily long commutes for those who did have low-paying service jobs (Harvey 'Neoliberalism'155).

In the United States, people fared no better as the public-housing system there too was systematically dismantled during the Reagan Era. During that same era, the 1980s, prisons 'effectively became the country's main public housing program' (Wacquant 160). LeBaron and Roberts argue that 'as social welfare programs have been scaled back and rendered more punitive over the past several decades, and as levels of inequality and poverty have risen, collective means of governing social marginality have largely been replaced by individualized, privatized, and severe ones. States, in conjunction with the private sector, have carried out this set of social policy changes through a range of directly and structurally coercive means, many of which overlap' (26). Prisons followed the rules of the increasingly privatised and marketised state, furthering the neoliberal political and economic agenda, which subjected the functions of the state to the task of value appropriation. Despite the doubling of the prison population in England and Wales over the past twenty years, most individuals fail to appreciate that this development is 'part of the broader reconstitution of the nature of the state and society under neoliberalism' (28).

The Thatcher government's determination to promote private

enterprise and expand the free market into public services extended itself into prison privatisation in the late 1980s. Thirty years later the UK has emerged as having the most privatised prison system in Europe, with 11.6% of its prisoners held in private prisons, a figure that rivals that of even the US (Prison Abolition 2014, 'What is the Prison Industrial Complex?'). Today multinational companies such as Serco and G4S profit from keeping their prisons full, making investment in rehabilitation run counter to their business plan. Prison no longer grants a reprieve from the requirement of employment, as thousands of prisoners spend their days now nominally paid for packing goods into boxes for private sector companies like Amazon. The tightening of immigration rules over the past thirty years has also been a boon to the private prison industry. The private sector run half of the immigration removal centres for the Home Office that forcibly house people seeking political asylum, those who are considered to be illegal immigrants and any other 'unauthorised' arrival of persons into the country. This is by no means the only vulnerable population sought out by this growing sector; the poor, minorities, gay communities, and individuals with mental health issues make up a disproportionate number of the prison population. Those most likely to spend some of their lives under a form of detention are not coincidentally the same people who suffer the greatest effects of poverty, racism and other forms of oppression (Prison Abolition 2014, 'What is the Prison Industrial Complex?').

Institutional forms of discrimination also play their part. Starting in the late 1990s, a large number of Muslims from Asia, the Middle East and North Africa were coming into Britain primarily as economic migrants. Their public perception changed radically after the events of 9/11 and 7/7. The Cambridge Institute of Criminology Prisons Research Centre's report of November 2011 noted in its assessment of staff-prisoner relationships at Whitemoor prison, that the facility housed 'several prisoners convicted of terrorist offences' and that its 'younger prisoner population' were the product of 'a fragmented religious and secular society', and thus were more prone to political 'radicalisation' (Liebling, Arnold and Straub iv). This, 'as well as the risk of violence, presented new challenges to staff, managers and prisoners at Whitemoor' (iv). The number of Muslims in British prisons has doubled in the decade coinciding with the events of 9/11 and 7/7 to 12,000. The rate of increase of Muslim inmates in British prisons is eight times faster than that of the overall prison population, and the numbers show a clear overrepresentation of Muslim convicts: Muslims, who make up roughly 4.7% of the British population as a whole, now make up 14% of the British prison population (compared to just 6% in 1997). The dramatic figures released in a recent Ministry of Justice report have prompted calls 'for ministers to investigate whether police and the courts are treating Muslims more harshly, with some suggesting the rise is due to Islamophobia' (Morris).

This call comes at a time when the proportion of Muslims in some jails has risen to more than one-third of inmates. In Whitemoor, a Category A prison in Cambridgeshire, Muslims make up a staggering '43 per cent' of inmates (Morris). What is remarkable to examine here is the neoliberal rhetoric that has emerged around this group's mass incarceration. The elite Anglo-American neoliberal think-tank Gatestone Institute published an article on the Whitemoor prison, 'Britain: Muslim Prison Population Up 200%', intimating that it was a typical British prison housing an average number of Muslim convicts. Whitemoor is far from typical. It houses around 500 of the most dangerous prisoners in the UK. The prison has a Dangerous Severe Personality Disorder unit and a Close Supervision Centre, which acts as a prison inside the prison to confine the most threatening members of its population. Gatestone's article on Whitemoor, which makes repeated reference to the opinions of non-Muslims and prison officers inside Whitemoor, relies heavily on the Cambridge Institute report prepared for the Ministry of Justice. It is they who described Islam as an 'organised gang' and a 'protection racket', which 'glorified terrorist behavior and exploited the fear related to it' (Liebling, Arnold and Straub iv). Prison guards are quoted as saying 'there were "proper Al-Qaeda" members in the prison who were regarded with "awe" by younger inmates' (Kern). Soeren Kern, the article's author, is also quick to note that some prisoners described Whitemoor in the report as a 'recruiting drive for the Taliban' and claimed that the prison itself is a 'fertile ground for hatred and a new generation of extremists' (qtd. in Kern). Whitemoor's prison guards by contrast are presented in the Cambridge Institute report as weak in comparison to a 'powerful and growing Islamic prison population' and as such have chosen to adopt a policy of general 'appeasement' towards them, though it was 'particularly convicted terrorists who were feared to be recruiting future extremists' and were implied to be feared by non-Muslim staff and convicts alike (Liebling, Arnold and Straub iv).

Kern chooses not to look solely at the Cambridge Institute report for background to his report, but also consults a July 2013 issue of the prisoner's magazine, *Inside Time*, to sustain his argument. Kern refers to the comments of a 'long serving prisoner' at a completely different high-security prison, Long Lartin, who has this to say:

> We are able to cook our own food here but if we attempt to cook pork in the communal kitchen it is deemed dangerous, even a threat to your life. The kitchen is usually occupied by 90% Muslims and we have been told if we cook pork we will be stabbed. There have been incidents here where people have been targeted and pressured and bullied into converting to Islam (Kern).

What is incredible about this commentary is that it represents a total historical inversion of the power dynamics leading up to the events that prompted the Mutiny of 1857. Once again the issue centres on the maintenance of religious norms, but on this occasion it is the white Christians rather than their Muslim-Asian counterparts who feel threatened. Here the perception is that Muslims are the powerful occupiers of this territory and it is their weaponry and will that is compelling the action leading to a potential crisis in terms of cultural hierarchy, as Islamic religion threatens to gain the upper hand, the statistical advantage and most significantly the ability to generate legions of insurrectionists through the subversion of Britain's own, literal institutional structures. Meanwhile, those put in charge of preserving the institution have either resorted to appeasement in the face of this threat, or to self-recrimination in suggesting that Islamophobia has contributed to this carceral phenomenon. Both strategies of containment threaten the neoliberal hegemon and therefore warrant immediate discipline and redress.

This neoliberal hegemonic discourse refuses to admit that Muslim imprisonment may correspond not to religious but rather class biases, insofar as higher rates of incrimination are linked with the prevalence of poor-performing state schools, unemployment and low-skilled jobs, and family breakdown in predominantly poor Muslim areas of the country. Such factors, rather than religious radicalisation, are far more likely to cause societal disintegration and to instigate the increasing numbers of Muslims behind bars. From the neoliberal state perspective these individuals are a cause for concern from the moment they become part of the youth population and are institutionally monitored as a matter of course. According to this logic their offences therefore are ontological rather than sociological in nature, and thus failure to 'contain' such a population inherently threatens the surrounding population with whom they share 'confined' urban space.

As the insecurities and inequalities generated by neoliberalism's social and economic policies mount for this predominantly Asian Muslim population, the white working-class individuals who surround them fail to recognise the fact that they too will ultimately be dealt with through increasingly punitive means by the neoliberal state, which will be forced to take action against a wider and wider portion of the population in order to conceal a fundamental paradox in the way it continues to operate. Free-market society's attempts to manage the crisis of social reproduction through debt, and through a punitive law-and-order regime, actually deepen social and economic insecurities and inequalities by generating ever greater numbers of individuals who must be incarcerated for failing to meet their societal obligations. Prison then, both in its public and private manifestations, can be seen as an apparatus that coercively manages poverty and social marginality, deemed ancillary to the profit-driven labour market, by criminalising non-market forms of social reproduction and coercively managing the problems associated with rising levels of poverty. The prison then becomes the logical warehouse for a new neoliberal subject born through a symbiosis of economic instability and market discipline that has become a defining feature of the neoliberal era.

Most citizens will not be able to readily equate the neoliberalism they are experiencing now to their great determinant, which is at base a function of a neocolonial economic experiment that was global in its application. Few will realise that such neoliberalism

> was first road-tested in Chile after General Augusto Pinochet's coup d'etat, then in New York City by the 1975 'coup d'etat by financial institutions against the democratically elected government,' and finally in the U.K. by the International Monetary Fund to reverse the course of Keynesian policies. These trial runs 'established a principle that, in the event of a

conflict between the integrity of financial institutions and bondholders on the one hand and the well-being of the citizens on the other, the former would be given preference' (Tayyab 472, quoting Harvey, *A Brief History* 29).

The disparity in consequence between the two classes relates back to the threat of incarceration that the young Indian businessman casually referred to above, if we consider that throughout the past 250 years it is possible to trace a concordance between domestic incarceration and its imperial counterpart in terms of both technique and application, and indeed that the two together act as a barometer of the need for new forms of social institutionalisation to emerge in periods of ungoverned capitalism. Through this lens it is possible to detect an indirect colonial resonance within his remarks, insofar as the modern inception of India's system of incarceration materialises as a direct result of the Mutiny of 1857. 'The revolt of 1857–8 thus marked an important moment in the colonial history of incarceration both as a mode of control and as a social institution' (C. Anderson 2). Between 1857 and 1858 over one hundred thousand troops, or just over two-thirds of the Bengal army, participated in the Mutiny. Prisons became a key site of rebellion against the British, because the prison was viewed by a segment of North India's population as a fundamentally alien institution to their native culture, which violated the norms of its society and thus was a symbol for the broader injustices visited upon them by the British colonial administration. As such prisons became popular 'sites of rebellious activity' and thus the Mutiny 'left a serious penal crisis in its wake, especially in the North-West Provinces where the rebels set thousands of prisoners free and damaged or destroyed dozens of jails' (16).

Despite Britain's eventual success in quelling the Mutiny in 1858, its brutality and insistence on mass incarceration for those presumed to be involved in acts of rebellion inadvertently helped to further politicise India's jails and prisons. This trend towards the overt politicisation of carceral spaces continued in India through the late nineteenth and early twentieth century, establishing them as critical sites for anti-colonial agitation, crucial to the cause to rest broader social, economic and political powers from their British rulers and ultimately to gain independence from them. As the movement for independence began to seriously coalesce, 'the notion that India itself was one vast prison became embedded in anti-colonial discourses, imprisonment took on a new metaphorical meaning that gave it enhanced significance' (179).

What India lacked however in waging these struggles was the illusion of a class, religious and racial unity Britain was able to ideologically utilise both at home and abroad to eventually conquer their rebellion. In contrast India's inability to galvanise its people in a similar manner during the course of the rebellion is somewhat evidenced by the fact that 'the mutineer-rebel sympathies lay with their high-caste or high status brethren and not with the general prison population' (A. Anderson 178). It can also be argued that the elitism on the part of those organising the rebellion ultimately hindered the success of their cause to obtain national independence for a further century, and moreover the will to rule India in a truly democratic way in the postcolonial period. Such an attitude paved the way for plutocratic control of the state in the twenty-first century and allows such an elite to consider itself largely beyond the reach of criminal apprehension based on their powerful social status in the present era.

Finally, in reflecting on the historic legacy of the Mutiny, it is crucial to recall that both the Mutiny and its cessation were military-style operations, and therein utilised common tactics to wage their campaigns. It's also crucial to remember that it was a corporation, and not a state apparatus, that was responsible for instituting and maintaining control of India at both a civic and carceral level. As new forms of colonial domination are being instituted as part of a heavily militarised globalisation process, it is helpful to review the actions of the East India Company as a forbearer in instituting such an aggressive approach to quelling resistance in the territory it came to forcibly occupy. There are many elements linking the uprising of the Islamic resistance the US faces currently with the Sepoy rebellion of 1857. Paul Gilroy contends that 'the ambiguities and defect of past colonial relations persist', and 'the enduring consequences of empire' are 'implicated in creating and amplifying many current problems' (Gilroy, *Postcolonial Melancholia* 3). William Dalrymple argues that 'it is one thing to conquer a country. It is quite another to stay there and try to force-feed your ideas onto a part of the world that has its own traditions. It is when empires strive to impose their ideals onto the conquered at bayonet point that even the most powerful occupying armies find themselves provoking violent resistance' (47). What is clear is that the global position of the United States in the twenty-first century, as successor to the European Empires that were defeated and transformed in the twentieth century, has allowed old imperialism to become an object of nostalgia, and novel forms of colonial rule to emerge that go unrecognised as an iteration of these past forms. These new forms of imperialism, moreover, can only be 'enforced by the economic and military means at the disposal of a unipolar global order' (Gilroy, *Postcolonial Melancholia* 3).

Seen through this perspective, 11 September 2001 can be understood in a way similar to its predecessor, the Sepoy Rebellion, as the symbolic birth-date for a new imperial state order, where concepts of nationality, law, power and history line up in such a way as to expand US geopolitical control of the globe, in the name of its sovereign right to defend itself against terrorism on whatever ground that challenge is to be met. America has designed its military campaign to conform seamlessly to the economic machinery of capitalism, which is made weightless and invisible when confronting the imperial groundwork placed before it by its imperial partners, most notably Britain. The blueprint for operations remains something largely mystified in the eyes of the general public in these two nations. In the era of postmodernism we suffer from a historical amnesia that is in no way symptomatic of the natural passage of time, but the product of wilful forgetting orchestrated by those who would seek to manipulate our ideals to conform to the bounds of nationalism and racism.

Western reaction to 11 September 2001 echoed the reaction of the British to the Sepoy Rebellion, insofar as the outrage came from the widespread disbelief that those of a 'lower' race had the audacity to attack and kill American civilians, and to destroy in the process one of the most potent symbols of the American way of life, by striking at the epicentre of global trade, bastardising the technology that circulates an elite global workforce and in the process eviscerating the Geneva Convention. 'Indeed, the Bush Administration's "war on terror" might be thought to have brought the slumbering giants of Christendom and the Orient back to life' (Gilroy, *Postcolonial Melancholia* 20). A key incident that took place around the Sepoy Mutiny confirms 9/11's historical resonance with the Indian Mutiny of 1857. Like Saddam Hussein, the Mughal Emperor 'was put on trial and charged—quite inaccurately—with being the evil genius behind an international Muslim conspiracy stretching from Constantinople, Mecca and Iran to the walls of the Red Fort in Delhi' (Dalrymple 47). Contrary to all the evidence that the uprising broke out first among the overwhelmingly Hindu Sepoys, the British prosecutor argued that 'to Musalman intrigues and Mohammedan conspiracy we may mainly attribute the dreadful calamities of the year 1857' (qtd. in Dalrymple 47). William Dalrymple describes this historical assessment of events as wholly resonant with 'the ideas propelling more recent adventures in the East', which similarly display 'a bigoted oversimplification of a complex reality' (47). Far from being an international

Muslim conspiracy, the Mutiny set off a chain of events not dissimilar to the occupation of Iraq, which simultaneously required 'the activation of racist xenophobia to recalibrate the boundaries of legitimate membership in society' at home, and the 'acceleration of militarization and use of direct violence both locally and globally' abroad to demonstrate the Coalition's pre-emptive power over any potential threat of political insurgency that might (once again) surface on the part of what was widely perceived as a marginal society (Tayyab 487).

The Coalition's invasion into a peripheral (economic) zone was predicated on a desire to hollow out its nationalised enterprises and replace their ownership with private contract firms. They would then use the excuse of ongoing political crisis to reinforce the priority of protecting the interests of these corporations in the region, over both the wellbeing of native populations and even that of their own Coalition troops. One decisive way to view the invasion is to see it as a financial coup and a triumph of neo-colonial banking practices, which involved radically limiting public understanding of the conflict and allowing domestic fear and xenophobia to rise exponentially so that the average individual would be convinced that military forces could and should be brought in to ostensibly break the back of terrorism, the enemy of global democracy. In reality, however, Iraq was only ever an adversary of finance capitalism; the threat being Saddam Hussein's determination to trade his oil in Euros as opposed to American Dollars. It is then possible to observe that the Coalition's military policy towards Iraq involved a trade-off between economic privateering and collateral damage.

The explicitly neoliberal economic ambitions of this military campaign were spelled out on 19 September 2003, when Paul Bremner, head of the Coalition Provisional Authority, 'promulgated four orders that included the full privatization of public enterprises, full ownership rights of foreign firms of Iraqi businesses, full repatriation of foreign profits', as well as 'the opening of Iraq's banks to foreign control, national treatment of foreign companies' and 'the elimination of nearly all trade barriers' (Harvey 'Neoliberalism'146). Bremner's sweeping privatisation orders were to be applied generally and immediately across 'all public services, the media, manufacturing, services, transportation, finance and construction', with the only exemption being the oil industry (146). Any industrial opposition to such policies was curtailed through the banning of unions and the right to strike in key sectors. Any political opposition was eliminated 'when the interim Iraqi government appointed at the end of June 2004, was accorded no power to change or write new laws: it could only confirm the decrees already promulgated' (146). An Iraqi member of the Coalition Provisional Authority protested the forced imposition of 'free market fundamentalism', describing it as a 'flawed logic that ignores history' (146–7). Therefore, David Harvey argues, 'the insurrection that followed can be in part interpreted … as Iraqi resistance to being driven into the embrace of free market fundamentalism against their free will' ('Neoliberalism' 147).

Over a little more than a decade we have had critique after critique of the war on terror as a campaign rooted in religious fundamentalism, with very little being said about al-Qaeda as a resistance organisation set up to counter the free-market fundamentalism of the West. This fundamentalism was expressed throughout the Cold War period in a number of ways including the establishment of neo-colonial client relationships in the Middle East with Western powers, the installation of puppet regimes loyal to Western aims in the region and the adoption of adversarial geopolitical policies toward regimes hostile to a model of democracy that was synonymous with capitalism. Most critiques also fail to consider the possibility that al-Qaeda was presenting its own version of corporatism as a challenger/successor to the Anglo-American Empire's secular variety. Bruce Hoffman, a terrorism expert at Georgetown

University, explained in an interview with National Public Radio that al-Qaeda 'didn't function as a traditional or typical terrorist organization did … It functioned really like a multinational. On the eve of 9/11, for example, the State Department has stated that al-Qaida had 60 offices worldwide. I mean, in essence it was a multinational' (qtd. in Temple-Raston).

Al-Qaeda as a multinational had its beginnings in the late 1980s. Its inception followed the global trend toward the privatisation of state functions, in particular national defence. In an effort to generate his new private defence force, Osama bin Laden decided to commission the elite forces of the Arab mujahedeen to join his private army through the enticement of a starting bonus. In *The Looming Tower: Al-Qaeda and the Road to 9/11*, Lawrence Wright explains how 'new recruits, in return for filling out forms in triplicate and pledging secrecy and loyalty to bin Laden, received salaries of $1,000–$1,500 per month, a round-trip ticket home each year, a month of vacation, a health-care plan, and a buyout option of $2,400. From the beginning al-Qaeda presented itself as an attractive employment opportunity for men whose education and careers had been curtailed by jihad' (142).

At first bin Laden found that he was unable to win them over with the familiar anti-colonial rhetoric of an international Muslim brotherhood, acting together to resist the hegemony of the West. He soon realised that in order to reach his Saudi audience of young, recently disenfranchised men he had to appeal to them on economic terms, telling his hometown audience who were facing the sudden withdrawal of state guarantees for college graduate employment, many of whom had also fought in Afghanistan, 'that their lives were sold at a discount' by a Saudi leadership beholden to Western interests, values and mores that ran counter to support of a traditional Islam (Wright 150). Despite his expression of hostility toward the Saudi Royal family in these audiences, he nonetheless was keen to offer al-Qaeda's services to them in the form of 'a new mujahideen army made up of his colleagues from the Afghan jihad and unemployed Saudi youth' (157). He pitched the use of this nascent private army, al-Qaeda, to fight against Saddam Hussein's invasion, using 'the Saudi Binladin group's extensive earth moving equipment' to build 'trenches and sand traps' to fight a border war (157). Bin Laden's plan was to create a wholly Muslim defensive force for the Kingdom that would eliminate the need for American intervention in resolving a conflict he believed should solely concern the Muslim world.

In essence, bin Laden was staging a military bid to compete directly with Western powers for defensive management of the Kingdom. When that bid was rejected it elevated his initial ambition to dethrone Western enterprise from the Kingdom, into a plan to rid the whole of the Middle East from what he viewed as the West's neo-colonial occupation of Muslim lands. This plan would later derive into an even larger aspiration, not only to check the geographical reach of Western power, but also to infiltrate it in such a way over time that Islam and not the West would become the world's governing authority. Through the political activation of Muslim populations around the globe whose pattern of diaspora traced the flow of capital from East to West, dating back to the time of the West's rapid colonial ascendency in the nineteenth century, al-Qaeda aimed to reverse the world order to flow back in the favour of the Islamic East for the first time since the fall of the Mughal Empire.

Al-Qaeda's multinational plan to enact its own neo-colonial brand of global domination over the West is perhaps in a way not dissimilar to America's pathway to neo-colonial ascendency in the postwar period through its campaign of economic imperialism in Germany, Japan and South Korea, to name but an obvious few. Nor is it dissimilar to Britain's road to neo-imperialism which coincided with the sophisticated development of its heritage industry as a means of solidifying its postwar global identity as the standard bearer for how any would-be empire built on the back of commercial enterprise should conduct itself. Doreen Massey observes that what these neoliberal approaches share in common is a set of 'ghastly ironies' where the public

> are told ... that much of our power and our pleasure, and our very self-identification, lies in our ability to choose (and we are indeed bombarded every day by 'choices', many of them meaningless, others we wish we didn't have to make), while at the level that really matters – what kind of society we'd like to live in, what kind of future we'd like to build – we are told, implacably, that, give or take a few minor variations, there is no alternative – no choice at all ('Vocabularies of the Economy' 16).

The crises that justify the rigid logic of social governance are not-coincidentally always playing out at the margins of sovereignty, neatly displacing interest away from centralised power, wherein there is an imperative to maintain a necessary silence about the routine collusion of government power and capitalism. In both instances crisis is seen to be a productive, and not destructive, function, insofar as its manufacture of social insecurity steadily paves the way for the emergence of a more pliable public constituency.

Such political economies are necessarily paradoxical, as demonstrated through Margaret Thatcher's recovery of the 'Victorian values' of thrift, a heavy work ethic, morality and capitalism, at the same time as she was aggressively restructuring the welfare state through successive moves towards its wholesale privatisation. Thatcher also wanted to demonstrate a contemporary military might reminiscent of her Victorian predecessors. The Falklands Crisis of 1982 provided a perfect opportunity to re-enliven British nationalist sentiments through a sense of shared outrage at the Argentines' attempt to seize one of

Britain's few remaining areas of continuous colonial occupation. Thatcher's disproportionate fury over the Falklands Crisis was deeply reflective of a larger crisis. Britain's concurrent loss of empire and recognition as a dominant world power left it vulnerable to domination by the United States and the Soviet Union, or closer to home an emerging European Union that threatened to eclipse its remaining prestige through its assimilation into a new collective continental entity. Since 'the time of the 1982 Falklands War under the premiership of Margaret Thatcher (the advocate, famously, of "Victorian values"), resurgences in British nationalist sentiments have tended to precipitate a concomitant proliferation of the Raj' (Kohlke & Gutleben 371). Britain's ability to win back her colonial holding, by winning the war in the Falklands, made Britons once again aware of Britain's strength when called upon to react to a sovereign threat. Ironically, this restored pride allowed Thatcher to convince Britons that truly its best days lay *behind* it.

To understand why Margaret Thatcher's radical modernisation of Britain's post-imperial identity had to be profoundly reinforced by the 'heritage industry', we must recognise the work selective memory and targeted nostalgia perform in the enactment of nationalist ideologies. The celebratory atmosphere of imperial might of the 1880s was being revived to contribute to the 'enterprise culture' of the 1980s, which selectively recovered that era to emphasise Britain's greatness as an enduring sovereign nation. When Tony Blair became Prime Minister in 1997 he continued Thatcher's work of 'retrolution', or 'disguising the future as the past in order to make it palatable' (Ho 17). During the Blair era the country experienced a great many 'anxieties and confusion over the breakdown of traditional notions of Englishness' (17). Blair's government had to both interact with and intervene in 'the uneasy tension between Englishness as an ethnicity under siege and the supposedly more inclusive multicultural, but equally problematic "British" identity' (17).

What Blair inherited from Thatcher made this a juggling act of identity between Englishness and Britishness, because there was simply no room for multiculturalism to appear within the national equation at either level of self-understanding. 'This meant that all attempts to recapture, defend and perform Britain's centrality in the world and Englishness on the home-front' were predicated on a trifecta of Englishness, maleness and whiteness. These were then visibly attached to heritage, what Stuart Hall has called 'the Heritage,' undeniably constructed for those who 'belong' to a greater society which is 'imagined as, in broad terms, culturally homogenous and unified' (S. Hall 6). What remains unacknowledged within those categories of identity are the patriarchal hierarchy, imperial values, commercial needs and rule of force that necessarily subtend their esteemed formation. Bearing this in mind, a post-imperial identity might have been formulated to acknowledge the foundation of Britain's greatness and therefore be in nature one that was apologetic, inclusive and empathetic. Instead in the latter decades of the twentieth century, as postcolonialism was in the ascendant, contemporary British culture chose to mount a 'backlash against the feminization of Englishness and the English politics that the Victoria-as-Thatcher allegory represents' (36). Therefore Blair, Thatcher's successor, could not be seen as backward-looking but rather had to mould his public image to be conversant with the emerging New Lad culture of the 1990s. Indeed Blair's early relationship with Brown ostensibly mirrored the new paradigm of male-bonding and camaraderie in a post-industrial Britain as one centred lightly on heterosexuality, hedonism and sexism: 'Blair's babes' forming the young and pretty political pack he and Brown conspicuously travelled with.

The downside of this image era of post-imperial masculinity would become apparent by the end of Blair's political reign, wherein his chosen successor Gordon Brown, the former

Chancellor of the Exchequer, appeared to be exhausted, alienated, and under siege, drastically revising down the appearance of 'New' Labour as heralding an era of forward thinking and of economic prosperity not seen since the dissolution of Empire. Instead, the return of the old boom and bust economy would become the very pattern of events that would topple Labour's brand of 'novelty' government, which conspired to keep the British public sheltered from both past and present excesses. Its story about itself, moreover, made them complicit in the rewriting of Britain as a 'cool' place, and indeed actively solicited their participation in the retrovolution campaign to make nostalgia saleable in its support of the nation. What is cool is what must be endlessly and commercially summoned, without notice paid to a problematic Englishness. 'Cool Britannia' for the most part fetishised London 'without necessarily addressing it as a crisis zone of Englishness that still persists at the heart of the former empire' (Ho 41). Instead, for Blair, 'London's history of theatricality, musicality and spectacle, which had its zenith in the late nineteenth century, still exists in his conception of contemporary London' (41).

There is an underside to the story being scripted here. That underside is comprised of the feelings of discomfort, shame and perplexity that arise from being confronted with the physical realities of an imperilled Englishness, which simultaneously exhibits itself in occasions of nationalistic celebration and periodic eruptions of racist violence towards its perceived Others. Cool Britannia works only if its population participates in an active forgetting and disavowal of its feelings of diminished capacity and focusses instead on the celebration of 'girl power' in the same breath as it dubs the only black member of that English grouping (The Spice Girls) as 'Scary'. The violence and terror of London's past can be effaced by a tranquil and certain image of unity, of participation and of inclusion into a domain that displays its whiteness, only to occlude its appearance within the prospect of a shared Britishness. What is also occluded is the wealth of history Cool Britannia has to draw upon in the name of new and creative commerce, which has largely come from its colonial spoils, remnants of which inhabit every corner of its historical record. That we name her coolness as feminine also fixes her as a marker of imperialism, as a body whose temperature is gauged by discrimination, containing the nation within herself through a ritual excess of boundary, the loss of which will in time summon an excess of military violence through Blair's decision to engage in (commercial) partnership with America in the invasion of Iraq. The image sold then to the public of a missile being able to reach London from Iraq in forty minutes will be almost but not quite enough to rally public support. Ultimately, the coolness died in a strategy of containment, wherein New Labour showed itself finally to be Old Tory. As that mask falls so too does the concealment of Britannia's historical past, which can no longer be ignored, or appropriated without the bloody history of this territory coming into view, tearing asunder the recent Blairite government's set pieces of retrieval and re-enactment, and hastily replacing them on the stage with an older repertoire of violence and sacrifice in the name of national stability.

If New Britain were really imperial England, then it would be able to supposedly recapture the confidence of its domestic market, whilst at the same time maintaining property as a pleasure dome for the world's richest conglomerates. London would exist as a futuristic housing project aimed at those seeking tax haven, whilst at the same time existing on large hand-outs from the world's collapsing governmental apparatuses. Those at the highest echelons of power attempted once again to dazzle and astound audiences both domestically and abroad with the spectre of Britain's imperial legacy and the influence it still wielded internationally, if now perhaps as partner rather than leader. It would strive to convince both its inhabitants and visitors alike that it remained at home with such power; a power rooted firmly in its enduring social and racial classificatory systems, developed and perfected not coincidentally in the Victorian era and presently retooled to complement a new era in the free marketisation of identity, wherein Britain is once again defined as a nation of individuals as a opposed to being members of a collective society.

In recent years, Britain's new Conservatives have set out to implicitly revive Victorian England's classificatory social system and explicitly its discourses of social crisis as a threat to national identity. Like Thatcher before him, David Cameron adopted a definition of social mobility into his political rhetoric that hinged on a proprietary logic, adapted from Victorian liberal principles. Rhetorically, he echoes Thatcher's approach in addressing the British people by at once 'minimis[ing] the ramifications of class and the complex economic and cultural hierarchies [that] it enforces', and maximising the value of 'the free-market subject, who was ideally free of state intervention to make contracts and profit, to alienate his labor and the products of his and other's labor, and to buy commodities' (Hadley 11). Despite his modernised appearance, this proprietary subject is one firmly born out of the nineteenth century, whose societal 'progress parallels the political journey of property itself, becoming, in certain circles, constituted by increasingly abstract formulations of property—real, liquid, and finally what might be called, somewhat imprecisely, mental property' (11).

This is significant to our reading of Dickens's work insofar as his own social ascendancy can be traced to the rising value of mental property, 'which was like other sorts of private property, in that it accrued value and could be exchanged, and unlike it, in that it was presumed to be less burdened by the denotative and connotative of landed or even commercial privilege. More generally, because of its conception as internally generated, mental property was perhaps the most perfect expression of liberal private property in Victorian Britain' (Hadley 11). Mental property not only functions to individuate its Victorian liberal subjects, it also bestows upon them a mark of distinction complimentary to nineteenth-century liberal ideology. Dickens's success as a writer, and indeed the possibility of him ever being able to be one as a self-educated Cockney, is tied to his exceptional ability to apply his mental property to the subject of character in a way that both reified and subverted common understanding. Dickens's genius was not based on his investment in the narrative form, but rather his speculation on something much dearer to the social classificatory system of his age: character.

Elaine Hadley makes the case for character in Victorian Britain being literally tied to economic survival for the majority of its people. In the nineteenth century, character 'was a written testimonial by an employer of the qualities and habits of his employees — his industriousness, honesty, punctuality, sobriety' (15). Rather than merely becoming a descriptor of a person's moral and social attributes, character played a much more crucial role as a descriptor of a person's economic attributes. When placed before potential employers its job was to answer the question, 'to what extend is this person an employee, a worker, a unit of alienable labor?' (15). Character therefore forms a critical nexus wherein one's moral and social attributes cannot in any way be dissociated from a similar economic evaluation. Moreover as economic evaluation becomes increasingly 'inextricable from moral evaluation', it becomes possible to recognise that both are contingent on a historically specific form of interpolation situated, figuratively and literally, in property.

In Dickens's novels the characters are mutually dependent in a way that would have been illustrative of the class hierarchy established by Victorian liberalism, and readily accepted by his readership because their own moral, social and class recognition would be implicated in that same system in reality. Their gentleman employers would possess their character as 'an intrinsic measure, manifest in the self's acquisition of itself', whilst for the employees, 'respectability seems to be an extrinsic measure, through the estimation of others, one's social superiors, as is the character reference itself, stamped with the signature of one's employer' (Hadley 16). The gain and loss of respectability becomes the fulcrum of many of Dickens's stories, which contain within them class-specific dramas of people striving, rarely achieving and often failing to gain that invaluable imprimatur.

The failure that is documented time and again in Dickens's dramas is pointedly omitted from Thatcher's revision of them over a century later. Instead she favours her own narrative, which recalls all the behaviours and attitudes that promote the mobility of labour without any attempt to restructure the rigid class system making a property of individuals to be sold on their attributes (industriousness, punctuality, sobriety), and once again making of respectability at best a low-rent version of character. The class system works perfectly with Thatcher's new heritage industry because it is in part a vestige from an older system of status hierarchy based on the ownership of land, and this 'perhaps contributed to certain people's perceptions of the class system's timelessness' (Hadley 17). What the heritage industry and the class system share in common, as a result of this under-standing of class as part of the natural order of English society, is a defining envy for the aristocracy amongst the aggregates of individuals that fall below its concern. The economic mobility of the working classes seldom led onto class mobility. 'In the market economy they were required to carry their "character" with them from job to job, while the characters of their social superiors were relatively immobile. The mobility of the working-class character, however, created its own set of problems. When they were required to carry their characters with them, they continually ran the risk of losing them' (Hadley 35, footnote 18).

The Poor Law of 1834 classed individuals according to their lack of property and made of this designation something necessarily related to impropriety. The classificatory system over time and with continual usage became second nature to our understanding of society. As a result the poor were persistently surveyed to reveal the marks of their moral failure, proof of their inherent inability to become a proprietary individual, and in turn, to be of good character. Today 'welfare moms and urban delinquents' alike must face 'a similar mobility crises at work' to their nineteenth-century counterparts placed under the New Poor Law. In the present day they 'remain publicly visible *as classes* in order to sustain, through productive contrast, what amounts to the more stable, more private and thus more invisible social peculiarities' of neoliberal character (Hadley 24). Ruth Cain cannily observes that 'since the financial crisis of 2008, the portrayal of the able-bodied unemployed has only gotten worse, through 'political and journalistic scare stories' that focus their unremitting attention on 'the supposedly useless and proliferative poor and disabled portrayed as "benefit scroungers"'. Although 'it is hardly a novel political move to identify poverty with depravity and degeneracy', Cameron's Coalition government has focussed its attention 'not on putting an end to poverty as its predecessor did, but rather has set its sights on putting an end to the morally wayward poor themselves' (R. Cain). In 2012, the Conservatives launched a massive programme of stringent welfare-reform measures through the Welfare Reform Act. Its aims were promoted by an obliging British popular media who supported the Prime Minister's agenda through 'a marked proliferation of stories that highlighted the individual monstrosity and abjection, representative of an underclass deemed ever more irresponsible, parasitic and toxic' to the public account (R. Cain).

Britain once again had become gripped in a panic about its purported moral decline wherein class hatred could be justified through the public demonisation of the working-class or unemployed, as shiftless spendthrifts who on one hand consume conspicuously, and on the other make a visible property of their destitution. 'Visual markers of "inferiority", such as obesity and cheap clothing, have become perhaps the most loaded signifiers of social marginality or poverty and as such, people (usually women) demonstrating such stigmata of failure and irresponsibility are consigned to the useless/dangerous residuum, who refuse to self-improve' (R. Cain). In this neoliberal schema those who inhabit these underclasses are confined to a zone of economic illegitimacy through their own actions, and as such their lives of intense hardship and poverty should not warrant care or valuation. Here we arrive at a 'critical historical and legal moment in which the UK switches from social security to a conditional welfare régime backed up with increasing surveillance, moralising and punishment', wherein 'the precarious existence of the poorest becomes the stuff of criminality and individuals reduced to an advanced status of marginality' (R. Cain). The government's feinted moral outrage at their existence allows them to more easily dehumanise those who suffer most under their draconian reforms.

What the classes above them fail to recognise in the appearance of their suffering is the emergence of a new kind of sub-citizenship, made vulnerable by an increasingly precarious and decreasingly rewarding labour market, which can rapidly produce conditions of poverty even amongst the once-secure middle classes. What is awaiting Britain's most vulnerable individuals today can in time arrive at their own doorsteps as the product of a neoliberal economy. We must recall that the campaign companion stereotype to the benefit scrounger is the 'striver', and sadly it is his appearance that represents 'an equally mendacious attempt to revive the Protestant work ethic in a context where labour practices' will become increasingly pernicious as the global economy continues to stagnate and indeed deteriorate under the auspices of neoliberal monetary policies (R. Cain). There is an inherent unfairness to this picture that comes perhaps not due to a lack of planning, but rather a sophisticated effort to prevent this wealth from coming into the hands of upcoming generations of workers. We are in an era of rentier-capitalism that is tilting its way toward a revival of feudalism, wherein the right to hold property in fee once again becomes the universal means of extraction for service or labour from amongst the poorer classes.

Under the terms of this new rentier capitalism, Doreen Massey argues that those at the top of the wealth pyramid no longer engage in the production of goods and services but instead solicit their wealth by controlling an already-existing asset such as property or pension funds ('Vocabularies of the Economy' 14). The City of London therefore is in the business not of wealth creation, but rather wealth extraction on a global scale. In recent decades the upper-middle strata of rich societies have aspired to emulate rentier practices that were formerly only the purview of the aristocracy. They have done so through the rise of house prices that have allowed them to acquire unearned wealth through sale of their property or buy-to-let schemes. The housing boom in the UK more generally has had the effect of greatly exacerbating inequality. It has equally contributed to the North-South divide through the phenomenon of flight capital drawn into London from the coffers of Third World Nations. Passive wealth is also now routinely acquired through pensions invested in secondary share-markets. Unbridled speculation within these share-markets over the past decade has led to a massive redistribution of wealth from poor to rich, contributing to a huge rise in food prices and malnutrition around the world. It has led to unsustainable property booms fuelled by the world's super-rich manipulating the currency markets, which forms the underpinning of a new financial imperialism. Cavalier financial practices have led to instability and crisis, with dire repercussions for people around the world, as the speculative bubbles they generate inevitably burst. Meanwhile, the lower-middle class, working class and even the poor are geared towards an admiration for this system that largely undermines their wealth, because neoliberal social identity has been intentionally shaped to affirm triumphant involvement in the market. Modelled in this way, a large percentage of the public believe that their welfare and success require that they be pitted against each other at home, as well as internationally, in order to survive and thrive in a world in which the only relationships are ones of competition. As the situation worsens our subjectivities are constantly adjusted 'to fortify a financialised ideology, and to pacify many into at least acquiescence if not enthusiasm' (Massey, 'Vocabularies of the Economy'14).

William Robinson and Jerry Harris make the case that the current rhetoric of inclusion, consensus and consent belies the fact we are living largely in post-national global societies, which increasingly share in common a three-tiered social structure:

The first tier is made up of some 30–40% of the population in core countries and less in peripheral countries, those who hold 'tenured' employment in the global economy and are able to maintain, and even expand, their consumption. The second tier, some 30% in the core and 20–30% in the periphery, form a growing army of 'casualized' workers who face chronic insecurity in the conditions of their employment and the absence of any collective insurance against risk previously secured by the welfare state. The third tier, some 30% of the population in the core capitalist countries, and some 50% or more in peripheral countries, represents those structurally excluded from productive activity and completely unprotected with the dismantling of welfare and developmentalist states, the 'superfluous' population of global capitalism.

It can be observed through the tier structure that at any time anywhere from 50% to 70% of the population is subject to economic crisis. The only tier possessing a firm social basis is the top tier that can extend their largess to support the second tier. The final tier does not share in such hopes and can only be described as the disaffected parties of exclusion who must be surveyed at the level of control.

As the welfare state continues its progress towards dismantlement under the sway of neoliberal economic policies, devising strategies of social control becomes paramount to the rule of governments. The welfare state of yesteryear morphs over time into a police state, 'replete with the dramatic expansion of public and private security forces, the mass incarceration of the excluded population (disproportionately minorities), new forms of social apartheid maintained through complex social control technologies, repressive anti-immigration legislation, and so on' (Robinson and Harris). In this new social order those who are most vulnerable are made responsible for their own social subsistence and exercise of their own civil authority. For its part the state, and largely society as a whole, have abandoned the most marginalised communities to both care for and maintain themselves and their territory within the bounds of the polis. Political hegemony allows the remaining tiers to remain somewhat ignorant of the fragility of the world monetary system, despite the growing social tensions expressed within the third tier, which at times bubble up to touch the periphery of the second tier.

There appears at present to be no coherent plan on the part of the first tier to concede to some regulatory order for the global financial system, nor to respond adequately to the raw bargain set before those most vulnerable to its excesses. Again we see the pattern re-emerging that we saw during the Victorian era of globalised economics, insofar as over-accumulation at home requires that it be twinned with racialised social polarity abroad. Whilst there was always the need for internal colonies in London and elsewhere to play out these tensions within the metropole, the ruling classes of the time in Britain managed to significantly avoid the threat of revolution at home, despite its prevalence in other parts of Europe during the nineteenth century. Nonetheless on a worldwide scale, the contradictions and tensions unleashed by empire inadvertently generated new opportunities for emancipatory projects from the perspective of globalised labour, in particular in India. The rise of a transnational precariat has become the counter-trend of the rise of the world's super-rich, with the increasingly attenuated middle class largely sitting out the class struggle that is sure to characterise the twenty-first century. To better apprehend its likely outcomes, we have only to look to the shape of class development in the Victorian era and to chart the historical rise of the new global ruling class of that era whose wealth was begotten by empire.

So now we end as we began: with a tale of *at least* two cities, London and Bengal. Once again class is made to do battle on the global territory of racial hierarchy, when in fact the fight is one waged at home and within the British social classificatory system. Dickens's work did not differ significantly from his literary counterparts 'insofar as he banished troublesome characters or thorny issues to the colonies or other peripheries', where they could be made to regulate and contain certain wayward behaviours (Joshi 48). Immediately following the two-year period of the India Mutiny, Dickens however did not resort to the well-worn trope he had employed previously in his works, using the marginality of the colonies as a narrative escape route, such as he did in *Dombey and Son*, *Hard Times* and *Little Dorrit* to resolve his complicated plotlines. Notably in his celebrated work of 1859, *A Tale of Two Cities*, the very concept of the colonial and its relationship to the metropole is expunged from the novel's quasi-historical record. Dickens had been an avid follower of news surrounding the rebellion in India and contributed commentaries about it in *Household Words*, throughout the period of uprising. He even went so far as to commission a thirteen-part special report by John Lang entitled 'Wonderings in India' that was published in the journal 'between November 1857 and February 1858' (51). His sixteen-year-old son, Walter, had joined the East India Company and set sail for Calcutta on 20 July 1857, only a week before reports of the Mutiny arrived in London, which surely raised private concerns in him about the soundness of Britain's colonial enterprise. Nevertheless, Dickens chooses not only to bypass the subject of empire, but the nineteenth century altogether, in an unprecedented exploration of the eighteenth century in a continental context for his subsequent novel. What only passably united historical France with the recent events in India were the presence of the mob and the notion of working-class unrest that pervaded both societies.

This similarity touches upon the British working classes insofar as the colony had been a popular escape hatch for many from a life hemmed in by the strictures of the class system. The working classes craved freedom from the various bureaucracies that sought to capture them at this time: the workhouse, the prison and the factory. In leaving Britain they were able to consolidate their British identity, through positive contrast with the lesser racial classes that inhabited the colonial territories. The Mutiny initially threatened their class pre-eminence abroad, and only later, with the triumph of British forces over the Indian rebellion, was it restored. The Indians had to be beaten back by Britain not only militarily, but ideologically, in order to preserve the system of racial hierarchy that underwrote all colonial endeavour and indeed British identity as a whole. Britain had to decisively overcome the rebellion. If there were failings in India it was the fault of corporate misconduct and mismanagement on the part of the East India Company, which left British soldiers and civilians in poorly equipped garrisons. This vulnerability had to therefore be classified as a commercial one, as opposed to a racial one, and gendered in such a way that the men remained heroic throughout the struggle to regain control of the North-

West territories, even at the cost of the lives of their women and children. The British military also had to enliven the charge against the Indians on the part of India's British foot soldiers, who were previously at odds with the workings of the East India Company on the ground. This situation of mutual casualties allowed both a corporate and nationalistic allegiance to emerge amongst the fighting men who were in effect carrying out martial law in the territories.

An unwavering belief in British (racial) exceptionalism had been at the heart of the country's quest for status, wealth, territory, conquest and trade, and for a time it was Dickens who through his writings led the charge to question the basis of this nationalism, because of its failings to apply the spoils of colonial enterprise to uplift the British working classes and the deserving poor. His novels are populated with figures such as Jo, Stephen Blackpool and Amy Dorrit who have been crushed under the weight of uncaring and negligent domestic bureaucracy. What these institutions squandered from Dickens's point of view was the wealth inherent in their biological stock as Britons, which when properly summoned demonstrated an inherent nobility and even potential for greatness. Such nobility by contrast could not emerge from the bodies of savages, no matter how diligently or avidly they worked to adopt British customs and appearances. What Dickens failed to acknowledge in his writings is that the British administration of India's working classes abroad mirrored the uncaring and negligence visited upon the British working classes at home. The Indian Mutiny was an opportune way to forego such an understanding in favour of the chance to assert Britain's muscular Christianity against a 'heathen' race, in a way that would subdue any notion of affinity that may have previously surfaced between the working classes of each respective society.

The average Briton remained profoundly ignorant of the banal atrocities routinely visited upon India by the East India Company in league with the British government. Indeed they knew very little of the Asian sub-continent generally. What they were told, largely by the media, was that it did not bear thinking about. That was until the opportune time arose when it became useful as a means of stoking British nationalist sentiment, which had been flagging due to widespread discontent with both the government and the Company's mishandling of the empire's colonial holdings. *A Tale of Two Cities*, then, becomes a project to re-imagine Britain's nationalistic past and to retrieve from it, through a safer, continentally rendered contest, evidence that its sacrifices in the settlement of its colonial territories had been worthwhile. The Mutiny can thus be viewed as an opening for a reconfiguration of British identity; one that reinforced a sense of British virtue, and convinced the public that Britain shone best against the controlled backdrop of these dark foreign territories. It also demonstrated how the divisive nature of class system at home could be temporarily overcome in defence of the colonial territory abroad. What is missing from this account is another opportunity: one that invites in the possibility of any recognition of plurality within British identity itself and one that questions the basis of increasingly forceful policing, both at home and abroad, of marginalised populations.

Hence *A Tale of Two Cities* can be seen as a fantasy version of nationalism, one that focussed wholly on the inherent capabilities of the British people at the expense of a sustained engagement with the plurality of 'foreign' subjectivity, or the possibility of social propriety being the preserve of other nations apart from Britain. Dickens's tacit examination of the India Mutiny and explicit examination of the French Revolution share in common an inability to look critically at the role a socially disaffected Britain played in shaping the logic of these conflagrations, or how the projection of a naturalised class inequality within British society fuelled the necessity for such rebellion amongst the working classes adversely impacted by such ideology. As a consequence of the political expression of such discontent, the endurance of class immobility could no longer reasonably guarantee national security.

In a letter to William C. Macready, dated October 1855, Dickens wrote that Victorian society had 'no such thing as a middle class (for though we are perpetually bragging of it as our safety, it is nothing but a poor fringe on the mantle of the upper)' (qtd. in Suchoff 47). The solution, then as now, was to manoeuvre such energy time and again toward the international arena and make neo-colonial adventures the safety valve for the quelling of social discontent at home. In *A Tale of Two Cities* Dickens amply demonstrates this mechanism and also reinforces the belief that it has been historically tested and proven to be reliable.

What the population at home never thinks to question is how a nationalism based on exceptionalism similar to theirs could be visited upon them from diverse parts of the world and used as a means of rejecting the presence of their countrymen in foreign lands. Such a principle must go actively unacknowledged in these neo-colonial times, as it did in Dickens's own, through a combination of government spectacle and media persuasion to produce within the masses a popular sentiment against those within its domestic population, which can be made visible in their racial and class marginality. It is the fate of these bodies to become the colony within Britain's national borders and to serve as territory for 'governmental experiment and innovation, the useful or tactical ambiguities of martial law, and the systematic use of torture to obtain confessions' (Gilroy, *Postcolonial Melancholia* 21). In this way government-sanctioned terror becomes banal and the source of scintillation for those who believe their societal privileges protect them from a similarly egregious set of outcomes. History tells us, too, that such assumptions have proven to be false and savagery is hardly the purview of our foreign adversaries alone. It is these forces that make up the ills of our time and bring us back to an age where social category becomes destiny, so that we are once more at home with the Victorians.

Epilogue: Crony Capitalism and the *Mutuality* of the Market

And O there are days in this life, worth life and worth death. And O what a bright old song it is, that O 'tis love, 'tis love, 'tis love that makes the world go round!
– Charles Dickens, *Our Mutual Friend*

In autumn 2013, Prime Minister David Cameron gave a Lord Mayor's Banquet speech reminiscent of *Our Mutual Friend*'s Mr. Podsnap. A regal Cameron, wearing white tails and tie, got up to address his rarefied audience; in front of him stood a golden speech stand, surrounding him were several expensive-looking glasses, chalices filled with wine and what appeared to be a totemic silver horse. To his side was a lady sitting on a golden throne, wearing a massive jewelled necklace (Weisenthal). As Cameron rose to speak from a golden throne, to read his notes from his golden speech, there was not the slightest hint of irony that the speech he was about to give was about his personal commitment to the cause of permanent austerity, nor that it should be directed at an audience comprised of various dignitaries, foreign diplomats, captains of industry and directors of large City firms who were the least likely to be the recipients of cuts to public spending. Cameron's announced plan for Britain's economic success was based on the legacy of three historical revolutions crucial to the progress of capitalism: the agricultural revolution, the industrial revolution and the financial revolution of the 1980s. Cameron implored his audience not to forget that these revolutions were only made possible in cooperation with Britain's core institutions: liberal governance, common law and the armed forces. All have been put in the service of defending property rights, access to markets, making economic profiteering correspond with the rule of law and ensuring 'equality for all before the law' amongst those who are apprehended as British subjects. Cameron asserted, 'these things are not incidental to our economic strength – they are absolutely key to it ... they form the golden thread of conditions which allow countries to thrive over the long term' (Cameron).

Cameron's metaphor of a 'golden thread' sat well with both present company and related moneyed objects whose congruence when placed in concordance with one another sanctified Cameron's speech. Cameron, uncannily like the fictional Mr. Podsnap before him, appeared 'a corpulent straddling epergne', delivering 'this address from an unsightly silver platform in the centre of the table ... All the big silver spoons and forks widened the mouths of the company expressly for the purpose of thrusting the sentiment down their throats with every morsel they ate' (Dickens, *Our Mutual Friend* 135; ch. 11). Cameron's own vulgar ornamentation referred well to his economic promise to keep authority over that 'golden thread' firmly in the hands of those in attendance, promising 'to build a leaner, more efficient state' for those who are least likely to be its recipients, or more accurately its direct recipients, who instead had their state welfare cheques handed to them in the form of tax breaks, unregulated bank bonuses, bank bailouts and off-shore accounting. By contrast, those who form the majority population outside of this gilded circle would need to do more with less. 'Not just now, but permanently.' This permanent austerity for them will mean cuts to education, welfare and the NHS. Even free school meals are threatened, because government findings show '64 per cent of children on free school meals don't get 5 good GCSEs with English and Maths', as though basic sustenance on the school dinner table equated directly with league tables. Cameron's proposal to put 'an end to the poverty and wealth traps' was addressed not to aid the poor themselves, but rather to come to the aid of a welfare system that for too long had been plagued by the appearance of its doleful recipients.

His proposed solution to head off this threat was 'capping welfare, so that no family is better off on benefits than in work' no matter how poorly paid that work may in reality be (Cameron). What Cameron's claim elides is the fact that 'the overwhelming majority of people who claim unemployment benefits each year spend at least three-quarters of their time in work' (Mulheirn). Indeed the great majority of welfare recipients are already in poorly paid, casualised work situations and as a result must continue to use benefits to supplement their wages to achieve a basic standard of subsistence. Cameron assured his audience that he was 'also very focused on supporting the voluntary sector to work alongside the State in fighting poverty and building this economy where everyone can take part'. Indeed they will have to do so in order to keep their benefits at all with the new welfare policy devised by Work and Pensions Secretary Iain Duncan Smith, which came into effect in April 2014. Under the new policy, which is 'estimated to cost the government £300 million to implement', anyone unemployed for more than six months seeking to maintain their job-seekers' allowance and housing benefits 'must work 35 hours in either unpaid private-sector work placements, or in the voluntary sector' (BBC News, 'Osborne Plans Community Work for Unemployed'). This near-to-full-time labour would be performed in exchange for what amounts to 'in effect £2 an hour' (Wintour, 'Some Benefits Claimants'). This scheme effectively guarantees that the poorest in society are forced to earn far less than the minimum wage in their equivalent of take-home benefits, through coerced and unremunerated labour. The new policy toward the poor is starkly reminiscent of the 1834 Poor Law, insofar as it bonds itself to the principle that those supported by the state should be kept in a condition more miserable than that of the lowest-paid labourer. After 180 years it appears that social policy has come full circle to make work pay, if not for the individual, then for the state and private enterprise who will continue to devise novel ways to extract value from this dependent population.

Cameron's generous plans to support private enterprise could not be more sharply contrasted with his harsh new welfare policies. He lauds everyone in attendance who contributes to 'a bigger and more prosperous private sector' and presumes it is they who happily 'generate wealth and pay for the public services we need' (Cameron). This presumption ignores the fact that the British, entrepreneurial class, whom Cameron affectionately and perhaps aptly refers to as 'buccaneers', i.e. pirates, come into the marketplace with a spirit towards governance 'that rewards people with the ambition to make things, sell things and create jobs for others up and down the country'. His praise obscures the fact that many of these same entrepreneurial buccaneers force their workers to rely on public assistance due to the poverty wages they offer to them. Nevertheless, Cameron insists that the much-needed 'fundamental culture change in our country' is not one that alleviates their hardships through a living wage, but rather one that readily accedes to the voracious demand for hand-outs on the part of corporations. These concessions include 'cutting corporation tax to 20 per cent' and eliminating unnecessary government bureaucracy, specifically its regulatory functions, 'saving businesses £1 billion'. Cameron insists he is backing innovative industries that 'will revolutionise world markets by removing barriers 'to enable new entrants and disruptive business models to develop at pace over the next five years'. The words 'revolutionise' and 'disruptive' give way to a description of a purely neoliberal economic ideology when Cameron boasts, 'we're not just putting enterprise at the heart of our economic policy. We want to make sure it is boosted everywhere. Promoted in schools. Taught in colleges. Celebrated in communities. Recognised properly in the honours system. And yes, supported abroad.'

Through his celebration of enterprise, Cameron aims to foster simultaneously a corporate boosterism, a new era of utilitarian state education and a multitude of neocolonial relationships abroad with 'China, Oman, Qatar, United Arab Emirates and Kuwait', from whom Britain can draw profitable resources well into the future. Therein Cameron, in his closing remarks, manages to chime his speech both to coincide with a nod to Britain's imperial past, as well as offer a guarantee to his audience of a future in which such utilitarian initiatives will be undertaken by the masses. Finally, Cameron urges his audience to remain 'confident that ... the City of London – the great innovator that has led the way in finance for centuries' – can now 'support a Great Britain whose innovation and creativity can lead the world for generations to come', by virtue of the fact that such utilitarianism will never be seriously practised amongst Britain's elite. Within that same rarefied lineage it is also possible to surmise that enterprise is here coded in a language of neocolonial financial domination, rather than cooperation with other nations. 'By doing this, we needn't look at the global race with fear' because we already know that the buccaneer class of Britons are more enterprising and clever than their foreign competitors. As for the average Briton, they can anticipate a nullified 'state we can afford', 'an economy where everyone' not only 'can take part' but will be forced to do so at whatever rate of pay the market allows. Ultimately they will be expected to participate in 'an economy based on enterprise at home and abroad', where resourcefulness will be key to survival as a culture of state-help progressively diminishes into one of self-help, not only for Britons themselves, but their neocolonial client populations as well. For Cameron and his privileged cronies in attendance, 'that's how we build something better'.

Amongst this most esteemed gathering stood one Ruth Hardy, present in the capacity of waitress. Hardy, in addition to pursuing her presumably unpaid journalism internship, also finds time to work evenings and weekends at an events company, most likely on a zero hours contract. Hardy boasts, 'the company is great and the hours are flexible, which allows me to combine it with my main job of an internship' ('It was hard to stomach David Cameron'). Nonetheless she concedes that as an aspirational twentysomething 'it's tough, and I've been in a state of semi-tiredness for the last two months'. Still Hardy remains grateful to be privileged enough 'to work at interesting events' where she gets to admire 'the fanciness of the Guildhall banquet' which she describes as 'breathtaking'. The politics behind her financial situation, as compared to those soon to be in her midst, fails to dawn on Hardy initially, nor does it her colleagues, who appear on the whole to have little grasp of the political hierarchy that determines their financial situation: 'as one of my colleagues said: "I thought Boris Johnson was the lord mayor, that's the only reason I agreed to work!"'.

What Hardy and her colleagues fail to recognise is that it is Johnson, and not Cameron, who is responsible for the conditions in which they presently labour. Johnson insisted in his speech to the Conservative Party Conference on 1 October 2013 (one month prior to Cameron's Banquet Speech delivered on 11 November 2013):

you've got to make sure that kids growing up in London are able to take the opportunity that our city offers and at the same time we must make sure they don't dismiss some jobs as quote/unquote 'menial', which is a word I sometimes hear, and that they see them, those jobs that London creates in such abundance, in the same way that … East Europeans see those jobs, as stepping stones, as a beginning to a life in work that can take them anywhere (Johnson).

And indeed for these servers it has taken them all the way to the Lord Mayor's Banquet to serve its privileged guests who enjoyed a champagne reception, and then were served a starter ('a celebration of British mushrooms'), a fish course and a main course of fillet of beef, all served with wine of course. Thus they were positively surfeited before Cameron's speech. Afterward, they were rewarded with a final course of dessert, coffee, dessert wine, port, brandy and whisky served by Hardy and her colleagues. Their work for the evening however was far from done. Rather, in a scene reminiscent of 'Downton Abbey' according to Hardy herself, the servers retreated downstairs to a steam-filled kitchen, where they were tasked with polishing a hoard of silverware. The striking contrast between the two levels of society was not lost on her, nor her colleagues; having met the challenges of the dinner service, most were already at the point of exhaustion as they were forced to combine two or three low-paid jobs to survive. It made little difference whether they were Britons or Eastern Europeans. This round the clock labour over time laid heavily on their persons regardless of their migration status. Boris Johnson, by contrast, could not be more pleased with this arrangement to service the needs of London as a city that never sleeps,

> A city with more American banks in it than there are in New York for heaven's sake. A 24 hour city in which there are 100,000 people working in supplying us all with coffee in the coffee bars of London, how about that? We have more baristas than barristers, there are quite a few barristers as well (Johnson).

It is likely that Hardy and her peers fall into the swelling ranks of the baristas who supply those far fewer British barristers and multinational corporate bankers with their desire for a caffeine fix, with none falling under the impression that such work 'can take them anywhere'. Instead of lending a helping hand to this legion of workers, Johnson insists we need to aid their corporate employers such as Starbucks and Costa by going forward with a low tax on enterprise. Johnson's solution to London's housing crisis for this low-wage working population similarly sets its sights not towards them, but rather the elite few by comparison they casually and invisibly serve each and every day 24/7. Johnson, in this same speech, argues against 'a mansion tax', 'because it would inhibit the very homes programme that we need to get going and we want to build ... hundreds of thousands of more homes' presumably to further cater to the tastes of this economically privileged class of key worker. It is these sorts of barriers, Johnson argues, we need to remove to ensure 'competitiveness in our country', with equality the providence of the rich.

Johnson, alongside Cameron, finds himself amongst 'the heads of tribes', who are rarely challenged in their societal perspective and assemble together in conference to make certain that others of a different mind are not granted influence. Their twenty-first-century century perspective echoes that of a nineteenth-century Mr. Podsnap, who cannot easily suffer the challenge of 'a stray personage of a meek demeanour' who intrudes upon his ancestral domain and dares to make 'reference to the circumstance that some half-dozen people had lately died in the streets, of starvation', a remark that 'was clearly ill-timed after dinner' (Dickens, *Our Mutual Friend* 143; ch. 11). Mr. Podsnap's utter disbelief that such a thing could happen in London is reflected in one contemporary Department of Work and Pension official's assertion that food banks have grown in Britain by virtue of 'aggressively marketing their services', rather than as a result of their vast and arbitrary censure of welfare benefits (Fisher). Most going to food banks have had benefits stopped for alleged breaches of job-centre rules, because they have been financially penalised by the bedroom tax, or they have simply had their working tax credits removed (Butler). The spike in food poverty has been well documented in the charity sector, but the government itself has refused to acknowledge the legitimacy of their inquests into the matter. Should evidence be obtained in this way to prove the plight of these individuals, they, like their fictitious predecessor Mr. Podsnap, would likely conclude that 'it was their own fault' (Dickens 143).

Nevertheless it is plain to see that starvation had 'in fact been forced upon them, and they would rather not have been starved upon the whole, if perfectly agreeable to all parties' (Dickens, *Our Mutual Friend* 143; ch. 11). Clearly it was not agreeable to the Conservative party. They, like Mr. Podsnap, would argue vehemently that 'there is not a country in the world, sir, where so noble a provision is made for the poor as in this country' (143). Their noble provisions, to the contrary, rendered their situation even worse and generated appalling conditions for those forced to endure their means. They appear instead to have no idea of the location of hardship, despite its proximity to their political stance. When challenged to identify its material dwelling, they seize upon the opportunity to exercise their distaste for anything resembling socialism or the possibility that these food banks, rather than being the preserve of the charity and religious sector to maintain, should in fact be centralised by the government to supply their revenues and structure. Here again we find ourselves in the company of Mr. Podsnap, who refuses to countenance 'centralization' because it is 'Not English' (143). To which one might ask, 'was dying of destitution and neglect necessarily English?' (143). To that Mr. Podsnap counters that Providence itself 'declared that you shall have the poor always with you', and that this relationship cannot be altered by government policies, and that it is not for the privileged likes of him 'to impugn the workings of Providence', which has in its wisdom placed him at the top rung of society (Dickens, *Our Mutual Friend*, 143-144; ch. 11).

It would appear that Mr. Johnson and Mr. Cameron share in common with the fictional Mr. Podsnap an audience (the heads of tribes) and an understanding with regard to knowing the intentions of Providence. Reading between the lines they also appear to bridle at the notion of societal interference, adhering to a liberal philosophy of governing a competitive national milieu skewed in the direction of those prepared to take greatest benefit from its administration. Hardy's next series of comments are the most telling in that regard, when she, perhaps like her meek male predecessor, presumes that perhaps 'Cameron didn't see the irony' or more accurately the individuals themselves, who provide creature comforts to these rich patrons, formulating amongst themselves no less than an 'army of waiting staff, cleaners, chefs and porters who were also present at the banquet'. Here again Hardy remarks on the presence of two worlds in attendance, 'rich people, who understood the necessity for austerity', and the poor who serve them, for whom 'this message might not be as easily comprehended by those who hadn't just enjoyed a four-course meal'. Such sentiments resonate disturbingly with Cameron's comments on the need to apply austerity to the provision of free school meals, based on their lack of correlation to improved test scores. Those who fail to achieve despite the meagre food in their bellies are presumably destined to join the legions 'on the minimum wage, for whom austerity has had a catastrophic and wounding effect', through the literal guarantee on the part of the rich to a 'leaner, more efficient, more affordable state' where 'a way of trimming down the administrative excesses of some public services' means a literal trimming away of the fat that sustains an economically vulnerable population. In the context of the current tough living conditions, which are creating hunger both in the capital and provincial areas of Britain, Hardy speculates that in response, perhaps at the banquet 'next year there will only be three courses, or the dessert wine will be ruthlessly culled' in solidarity to those less fortunate. Perhaps not, as a white-tied Cameron appears to be enjoying the banquet this year, despite the fact that 'the number of people using food banks has tripled in the past year'. Instead it is the rich who get hand-outs from the state: as someone on the shift with Hardy said, 'It gets annoying that we always serve free food to the people who really don't need free food'.

Following this is a nod to the neofeudalism portended by Cameron's political creed. Hardy remarks cannily: 'I have a fundamental problem with a man who sits on a golden throne and lectures us about spending less, like a modern-day, white-tie clad sheriff of Nottingham. And all around him, the insidious stain of austerity creeps across the country, manifesting in the bedroom tax, rising tuition fees and the closure of public services that vulnerable people depend on.' Hardy senses in these remarks that the condition of serfdom such a system of austerity implies, is one that carries with it a lifetime sentence: 'each of us has just one chance at existence, and so many people's lives are being blighted by these cuts. If this is the cruel and damaging reality of permanent austerity, then we should be telling Mr Cameron we don't want it.'

'The aspirations of an age usually tell us more about its inner life than do its ... achievements' (Clausen 404). What will endure are the 'ideas and ambitions' of 'a small minority of the population' who have a hand in enacting government and governing commerce (404). Today it is that same elite minority that is responsible for reviving a phraseology we have not witnessed being taken seriously since the Victorian era. The language of 'character', 'independence' and 'respectability' once again are being enunciated by the middle classes of contemporary Britain to chime with the neoliberal message that opportunities for social advancement are possible for those willing to take advantage of them. Today we face a situation where the aristocracy has pride of place in government, through the likes of Cameron and Johnson, and the British monarchy are experiencing an era of unprecedented popularity proportionally comparable to the reign of Queen Victoria. At the same time in Britain's postindustrial society, we are witnessing an economically ascendant middle class, which has taken hold of the aristocracy's moral discourse and fashioned it into a mantle for their own conduct. Meanwhile, the working classes find themselves under constant scrutiny; loudly excoriated by their class superiors for their perceived lack of moral values and antisocial behaviour. In the same breath they are assured that social mobility remains in their reach provided they behave reasonably and work diligently to accumulate wealth. It is through such a philosophy that the Conservatives are able to congratulate themselves as being 'on the side of hardworking people' (Cameron).

Returning to the context of Victorian Britain, this liberal rhetoric of self-help could very easily have Dickens as its poster child; his biography making the case for the promise of class ascendency to be fulfilled even amongst those that began life by being poorly educated and financially burdened. Dickens himself did not perceive the equation of poverty to wealth in quite that fashion, but rather believed that both rich and poor filled the roles of consumer and consumed until they became almost interchangeable states for the individual under the dictates of capitalism; this as a consequence of their becoming progressively ensnared in the cycle of production and consumption. For Dickens it is clear that an individual who 'has fallen into the world of production and consumption, is not born; he is made' (Houston, '"Pip" and "Property"' 18). To this peculiar manufacture, he owes both his debt and his burden as one of the powerless masses charged with underwriting the excesses of the powerful few. Gail Turley Houston observes that 'one of the most important perceptions of Dickens's fiction is of Victorian society as one in which 'the weak support the strong, the starving underwrite the satiated, the poor prop up the rich, the children sustain the parents, the female upholds the male' (13). Together they bring the rapaciousness of the market to play in the sum of social relations, a condition that can only be temporarily ameliorated through self-sacrifice and self-abnegation in regard to the acquisition of money and position.

Employing such a theorem, Dickens attacks mid-Victorian political economy and its laissez-faire foundation through a great series of his novels including *Oliver Twist, Dombey and Son, Hard Times, Little Dorrit, A Christmas Carol* and *Our Mutual Friend*. As Fulweiler points out, 'That Dickens should introduce Darwinian thought into his fictional critique after 1859 seems surprising in light of the laissez-faire origin of *The Origin*' (51). In their recent book, *Darwin: The Life of a Tormented Evolutionist*, Adrian Desmond and James Moore insist that Darwin's view of nature was in sympathy with the 'competitive, capitalist, Malthusian dynamics of a poor-law society' (267). They write that Darwin was a convinced Whig 'in an age when Whig government was building workhouses and the poor were burning them down' ... moreover Darwin's 'notebooks make plain that competition, free trade, imperialism, racial extermination, and sexual inequality were written into the equation from the start' in the formulation of his new biological proposition (1). Despite the fact that *Our Mutual Friend* draws its narrative structure from similar outlines, and is saturated with motifs of Darwinian biology, ultimately Dickens employs these features in order to display their defect.

Each of Dickens's characters responds to Darwin's inadequacy with a demonstration of their own shortsightedness about how to confront the terms of their relationship to accumulation. On the top end of the equation, 'Mr. Podsnap's value in Mr. Podsnap's eyes is exactly determined by the amount of wealth he has, just as his possessions are valuable to him because they are worth so much cash' (J. H. Miller 69). At the very bottom, 'Betty Higden concentrates her waning energy on avoiding the workhouse and on protecting the burial money she has sewn in her dress' (69). It says everything about her implication into a system of capitalism, that her 'central aim is the desire for financial independence', thus creating strange political bedfellows between her and Mr.

Podsnap. Dickens's writing suggests that both of their conditions are predicated on acquisition and hoarding of one kind or another contributing to their own demise. Money for Dickens has made of life's worth only that which can be counted, weighed, displayed, concealed or speculated upon at will. With life thus reduced to its base consistency, it then becomes possible to justify the naturalness of the competitive environment in which individuals must struggle against one another for the spoils of society and where there are quite naturally and indeed necessarily winners and losers. Interference in the pattern of this struggle presumes an omniscience that is frowned upon because it is seen as attempting to govern the very laws of nature itself. The fact that some of us are predators, whilst others are scavengers, speaks to the stuff we are made of, in a similar way that it reveals our true stuffing, that is to say the secret of our inheritance, which was for liberals largely a matter of birthright, and for radicals like Dickens largely a matter of one's moral will. For Dickens this is the true purpose of evolution. This question of inheritance for Dickens is as much about the question of accumulation as it is Darwin's biological schema, with one important distinction: its role in relation to capitalism and the choice of whether to wed oneself to the order of self-interest, or that of social-mutuality. The latter is the choice Dickens is advocating not just in *Our Mutual Friend*, but equally in every one of his mature novels. It is this pattern for society's evolution that Dickens purports to demonstrate, thus introducing a factor of self-governance, to compete as it were with the basic laws of nature.

Although Dickens made use of the explanatory powers of both natural selection and laissez-faire economics, and although he remained sympathetic to science, his ultimate aim in writing was to transcend and oppose the ideological paradigms of Malthus and Darwin in order 'to project a teleological and designed evolution in the human world toward a moral community of responsible men and women' (Fulweiler 53). By choosing to introduce a discourse of responsibilisation into the narrative of nineteenth-century liberalism, Dickens proposes to radically challenge its established limits to accommodate a continuous evolution for humanity that reflects a higher, perhaps even divine causality. For Dickens this iteration of Darwin's theory would provide the missing link en route to the anti-humanism that he envisioned might evolve for British society, in much the same way as it would do in later years for Michel Foucault. Both Dickens and Foucault take it upon themselves to think positively and generatively about the exercise of power under the terms of liberalism, and moreover, as radicals in their respective ways, attempt to faithfully render its forms rather than simply denouncing it as a means of unearthing its wide-reaching potential.

For Dickens as an author, this meant narrating a set of ideological coordinates between eighteenth-century mercan-tilism and nineteenth-century capitalism as a medium for the public's understanding of the progress of liberal ideology. For Michel Foucault, as a political philosopher, the task was perhaps a more direct one: to model the distinctions between eighteenth-century liberalism and its twentieth-century successor neoliber-alism with regard to understanding their structure of compe-tition. In Foucault's supposition, the fundamental issue neoliber-alism has with its predecessor, liberalism, 'is that whether you define the market by exchange or by competition you are still thinking of it as a sort of given nature, something produced spontaneously which the state must respect precisely inasmuch as it is a natural datum' (*The Birth of Biopolitics* 120). For neolib-erals this represents a fundamental misunderstanding of compe-tition within liberal thought, because for them it is absolutely not a given of nature. Competition as a contest, mechanism and source of material effects cannot be left to rely upon the interplay of natural appetites, instincts and behaviours as though these were pre-existing in nature. Rather, these elements must be understood as owing to 'a formal privilege', wherein competition assumes the mold of 'a formal game between inequalities' as opposed to 'a natural game between individuals and behaviors' (120). Liberalism must be revised to accept competition as something that produces its effects under certain conditions that have to be carefully orchestrated and artificially constructed. Pure competition understood is this way is by no means a primitive given, but rather a historical objective and a governmental art commanding of respect. In the twentieth-century revision of eighteenth-century liberal-economic theory, one must govern *for* the market, rather than *because* of it. To that extent we can see the relationship defined by eighteenth-century liberalism is completely reversed so that in essence the principles of a market economy come in time to supersede the traditional exercise of political power.

In order for this new relationship with market competition to be arrived at, the neoliberals had to subject classical liberalism to a number of transformations. Given liberalism's insistence that competition forms the natural basis of society, the problem of liberal policy was the development of concrete spaces in which the formal structure of competition could function. By contrast the problem of neoliberal policy was to act through perpetual surveillance, movement and interference to govern those spaces. Neoliberalism, then, may be thought of as a superseding form of liberalism and therein the problem is one of not of government, but rather technique, when it comes managing resources. In understanding the distinction in competition between liberalism and neoliberalism, it is helpful to consider it as a disagreement of nature versus nurture. Under the liberals there is only one true and fundamental social policy: government interference only to protect private property and inheritance. Under the terms of neoliberal economy, the one true and fundamental social policy becomes economic growth. Its revised doctrine assumes that 'economic growth and only economic growth should enable all individuals to achieve a level of income that will allow them the individual insurance, access to private property and individual or familial capitalization with which to absorb risks' (*The Birth of Biopolitics* 144). Victorian liberal principle was largely bent upon noninterference. Contemporary neoliberalism, by contrast, is determined to intervene on a perpetual basis so that competitive mechanisms can play a regulatory role in the market and thus achieve its fundamental objective, 'the general regulation of society by the market' (145). Whereas liberalism sought to expose its society to the dynamic of commodification, neoliberalism sought to expose it to the dynamic of competition. As a result, the *homo oeconomicus* sought by neoliberalism is not a man of exchange as he was conceived in the eighteenth century, nor a man of consumption of the nineteenth and mid-twentieth centuries respectively, but rather a man of enterprise for the late twentieth century and beyond.

Liberal authority is only partially based on belief in 'a spontaneous natural order as the many authors of the Natural codes declared in the eighteenth century' (*The Birth of Biopolitics* 161). Beyond that basis, it finds its foundation in a pseudo-spontaneous legal order, which 'presupposes juridical intervention by the state' and dictates that economic life 'take place in accordance with a juridical framework that fixes the regime of property, contracts, patents, bankruptcy, the status of professional associations and commercial societies, the currency and banking as creations', not founded in nature, but rather through legislation (161). Liberalism therefore relies on an ability to constantly adapt the legal order 'to scientific discoveries, to the progress of economic organization and technique, to changes in the structure of society, and to the requirements of contemporary consciousness' (161–2). Dickens's writing attempts to chart such adaptation of the economic to the social that exists from capitalism's beginning, as an arrangement of regulatory activities with rules that operate at various discreet levels, to allow certain forms, origins, dates and chronologies to dominate understanding. The conventions derived from this process go on to constitute social bodies, comprise religious prescription, formulate ethics, govern corporate regulation and ratify law. It is this continuous process that makes up the true evolution of capitalist society.

What we witness in the intervening era between the eighteenth century and the twentieth is a progression in the understanding of the market from an arena of exchange in the eighteenth century, to one of competition in the nineteenth century, and in the twentieth century one of enterprise. As capitalism attempted to absorb all of these values, the outward consumption initially prescribed by liberalism over time evolved to become a prescription for inward expenditure under the new terms of neoliberalism. In the eighteenth century, classical liberalism identified human labour as the source for both the manufacture and justification of private property. Under the constraints of neoliberalism, any special status for human labour was abandoned along with liberalism's 'older distinctions between production and consumption rooted in the labor theory of value' (Mirowski 59). What replaces such values is an understanding of the human being as 'an arbitrary bundle of "investments", skill sets, temporary alliances (family, sex, race) and fungible body parts' (59). Under these new vestiges of neoliberalism, 'there are no more "classes" in the sense of the older political economy, since every individual is both employer and worker simultaneously; in the limit, every man should be his own business firm or corporation' (59). Today we find ourselves at a historical juncture where the liberal market rooted in nature has firmly given way to the neoliberal market rooted in self-governance in a way that anticipates neoliberalism's core ethos.

There is no real concern for social mobility within the narrative of *Our Mutual Friend* as such. Rather the achievement

sought is 'a just social hierarchy, in which only the truly exceptional should be rewarded with social progression, while the
unexceptional hardly progress at all and indeed at times struggle
to maintain their current hierarchal level' (Goodlad, *Victorian
Literature* 166). That romance figures as a conduit to this end, is
based on the idea that romance validates upper-middle-class
values. Romance then is a norm to aspire to for those in the abject
working classes, who are usually denied such a luxury.
Commodified in this way, romance, i.e. normative desire,
becomes the language of capitalism at the historical moment of
its affective intersection with global free trade and the bounded
nation-state. It is the task of authors like Dickens to set Victorian
readers on a course to understanding and appreciation of how
production, and indeed reproduction, play out against a
backdrop of economic globalisation, and how to greet the system
of capital with if not outright adulation, then at least tempered
affection. In this way romance, like money, takes on a protean
capacity, whose fluctuations of fortune can potentially transform
the fate of us all, and the fact that it does so as a matter of course
increases our ardour for it all the more. 'What distinguished the
romance narration of global capitalism, then, was its imagination
of departure from centralized authority, which in turn evoked
transformation of experiences in space, and the sense of
belonging' that gave temporary refuge to the individual from the
violence and volatility of the self-regulating market (Çelikkol 14).
Meanwhile, capitalist ideology refashioned the operation of
erotic desire to better resemble the satisfaction that was meant to
be inherent to the purchase as it were of quality goods. As a
consequence the pursuit of romance only seems to expand the
system of capitalism by other means, because according with its
new capitalistic terms it is predicated on the circulation of
material wealth.

It is for this reason that Dickens is unable to build any political
capital for himself within his guises of author and journalist,

because his writing is in some way stranded at that level of description and critique, forever failing as it were to reach the shore of prescription, because simply put Dickens can see no way for man to divorce romance permanently from economics. As a consequence of this, he grants readers an unsatisfactory, temporary separation from it by at once lending character to the material things, and denying it to the subject just long enough for the spectre of their attachment to become ever-so-subtly visible. This referent, this 'golden thread', weaves its way forward to be included in Cameron's assumptions about social hierarchy, and indeed the necessity of continuous adaptation to the market where the material qualities of the enterprise becomes the desirable and governable outline for every man. Under the updated terms of capitalist neoliberalism, desire for the other, or for the object, gives way to the pursuit of self-love and self-aggrandizement. The pendulum of romance no longer swings between 'she loves me, she loves me not', as it did under the auspices of liberalism, but rather between self-love and self-hatred within the confined space of the atomised consumerist individual.

The irony of this new situation is that social mobility, as evidenced through personal or professional success, is crafted to resemble the look of 'hard work', when in fact it is most often the case that those putting their hand to social engineering are 'an unprecedented cadre of politicians and millionaire elites' who blithely aim 'to justify their position and success' by ascribing it to a combination of 'hard work and self-belief'. In reality, however, 'their quasi-aristocratic or aristocratic backgrounds' have virtually guaranteed their material triumph (Littler 68). Nevertheless they insist to their struggling, aspiring audiences that you have to want to win. Following on from such a neoliberal logic, one must conclude that those who fail to take hold of societal advancement are simply victim to their own failure of expectations. This same affective economy 'encourages an optimistic idea of a brighter future, whilst such attachments are simultaneously "actively impeded" by the harsh precarities and instabilities of neoliberalism' (66). Despite this painful contradiction, and through careful censure of the highly selective nature of the neoliberal quality of opportunity, the vast majority are encouraged to ignore the stark reality of their likelihood of achieving class ascension. Yet for all intents and purposes this ascension remains a distant prospect, one that moreover is receding even further from their grasp with every cut made to the social safety net; its remnant 'golden threads' given over to the welfare of monopoly corporations.

Cameron may talk of a meritocratic Britain, but his actions reinforce the entitlements of a privileged elite. It is the ease of privilege that allows this class to adopt an appearance of activity when it comes to setting goals, without the necessity of ever having to demonstrate their satisfactory completion. Under the terms of neoliberalism, aspiration takes the place of accomplishment. This same ethos goes a long way toward motivating the working-class majority, who are constantly goaded by the Conservative government to compete against one another for a much-sought-after pile of riches, waging a thankless campaign to do so based on the dubious virtue of so-called merit alone. 'Through neoliberalism meritocracy has become an alibi for plutocracy, or government by a wealthy elite' (Littler 69). Meanwhile those occupying the bottom rung of society are relentlessly blamed for their own failure to progress up the ladder of wealth.

This situation was anticipated in *Our Mutual Friend*, which sought to anatomise the struggle for class ascendency in Victorian Britain through its schema of relations and predicted failure for those creatures who sought their class evolution within the abiding social classificatory system. As Todd May suggests, 'inasmuch as we think of ourselves as consumers and entrepreneurs, and act in accordance with these self-conceptions, we are unlikely to open ourselves to close friendships. They will not appear to us as possibilities on our interpersonal horizon' (141). For Dickens it was only those who witnessed another abiding feature, that is to say the feature of their mutuality, who had any real chance of capturing a lasting friendship with one another. In *Our Mutual Friend*, friendship is not a neutral social archetype to be idealised or romanticised, but rather is understood as a powerful organising principle of society that while enmeshed within its norms, on rare occasions allows its pairing to cut across formal class structures, and in doing so glimpse the historically contingent limitations bound up within their division. The span of these joinings reminds us that there are many alternatives to society as it is. Indeed, 'so many things can be changed', and 'as fragile' as these affinities amongst us might be, the apparent strength of the distinctions amongst us upon closer inspection appear 'bound up more with circumstances than with necessities'. In the light of intimacy these appear more 'arbitrary than self-evident, more a matter of complex, but temporary, historical circumstances than with inevitable anthropological constraints' (Foucault, 'Practicing Criticism' 156).

In *Our Mutual Friend* Dickens experiments with friendship as an ethical instrument capable of allowing us to rearticulate 'agency as a social or transindividual phenomenon' (Rothenberg 722). It is in this sense that Dickens's narrative about 'friendship' opens up the possibility of conducting our relations to one another differently, so that we are concerned with the other for the sake of the other, as opposed to some sought return on investment for the time we have spent together with that person. Through this arrangement of class relations as asymmetrical, as opposed to complementary, class distinction is able to take on a multiplicity heretofore denied to it. 'By articulating agency as an ethical matter the novel helps us to see why the passage from a cultural particular to a politically viable universal must be forged again and again, without reliable guides to the results, and how politics is predicated on repressing this history' (Rothenberg 743). In this way Dickens's writing envisages a way to radically alter the liberal political paradigm for binding classes as a means of deriving calculated worth, by introducing instead the possibility of their existence as a unity of elective affinities capable of temporarily liberating themselves, whilst still remaining formally within the confines of a repressive social system. Today's neoliberal politics, like their liberal predecessor, strive to obscure the potential of such mutuality amongst the classes, who when brought into proximity with one another might work to create provisions within society capable of generating forms of social reproduction worthy of collective valuation.

Dickens was devoted to furthering this concept of class mutuality for the whole of his career, and indeed chose to end his civic vocation with *A Christmas Carol* as his final public reading in 1870:

His last reading of the little book took place in London at St James's Hall, on March 15, 1870. At the end of the performance, he told his audience: 'From these garish lights, I vanish now for evermore, with a heartfelt, grateful, respectful, and affectionate farewell' … With tears streaming down his face, Dickens raised his hands to his lips in an affectionate kiss and departed from the platform forever (Francis).

In essence he was departing from his great, multifarious audience on terms of appreciative friendship. What he left for them to reckon with for the national benefit was at an obvious level the moral redemption of the repugnant businessman Ebenezer Scrooge, and perhaps at a more subtle level the lingering offspring born of Scrooge's former Malthusian/Darwinian ideology. In the novel 'they were a boy and a girl', denied their natural course: 'where graceful youth should have filled their features out, and touched them with its freshest tints, a stale and shrivelled hand, like that of age, had pinched, and twisted them, and pulled them into shreds' (Dickens, *A Christmas Carol* 85). It was not only favourable form that had been denied to this boy and girl, but Holy Spirit as well: 'where angels might have sat enthroned, devils lurked, and glared out menacing' (85). In challenge to Darwin's theory, their odious mutation was said not to be born of the order of nature for indeed the scale of their perversity demonstrated clearly for all who wished to see that 'no change, no degradation, no perversion of humanity, in any grade, through all the mysteries of wonderful creation, has monsters half so horrible and dread' (85–6). Scrooge could hardly be said to be alone in his impulse to retreat at the appalling sight of them, and in brief loyalty to his liberal bearings 'he tried to say they were fine children, but the words choked themselves, rather than be parties to a lie of such enormous magnitude' (86). In the midst of their rhetorical rebellion, Spirit took on the act of speech and assigned the part to their rightful parentage, not God nor Spirit, but the Providence of Man. Before a silent Scrooge the time of their reunion was finally upon us: 'this boy is Ignorance. This girl is Want. Beware them both, and all of their degree, but most of all beware this boy, for on his brow I see that written which is Doom, unless the writing be erased' (86). It is here that we might finally comprehend that far from being a natural state, both the naming of their poverty and its dire outcome for society as whole were products of discursive practices founded in the political economy of the age. The origins of such rhetoric are not found in the proclamations of the Holy Spirit, but rather in a clever form of class manipulation wrought by the hands of city bankers, who not only 'deny' that fact, but also 'slander those who tell it ye'; this impoverished class have 'no refuge or resource' apart from 'prisons and 'workhouses' (86).

'The bell struck twelve', the banqueting of the rich ceased, and once more we found ourselves the unfortunate children of midnight, who 180 years later still repose to a shelter and benefit that austerely resumes their criminal definition (86). Within that same murky light the bankers look about themselves for the spectre of rebellion from their charges, but fail to see it manifest in the 'yellow, meagre, ragged, scowling, wolfish' faces of the poor who remain 'prostrate … in their humility' before the Lords of Finance, the Masters of the Universe (86). 'As the last stroke ceased to vibrate', both parties would do well to '[remember] the prediction of old Jacob Marley', and turn their eyes, to behold 'a solemn Phantom, draped and hooded, coming, like a mist along the ground, towards' them to demonstrate a clear consequence to their nefarious conduct (86). Read in this light and in comparison to the Phantom, the ignorant boy is but a cipher. Therefore he must be appreciated not as Doom's agent, but rather its messenger, portending a time when great poverty and great wealth will conspire in their 'avarice, hard-dealing, griping cares' to bring humanity to 'a rich end, truly' (Dickens, *A Christmas Carol*, 98). This outcome however can be vanquished, 'shrunk, collapsed, and dwindled down into a bedpost' if only we make the cause to live 'in the Past, the Present, and the Future' and not 'shut out the lessons that they teach' (108). Following this course, Dickens argues, might allow us to expunge the script of institutions, and tally in their place 'a new graceful capacity to garner enlightenment and fulfillment for the benefit of all' (108). Until such time as this happens, the majority of us are left to dwell on the paths of our ignoble displacement, reading our times and ourselves as both neoliberal and neoDickensian.

Works Cited

Ackroyd, Peter. *Dickens*. New York: HarperCollins Publishers, 1990. Print.

Adorno, Theodor W. 'On Dickens' *The Old Curiosity Shop*: A Lecture.' *Notes on Literature*. Ed. Rolf Tiedemann. Trans. Sherry Weber Nicholsen. New York: Columbia University Press, 1992. Print.

Ahmed, Nafeez. 'Inclusive Capitalism Initiative is Trojan Horse to Quell Coming Global Revolt.' *The Guardian*. 28 May 2014. Web. Accessed 28 May 2014.

Anderson, Amanda. *The Powers of Distance: Cosmopolitanism and the Cultivation of Detachment*. Princeton: Princeton University Press, 2001. Print.

Anderson, Benedict. *Imagined Communities: Reflections on the Origin and Spread of Nationalism, Revised Edition*. London: Verso, 2006. Print.

Anderson, Claire. *Indian Uprising of 1857–8: Prisons, Prisoners, and Rebellion*. London: Anthem Press, 2007. Print.

Barrow, Becky. 'Civil Servant Strike Brings Chaos to Key Public Services.' *Daily Mail Online*. Daily Mail and General Trust. 8 March 2010. Web. Accessed 27 July 2014.

Bartels, Emily C. 'Too Many Blackamoors: Deportation, Discrimination, and Elizabeth I.' *Studies in English Literature*. 46.2 (2006): 305–22. Web. Accessed 7 Aug 2013.

BBC News. 'England riots: "The whites have become black" says David Starkey.' *www.bbc.com*. 12 Aug 2011. Web. Accessed 29 Nov 2014.

—-. 'Osborne Plans Community Work for Unemployed.' *YouTube*. 30 Sept 2013. Web. Accessed 12 Dec 2013.

—-. 'Riot problems still an issue, Mayor Boris Johnson says.' *www.bbc.com*. BBC News. 6 Aug 2012. Web. Accessed 20 Oct 2013.

Benn, David Wedgwood. 'The Crimean War and its Lessons for Today.' *International Affairs*. 88. 2 (2012): 387–91. Web. Accessed 23 July 2014.

Bishop, Matthew and Michael Green. 'Victorian Giving.' *Philanthrocapitalism: How Giving Can Save the World*. London: Bloomsbury Press, 2009. *www.philanthrocapitalism.net*. n.d. Web. Accessed 4 May 2012.

Bloy, Marjie. 'Henry John Temple, Viscount Palmerston (1784-1865).' *www.victorianweb.org*. The Victorian Web. 15 March 2002. Web. Accessed 22 July 2014.

—-. 'General Comments on the Crimean War.' *www.victorianweb.org*. The Victorian Web. 16 May 2014. Web. Accessed 22 July 2014.

Bose, Shumi. 'Golden Boys: The Art of Elmgreen & Dragset.' *DesignCurial*. 14 Nov 2013. Web. Accessed 19 Oct 2014.

Bowen, John. *Other Dickens: Pickwick to Chuzzlewit*. Oxford: Oxford University Press, 2003. Print.

Bowler, Peter J. 'What Darwin Disturbed: The Biology That Might Have Been.' *Isis*. 99 (2008): 560–67. Web. Accessed 12 Jan 2013

Bradley, Kimberly. 'Elmgreen & Dragset.' *Artview*. Oct 2013. Web. Accessed 18 Oct 2014.

Butler, Patrick. 'Government dismisses study linking use of food banks to benefit cuts.' *The Guardian*. Guardian Media Group. 19 Nov 2014. Web. Accessed 2 Dec 2014.

Cain Jr., Jimmie E., *Bram Stoker and Russophobia: Evidence of the British Fear of Russia in* Dracula *and* The Lady of the Shroud. Jefferson NC: MacFarland, 2006. Print.

Cain, Ruth. 'The Philpott Trial, Welfare Reform and the Facialisation of Poverty.' *Critical Legal Thinking*. 19 April 2013. Web. Accessed 16 August 2013.

Caldwell, Christopher. 'Can David Cameron Redefine Britain's Tory Party?' *The New York Times*. The New York Times Company. 8 July, 2009. Web. Accessed 25 July 2014.

Cameron, David. 'David Cameron's Lord Mayor's Banquet

Speech: In Full.' *The Telegraph*. Telegraph Media Group. 11 Nov 2013. Web. Accessed 12 Dec 2013.

Capuano, Peter, J. 'Handling the Perceptual Politics of Identity in *Great Expectations*.' *Dickens Quarterly*. 27:3 (2010): 185–208. Web. Accessed 6 Sept 2013.

Cavendish, Richard. 'Lord Palmerston Becomes PM.' *History Today*. Vol. 55.2 (2005). Web. Accessed 24 July 2014.

Çelikkol, Ayse. *Romances of Free Trade: British Literature, Laissez-Faire, and the Global Nineteenth Century*. Oxford: Oxford University Press, 2011. Print.

Clarke, William. *The Lost Fortune of the Tsars*. New York: St. Martin's Press, 1994. Print.

Clausen, Christopher. 'How to Join the Middle Classes: With the Help of Dr. Smiles and Mrs. Beeton.' *The American Scholar*. 62.3 (1993): 403–418.

Colebrook, Claire. *Gilles Deleuze*. London: Routledge, 2002. Print.

Coutts. 'Coutts History.' *www.coutts.com*. n.d. Web. Accessed 4 May 2012.

Dalrymple, William. 'When East Fought West.' *Time International (South Pacific Edition)*. Time Inc. 2007.

DeLong, Brad. 'The Panic of 1825.' *The Week*. 14 Apr 2009. Web. Accessed 28 Nov 2014.

Deleuze, Gilles. *Logic of Sense*. London: The Athlone Press, 1990. Print.

Derrida, Jacques. *On Cosmopolitanism and Forgiveness*. London: Routledge, 2001. Print.

—-. *Spectres of Marx: The State of Debt, the Work of Mourning, & the New International*. London: Routledge, 2006. Print.

Desmond, Adrian J. and James Richard Moore. *Darwin: The Life of a Tormented Evolutionist*. New York: W.W. Norton & Company Inc., 1991. Print.

Dick, Alexander J. 'On the Financial Crisis, 1825–26.' *www.branch-collective.org*. BRANCH: Britain, Representation and Nineteenth-Century History. Web. Accessed 27 Nov 2014.

Dickens, Charles. *A Christmas Carol*. Fairfield: 1st World Publishing, 2004. Print.

—-. *Bleak House*. New York: Signet Classics, 1964. Print.

—-. *Great Expectations*. New York: Penguin Books 2010. Print.

—-. *Little Dorrit*. New York: Alfred A Knopf, 1992. Print.

—-. *Nicholas Nickleby*. Ware: Wordsworth Editions Ltd., 1998. Print.

—-. 'Nobody, Somebody and Everybody.' *The Works of Charles Dickens, Volume 20*. London: Chapman and Hall, 1911. Google eBook. Web. Accessed 19 Nov 2014.

—-. *Oliver Twist*. New York: Penguin Classics, 2007. Print.

—-. *Our Mutual Friend*. London: Penguin Classics, 1998. Print.

Donadio, Rachel. 'A Life Interrupted by Viewers Elmgreen & Dragset's "Tomorrow," at Victoria & Albert Museum.' *The New York Times*. 9 Dec 2013. Web. Accessed 23 Oct 2014.

Douglas-Fairhurst, Robert. 'Financial crisis: We should turn to Charles Dickens in hard times, not just Little Dorrit.' *The Telegraph*. 21 Oct 2008. Web. Accessed 28 Nov 2014.

Duncan Smith, Iain. 'Britain Cannot Afford the Spare Room Subsidy.' *The Telegraph*. 7 Mar 2013. Web. Accessed 29 Jan 2014.

Dugan, Emily. '"Big Lie" Behind the Bedroom Tax: Families Trapped with Nowhere to Move Face Penalty for Having Spare Room.' *The Independent*. 5 Aug 2013. Web Accessed 29 Jan 2014.

Dworkin, Dennis. 'Paul Gilroy and the Pitfalls of British Identity.' Conference Paper. *Institute for Arts and Humanities at the University of North Carolina at Chapel Hill* for the event *Paul Gilroy*. 17–19 Jan 2008. Web. Accessed 27 Aug 2013.

Dzelzainis, Ella. 'Introduction.' *Victorian Network*. 4:1 (2012) 1–7. *www.victoriannetwork.org*. n.d. Web. Accessed 29 Dec 2013.

Economist. 'The Exhibition – The Crystal Palace.' 18 May 1851. 5, 29. Print.

—-. 'Breaking the Chains.' *The Economist*. 22 Feb 2007. Web. Accessed 4 Oct 2013.

—-. 'The Slumps that Shaped Modern Finance.' *The Economist*. 14 April 2014. Web. Accessed 27 Nov 2014.

Elmgreen, Michael and Ingar Dragset. 'The Welfare Show.' Online Video. n.d. *serpentinegalleries.org*. Serpentine Gallery. Web. Accessed 21 Oct 2014.

—-. 'Tomorrow.' *Victoria and Albert Museum*. 2014.

Esterhammer, Angela. 'Improvisation, Speculation, Risky Business: Fiction and Performance, 1824–1826' *Essays in Romanticism*. 21.1(2014): 1–16. Web. Accessed 20 Mar 2014.

Ferguson, Niall. *The House of Rothschild: The World's Banker 1849–1999*. New York: Viking Penguin, 1999. Print.

Figes, Orlando. 'In Ukraine, Putin is running rings around the west.' *The Guardian*. The Guardian Media Group. 9 May 2014. Web. 15 May 2014.

—-. *The Crimean War: A History*. New York: Picador, 2012. Print.

Fisher, Lucy. 'Christian charity hits back over Tory attacks on food banks.' *The Guardian*. Guardian Media Group. 19 Apr 2014. Web. Accessed 2 Dec 2014.

Foucault, Michel. 'Practicing Criticism.' *Politics, Philosophy Culture: Interviews and Other Writings of Michel Foucault*. Ed. L.D. Kritzman. London: Routledge, 1990. Print.

—-. *The Birth of Biopolitics: Lectures at the Collège de France, 1978–1979 (Lectures at the College de France)*. London: Picador, 2010. Print.

Francis, Clive. 'Ten Things You Never Knew About Charles Dickens's *A Christmas Carol*.' *The Telegraph*. 5 Dec 2012. Web. Accessed 24 Dec 2013.

Freeland, Chrystia. *Plutocrats: The Rise of the New Global Super-Rich and the Fall of Everyone Else*. New York: Penguin, 2012. Print.

Fulweiler, Howard A. '"A Dismal Swamp": Darwin, Design and Evolution in *Our Mutual Friend*.' *Nineteenth-Century Literature*. 49:1 (1994): 50–74. Web. Accessed 12 Jan 2013.

Gallagher, Catherine. 'The Bioeconomics of *Our Mutual Friend*.'

Subject to History: Ideology, Class, Gender. Ed. David Simpson. Ithaca: Cornell University Press, 1991. Print.

Gallagher, Catherine and Stephen Greenblatt. *Practicing New Historicism*. Chicago: University of Chicago Press, 2001. Print.

Ghosh, Amrita. 'Carlyle, Mill, Bodington and the Case of 19th Century Imperialized Science.' *Journal of Philosophy: A Cross-Disciplinary Inquiry*. 4.9 (2009): 26–33. Web. Accessed 14 Oct 2013.

Gilbert, Jenny. 'IoS exhibition review: Charles Dickens Museum, Doughty Street, London.' *Independent on Sunday*. 16 Dec 2012. Web. Accessed 7 Dec 2013.

Gilbert, Pamela K. *Mapping the Victorian Social Body*. Albany: State University of New York Press, 2004. Print.

Gilmour, Robin. *The Idea of the Gentleman in the Victorian Novel*. London: George Allen & Unwin, 1981. Print.

Gilroy, Paul. '1981 and 2011: From Social Democratic to Neoliberal Rioting.' *South Atlantic Quarterly*. 112.3 (2013): 550–8. Web. Accessed 14 Oct 2013.

—-. *Postcolonial Melancholia*. New York: Columbia University Press, 2005. Print.

Golbort, Sarah. *Imaginary Gentlemen: Performing Masculinity in Dickens's Bildungsromane* Great Expectations *and* David Copperfield. MA Thesis. Mt. Pleasant. Central Michigan University, 2012. Web. Accessed 12 Oct 2013.

Goodlad, Lauren M. E. 'Beyond the Panopticon: Victorian Britain and the Critical Imagination.' *PMLA*. 118.3 (2003): 539–56. Web. Accessed 14 Jan 2014.

—-. *Victorian Literature and the Victorian State: Character and Governance in a Liberal Society*. Baltimore: Johns Hopkins University Press, 2003. Print.

Greeley, Horace. 'The Crystal Palace and its Lessons: A Lecture.' Harvard Library, 1852. Print.

Grossman, Jonathan H. 'The Absent Jew in Dickens: Narrators in *Oliver Twist, Our Mutual Friend* and *A Christmas Carol*.' *Dickens*

Studies Annual: Essay on Victorian Fiction. 24 (1996): 37–57. Web. Accessed 2 Dec 2012.

Hadley, Elaine. 'The Past is A Foreign Country: The Neo-Conservative Romance with Victorian Liberalism.' *The Yale Journal of Criticism.* 10.1 (1997): 7–38. Web. Accessed 29 Dec 2013.

Hall, Catherine. 'Troubling Memories: Nineteenth Century Histories of the Slave Trade and Slavery.' *Transactions of the RHS.* 21 (2011): 147–69. Web. Accessed 7 Sept 2013.

Hall, Stuart. 'Un-settling "the heritage", re-imagining the post-nation: Whose heritage?' *Third Text.* 19 Jun 2008. Web. Accessed 15 Jan 2015.

Hammond, Matthew. 'Expecting the Event: Dickens and Deleuze.' *Deleuze and Literature.* Conference Paper. University of Warwick Department of Philosophy. 20 March 2006. Web. Accessed 5 Nov 2012.

Hardy, Ruth. 'It was hard to stomach David Cameron preaching austerity from a golden throne.' *The Guardian.* The Guardian. 13 Nov 2013. Web. Accessed 14 Nov 2013.

Harris, John. 'Generation Y: Why Young Voters are Backing the Conservatives.' *The Guardian.* Guardian Media Group. 25 June 2013. Web. Accessed 27 Sept 2013.

—-. 'The Tories Are Creating a Hostile Environment – Not Just for Migrants.' *The Guardian.* The Guardian. 13 Oct 2013. Web. Accessed 13 Oct 2013.

Harvey, David. *A Brief History of Neoliberalism.* New York: Oxford University Press, 2007. Print.

—-. 'Neo-Liberalism as Creative Destruction Geografiska Annaler.' *Human Geography: Geography and Power, the Power of Geography.* 88. 2 (2006): 145–58. Web. Accessed 15 Oct 2013.

Heady, Emily. 'The Polis's Different Voices: Narrating England's Progress in Dickens's Bleak House.' *Texas Studies in Literature and Language.* 48.4 (2006): 312–39. Web. Accessed 14 Jan 2014.

Henry, Nancy and Cannon Schmitt. 'Introduction: Finance,

Capital and Culture.' *Victorian Investment: New Perspectives on Finance and Culture*. Ed. Nancy Henry and Cannon Schmitt. Bloomington: Indiana University Press, 2008. Print.

Herbert, Christopher. 'Filthy Lucre: Victorian Ideas of Money.' *Victorian Studies*. 44.2 (2002): 185–213. Web. Accessed 13 Feb 2013.

—-. 'The Occult in *Bleak House*.' *NOVEL: A Forum on Fiction*. 17.2 (1984): 101–115. Web. Accessed 13 Jan 2014.

Higbie, Robert. *Dickens and Imagination*. Gainesville: University Press of Florida, 1998. Print.

Himelfarb, Ellen. 'Elmgreen & Dragset's retrospective at the National Gallery of Denmark explores loneliness and solitude in contemporary culture.' *Wallpaper*. 29 Sept 2014. Web. Accessed 19 Oct 2014.

Ho, Elizabeth. *Neo-Victorianism and the Memory of Empire*. New York: Continuum, 2012. Print.

Houston, Gail Turley. *From Dickens to Dracula: Gothic, Economics, and Victorian Fiction*. Cambridge: Cambridge University Press, 2005. Print.

—-. '"Pip" and "Property: The (Re)production of the Self in *Great Expectations*.' *Studies in the Novel*. 24: 1 (1992): 13–25. Web. Accessed 5 Nov 2012.

Hutchings, Peter, J. *The Criminal Spectre in Law, Literature and Aesthetics*. London: Routledge, 2001. Print.

Jacobs, Jane M. *Edge of Empire: Postcolonialism and the City*. London: Routledge, 2002. Print.

Jaffe, Audrey. 'Trollope in the Stock Market Irrational Exuberance and the Prime Minister.' *Victorian Investment. New Perspectives on Finance and Culture*. Bloomington: Indiana University Press, 2008. Print.

Jarvie, Paul A. *Ready to Trample on All Human Law: Financial Capitalism in the Fiction of Charles Dickens*. Oxford: Routledge, 2005. Print.

Jenkins, Simon. 'To Mock President Putin's Pride and Test His

Paranoia is Folly.' *The Guardian*. Guardian Media Group. 24 Jul 2014. Web. Accessed 25 Jul 2014.

Jennings, Will. 'A deftly-curated "house": Tomorrow by Elmgreen & Dragset at the V&A Museum.' *One Stop Arts*. 29 Sept 2013. Web. Accessed 22 Oct. 2014.

Johnson, Boris. 'Boris Johnson's Speech to the Conservative Conference: Full Text and Audio.' *The Spectator*. 1 October 2013. Web. Accessed 12 Dec 2013.

Johnston, Judith. 'Women and Violence in Dickens's *Great Expectations*.' *Sydney Studies*. 18 (2008): 93–110. Web. Accessed 5 Nov 2012.

Joshi, Priti. 'Mutiny Echoes: India, Britons, and Charles Dickens's *A Tale of Two Cities*.' *Nineteenth-Century Literature*. 62.1 (2007). Web. Accessed 21 August 2013.

Judd, Denis. *Empire: The British Imperial Experience, 1765 to the Present*. New York: Basic Books, 1996. Print.

Kaminsky, Laura Graciela and Pablo Vega-Garcia. 'Varieties of Sovereign Crises: Latin America, 1820–1931.' Department of Economics, George Washington University. 30 Sept 2013. Web. Accessed 27 Nov 2014.

Kelley, Alice Van Buren. 'The Bleak Houses of *Bleak House*.' *Nineteenth-Century Fiction*. 25.3 (1970): 253–68. Web. Accessed 13 Jan 2014.

Kern, Soeren. 'Britain: Muslim Prison Population Up 200%.' *gatestoneinstitute.org*. The Gatestone Institute. 2 Aug 2013. Web. Accessed 2 Dec 2014.

Klaver, Claudia C. *A/moral Economics: Classical Political Economy and Cultural Authority in Nineteenth Century England*. Columbus: The Ohio State University Press, 2003. Print.

Klein, Christopher. '10 Things You May Not Know About the Boston Tea Party.' *www.history.com*. History Channel. 14 Dec 2012. Web. Accessed 12 Mar 2013.

Knezevic, Borislav. *Figures of Finance Capitalism: Writing, Class and Capital in Mid-Victorian Narratives*. London: Routledge,

2003. Print.

Kohlke, Marie-Luise and Christian Gutleben. *Neo-Victorian Tropes of Trauma: The Politics of Bearing After-Witness to Nineteenth-Century Suffering*. Amsterdam: Editions Rodopi, 2010. Print.

Kuskey, Jessica. 'The Body Machinic: Technology, Labor, and Mechanized Bodies in Victorian Culture.' *English – Dissertations*. (2012): Paper 62. Web. Accessed 19 May 2013.

Lanchester, John. 'Why the Super-Rich Love the UK.' *www.guardian.com*. Guardian Media Group. 24 Feb 2012. Web. Accessed 3 Dec 2012.

LeBaron, Genevieve and Roberts, Adrienne. 'Confining Social Insecurity: Neoliberalism and the Rise of the 21st Century Debtors' Prison.' *Politics & Gender*. 8.1 (2012): 25–49. Web. 3 Dec 2012.

Lesjak, Carolyn. *Working Fictions: A Genealogy of the Victorian Novel*. Durham: Duke University Press, 2006. Print.

Levine, Gary Martin. *The Merchant of Modernism: The Economic Jew in Anglo-American Literature, 1864–1939*. London: Taylor & Francis, 2002. Print.

Levine, George. *Darwin and the Novelists*. Chicago: University of Chicago Press, 1988. Print.

Lewis, Susan S. 'The Artist and Architectural Patronage of Angela Burdett-Coutts Volume 1.' PhD Thesis. Royal Holloway, University of London. June 2012. Web. Accessed 12 Nov 2014.

Liebling Alison, Helen Arnold and Christina Straub. 'An exploration of staff – prisoner relationships at HMP Whitemoor: 12 years on.' *Cambridge Institute of Criminology Prisons Research Centre*. National Ministry of Justice. Nov 2011. Web. Accessed 2 Dec 2014.

Littler, Jo. 'Meritocracy as Plutocracy: The Marketising of "Equality" under Neoliberalism.' *New Formations*. Vol. 80–81 (2013): 52–72. Web. Accessed 12 Dec 2013.

Logan, Peter. 'Dickens Month on Masterpiece.' *The Inquirer*. 1 Apr 2012. Section H, 4. Print.

Manning, Sanchez. 'Britain's Colonial Shame: Slave-Owners Given Huge Payouts after Abolition.' *The Independent.* The Independent. 24 Feb 2013. Web. Accessed 7 Sept 2013.

Marcus, Steven. 'Homelessness and Dickens.' *Social Research.* 58.1 (1991): 93–106. Web. Accessed 13 Jan 2014.

Marx, Karl. *Das Kapital.* Washington, D.C.: Regnery Publishing, 2009. Print.

—-. 'A Superannuated Administration. Prospects of the coalition ministry, &c.' *New-York Daily Tribune.* 3677, 28 Jan 1853. www.marxengels.public-archive.net/. Web. Accessed 13 Dec 2013.

Marx, Karl and Friedrich Engels. 'Karl Marx to Friedrich Engels, 18 June 1862.' *Karl Marx, Friedrich Engels: Collected Works Volume 41.* London: Lawrence and Wishart, 1975–2004. www.mecollectiveworks.files.wordpress.com. Web. Accessed 2 Sept 2013.

Mason, Paul. 'Financial Sanctions on Russia: Big or Nothing?' *blogs.channel4.com.* Channel 4 News. 22 July 2014. Web. Accessed 22 July 2014.

—-. 'Iraq, Syria, Egypt, Ukraine: What Happens Next in a World without Framework?' *blogs.channel4.com.* Channel 4 News. 24 June 2014. Web. Accessed 12 July 2014.

Mason, Tony. 'England 1966 Traditional or Modern?' *National Identity and Global Sports Events: Culture, Politics, and Spectacle in the Olympics and the Football World Cup.* Eds. Alan Tomlinson and Christopher Young. Albany: State University of New York Press, 2006.

Massey, Doreen. 'London Inside-Out.' *Soundings: A Journal of Politics and Culture.* 32 (2006): 62–71. Accessed 11 Oct 2013.

—-. 'Vocabularies of the Economy.' *After Neoliberalism? The Kilburn Manifesto. Soundings.* (2013) 3–17. Web. Accessed 13 Jun 2013.

May, Todd. *Friendship in an Age of Economics: Resisting the Forces of Neoliberalism.* Lenham: Lexington Books, 2012.

McFarlane, Gary. 'A Respectable Trade? Slavery and the Rise of Capitalism. A review of Hugh Thomas, *The Slave Trade: The History of the Atlantic Slave Trade 1440-1870* (Picador, 1997) £25.' *International Socialism*. Issue 80. Sept 1998. Web. Accessed 7 Oct 2013.

McMillan, Michael. 'The West Indian Front Room: Reflections on a Diasporic Phenomenon.' *Small Axe*. 28. 13. 1 (2009): 135–56. 28 March 2009. Web. Accessed 7 Oct 2013.

Michie, Helena. 'Under Victorian Skins: The Bodies Beneath.' *A Companion to Victorian Literature and Culture*. Ed. Herbert F. Tucker. Oxford: Blackwell, 1999. Print.

Miller, Joseph Hillis. *Victorian Subjects*. Durham: Duke University Press, 1991. Print.

Miller, Shari. 'Revealed: Samantha Cameron is Descended from Aristocratic Slave Owner.' *Daily Mail*. Daily Mail and General Trust. 12 May 2013. Web. Accessed 7 Oct 2013.

Mirowski, Philip. *Never Let a Serious Crisis Go to Waste: How Neoliberalism Survived the Financial Meltdown*. London: Verso, 2013. Print.

Mohanram, Radhika. *Imperial White: Race, Diaspora, and the British Empire*. Minneapolis: University of Minnesota Press, 2007. Print.

Moore, Grace. *Dickens and Empire: Discourses of Class, Race and Colonialism in the Works of Charles Dickens*. London: Ashgate Publishing Ltd., 2004. Print.

Morris, Nigel. 'Number of Muslims in prison doubles in decade to 12,000.' *The Independent*. 28 March 2014. Web. Accessed 12 Dec 2014.

Mulheirn, Ian. 'The Myth of the "Welfare Scrounger."' *New Statesman*. New Statesman. 21 March 2013. Web. Accessed 21 Dec 2013.

Nayeri, Farah. 'Dickens's Revamped London Home Reopens for Christmas.' *Bloomberg.com*. Bloomberg L.P. 22 Dec 2012. Web. Accessed 5 Dec 2013.

Neal, Larry. 'The Financial Crisis of 1825 and the Restructuring of the British Financial System.' *Review.* Federal Reserve Bank of Saint Louis. May/June (1998): 53–76. Web. Accessed 12 Dec 2014.

Newton, Lucy. 'Change and continuity: the development of joint stock banking in the early nineteenth century.' *Centre for International Business History.* University of Reading, Henley School of Management. 2007. Web. Accessed 2 Dec 2014.

Novak, Daniel. 'If Re-Collecting Were Forgetting: Forged Bodies and Forgotten Labor in Little Dorrit.' *Novel: A Forum on Fiction.* Vol. 31.1 (1997): 21. Web. Accessed 12 May 2012.

O'Quinn, Daniel. 'Who Owns What: Slavery, Property, and Eschatological Compensation in Thomas De Quincey's Opium Writings.' *Texas Studies in Literature and Language.* 45.3 (2003): 262–92. Web. Accessed 7 Sept 2013.

Orbell, John. 'Baring, Thomas (1799–1873).' *Oxford Dictionary of National Biography.* Oxford University Press. Oct 2006. Web. Accessed 20 June 2014.

Owen, Glen. 'The Coalition of Millionaires: 23 of the 29 Member of the New Cabinet are Worth more than £1m… and the Lib Dems are Just as Wealthy as the Tories.' *Daily Mail Online.* Daily Mail and General Trust. 23 May 2010. Web. Accessed 25 July 2014.

Perera, Suvendrini. *Reaches of Empire: The English Novel from Edgeworth to Dickens.* New York: Columbia University Press, 1991. Print.

Philo, Gregory. 'Capital's role in the economic crisis.' *The Guardian.* Guardian Media Group. 12 Aug 2013. Web. Accessed 4 Oct 2013.

Philpotts, Trey. *The Companion to Little Dorrit.* Mountfield: Helm Information, 2003.

Plotz, John. *Portable Property: Victorian Culture on the Move.* Princeton, NJ: Princeton University Press, 2008. Print.

Polanyi, Karl. *The Great Transformation: The Political and Economic*

Origins of Our Time. Boston: Beacon Press, 1944. Print.

Pool, Daniel. *What Jane Austen Ate and Charles Dickens Knew: From Fox Hunting to Whist – the Facts of Daily Life in Nineteenth-Century England.* New York: Simon and Schuster, 1994. Print.

Poon, Angelia. *Enacting Englishness in the Victorian Period: Colonialism and the Politics of Performance.* Aldershot: Ashgate, 2008. Print.

Poovey, Mary. 'Writing About Finance in Victorian England Disclosure and Secrecy in the Culture of Investment.' *Victorian Investment: New Perspectives on Finance and Culture.* Bloomington: Indiana University Press, 2008. Print.

Prison Abolition 2014. 'What is the Prison Industrial Complex?' *prisonabilition.org.* n.d. Web. Accessed 2 Dec 2014.

Rediker, Marcus Buford. *The Slave Ship: A Human History.* New York: Penguin, 2007. Print.

Reid, Kristy. 'Exile, Empire and the Convict Diaspora: The Return of Magwitch.' *Creativity in Exile.* Ed. Michael Hanne. Amsterdam: Rodopi, 2004. Print.

Rhodes, James. 'Remaking Whiteness in the "Postracial" UK.' *The State of Race.* Ed. Nisha Kapoor, Virinder Kalra and James Rhodes. London: Palgrave Macmillan, 2013. Print.

Richards, Thomas. *The Commodity Culture of Victorian England: Advertising and Spectacle, 1851–1914.* Stanford: Stanford University Press, 1991. Print.

Robins, Nick. 'Loot: In search of the East India Company, the World's First Transnational Corporation.' *Environment and Urbanization.* 14 (2002): 79–88. Web. Accessed 24 Mar 2013.

Robinson, William and Jerry Harris. 'Towards a Global Ruling Class? Globalization and the Transnational Capitalist Class.' *Science & Society.* 64.1 (2000): 11–54. Web. Accessed 15 Mar 2013.

Rosen, Michael. 'Bedroom Tax Plans are a Levy on the Grief of the Poor.' *The Guardian.* The Guardian Media Group. 14 Jan 2014. Web. Accessed 15 Jan 2014.

Rothenberg, Molly Anne. 'Articulating Social Agency in *Our Mutual Friend*: Problems with Performances, Practices, and Political Efficacy.' *ELH* 71:3 (2004): 719–49. Web. Accessed 25 Dec 2013.

Roy, Arundhati. *Ordinary Person's Guide to Empire*. New Delhi: Penguin Books, 2005. Print.

Rushdie, Salman. 'Charles Dickens at 200.' *The Charlie Rose Show*. Waltham: CQ Transcriptions. 26 Dec 2012.

Said, Edward W. *Culture and Imperialism*. London: Vintage Books, 1994. Print.

Schlicke, Paul. *The Oxford Companion to Charles Dickens: Anniversary Edition*. Oxford: Oxford University Press, 2011. Print.

Sherwood, Marika. 'Atlantic Trade and Arab Slavery.' *New African*. 521.10 (2012): 30–31. Web. Accessed 9 Sept 2013.

Shin, Hisup. 'Tarrying with Sensuous Materiality: A Study of the Interplay between Objects and the Human Body in Dickens.' *rhizomes*. 05 fall 2005. Web. Accessed 12 May 2012.

Sicher, Efriam. 'Reanimation, Regeneration and Re-Evaluation: Re-Reading *Our Mutual Friend*.' *Connotations*. 19.1-3 (2009–10): 36–44. Web. Accessed 12 May 2012.

Smith, Grahame. *Dickens, Money, and Society*. Berkeley: University of California Press, 1968. Print.

Smith, Sydney. *The Edinburgh Review, Volumes 94–95*. London: A. and C. Black Publishers Ltd., 1851. Google eBook. Web. Accessed 17 Jan 2014.

Solow, Barbara L. 'Capitalism and Slavery in the Exceedingly Long Run.' *British Capitalism and Caribbean Slavery: The Legacy of Eric Williams*. Ed. Barbara Lewis Solow & Stanley L. Engerman. Cambridge: Cambridge University Press, 2004. Print.

—-. 'The British & the Slave Trade.' *The New York Review of Books*. 12 Jan 2012. Web. Accessed 4 Oct 2013.

Sparrow, Andrew. '"Go home" campaign against illegal

immigrants could go nationwide.' *The Guardian*. The Guardian Media Group. 29 Jul 2014. Web. Accessed 31 June 2013.

Soros, George. 'How the EU Can Save Ukraine.' *The Guardian*. Guardian Media Group. 29 May 2014. Web. Accessed 29 May 2014.

Steinlight, Emily. 'Dickens's "Supernumeraries" and the Biopolitical Imagination of Victorian Fiction.' *Novel: A Forum On Fiction*. 43.2 (2010): 227–50. Web. Accessed 13 Mar 2013.

Suchoff, David Bruce. *Critical Theory and the Novel: Mass Society and Cultural Criticism in Dickens, Melville, and Kafka*. Madison: University of Wisconsin Press, 1994. Print.

Sussman, Herbert and Gerhard Joseph. 'Prefiguring the Posthuman: Dickens and Prosthesis.' *Victorian Literature and Culture*. 32.2 (2004): 617–28. *journals.cambridge.org*. Cambridge Journals Online. 1 Sept 2004. Web. Accessed 12 May 2012.

Sussman, Herbert. *Victorian Technology: Invention, Innovation, and the Rise of the Machine*. Santa Barbara: Praeger, 2009. Print.

Tamai, Fumie. 'Nationalism, and the Shadow of a Declining Empire: Dickens's Journalism and Speeches in the Mid-Fifties.' *Studies in Comparative Culture*. Vol. 52 (2000): 1–13. Web. Accessed 12 June 2013.

Tayyab, Mahmud. 'Debt and Discipline.' *American Quarterly*. 64.3 (2012):469–94. Web. Accessed 27 March 2013.

Temple-Raston, Diana. 'Al-Qaida's Paper Trail: A "Treasure Trove" For U.S.' *www.npr.org*. National Public Radio. 31 May 2011. Web. Accessed 11 Mar 2013.

Thornbury, Walter. *Old and New London: A Narrative of Its History, Its People, and Its Places*. London: Cassell Limited, 1892. Google eBook. Web. Accessed 17 Jan 2014.

Traps, Yevgeniya. 'Transporting Things: The Spiritual Life of Victorian Objects.' *Nineteenth-Century Gender Studies*. 6.3 (2010). Web. Accessed 3 Jan 2014.

Trocki, Carl A. *Opium, Empire and the Global Political Economy: A Study of the Asian Opium Trade*. London: Routledge, 1999. Print.

Tuohy, Brian. 'There is a history of match-fixing at the World Cup.' n.d. *SportsonEarth.com*. Web. Accessed 5 Oct 2014.

University of York. 'Lessons from the past: York academics investigate 1966 World Cup.' *www.york.ac.uk*. 6 Mar 2014. Web. Accessed 4 Oct 2014.

V&A. 'A Brief History of the Museum.' *www.vam.ac.uk*. V&A website. n.d. Web. Accessed 23 Oct 2014.

—-. 'Elmgreen & Dragset at the V&A: About the Exhibition." Online video. n.d. *www.vam.ac.uk*. V&A website. Web. Accessed 2 Dec 2013.

—-. 'Video: Elmgreen & Dragset.' Online Video. n.d. *www.vam.ac.uk*.V&A website. Web. Accessed 5 Dec 2013.

Vanden Bossche, Chris R. 'Class Discourse and Popular Agency in *Bleak House*.' *Victorian Studies*. 47.1 (2004): 7–31. Web. Accessed 14 Jan 2014.

Vercellone, Carlo. 'The Crisis of the Law of Value and the Becoming-Rent of Profit.' Eds. Andrea Fumagalli, Sandro Mezzadra. *Crisis in the Global Economy: Financial Markets, Social Struggles, and New Political Scenarios*. Semiotext(e), Cambridge: The MIT Press, 2010. Web. Accessed 22 Aug 2013.

Vesperoni, Alberto. 'War profiteering.' *FoKos Institute University Seigen*. (2014): 1–13. Web. Accessed 22 July 2014.

Wacquant, Loïc. *Deadly Symbiosis: Race and the Rise of the Penal State*. London: Polity, 2009. Print.

Wagner, Tamara S. *Financial Speculation in Victorian Fiction: Plotting Money and the Novel Genre, 1815–1901*. Columbus: The Ohio State University Press, 2010. Print.

— —. 'Imperialist Commerce and the Demystified Orient: Semicolonial China in Nineteenth Century English Literature.' *Postcolonial Text*. Vol. 6.3 (2011): 1–18.

Walvin, James. 'Slavery and the Building of Britain.' *bbc.co.uk/history*. The British Broadcasting Corporation. 17 Feb 2011. Web. Accessed 14 Jul 2014.

Watson, Lauren. 'Mimics, Counterfeits and Other Bad Copies:

Forging the Currency of Class and Colonialism in Great Expectations.' *Textual Practice*. 25:2 (2011): 493–511. Web. Accessed 4 Sept 2013.

Weisenthal, Joe. 'Here's David Cameron Calling for Permanent Austerity in Front of All Kinds of Ridiculous Gold Things.' *Business Insider*. 12 Nov 2013. Web. Accessed 16 Dec 2013.

Williams, Eric Eustace. *Capitalism & Slavery*. Chapel Hill: University of North Carolina Press, 1994. Print.

Wintour, Patrick. 'Some Benefits Claimants Face 35 Hours a Week at JobCentre.' *The Guardian*. Guardian Media Group. 30 Sept 2013. Web. Accessed 21 Dec 2013.

Wohl, Anthony S. 'Racism and Anti-Irish Prejudice in Victorian England.' *www.victorianweb.com*. The Victorian Web. Web. Accessed 11 Oct 2013.

Wolfreys, Julian. 'The Nineteenth-Century Political Novel.' *A Companion to the Victorian Novel*. Westport: Greenwood Publishing Group, 2002. Print.

Woodman, Ellis. 'Tomorrow — Elmgreen & Dragset at the V&A.' *BDonline.co.uk*. 30 Sept 2013. Web. Accessed 2 Dec 2013.

Wrathall, Claire. 'Elmgreen & Dragset on Creating a Brand New "Tomorrow" at the V&A.' *Modern Painters*. 30 Nov 2013. Web. Accessed 5 Dec 2013.

Wright, Lawrence. *The Looming Tower: Al-Qaeda and the Road to 9/11*. London: Vintage, 2007. Print.

Xu, Wenying. 'The Opium Trade and *Little Dorrit*: A Case of Reading Silences.' *Victorian Literature and Culture*. 25. 1 (1997): 53–66. Web. Accessed 2 Nov 2014.

Zwierlein, Anne-Julia. 'The Biology of Social Class: Habit Formation and Social Stratification.' *Nineteenth-Century British Bildungsromane and Scientific Discourse*. 10.2 (2012): 335–60. Web. Accessed 4 Sept 2013.

zero
books

Contemporary culture has eliminated both the concept of the
public and the figure of the intellectual. Former public spaces –
both physical and cultural – are now either derelict or colonized
by advertising. A cretinous anti-intellectualism presides,
cheerled by expensively educated hacks in the pay of
multinational corporations who reassure their bored readers
that there is no need to rouse themselves from their interpassive
stupor. The informal censorship internalized and propagated by
the cultural workers of late capitalism generates a banal
conformity that the propaganda chiefs of Stalinism could only
ever have dreamt of imposing. Zer0 Books knows that another
kind of discourse – intellectual without being academic, popular
without being populist – is not only possible: it is already
flourishing, in the regions beyond the striplit malls of so-called
mass media and the neurotically bureaucratic halls of the
academy. Zer0 is committed to the idea of publishing as a
making public of the intellectual. It is convinced that in
the unthinking, blandly consensual culture in which we live,
critical and engaged theoretical reflection is more important
than ever before.

ZERO BOOKS

If this book has helped you to clarify an idea, solve a problem or extend your knowledge, you may like to read more titles from Zero Books. Recent bestsellers are:

Capitalist Realism Is there no alternative?
Mark Fisher
An analysis of the ways in which capitalism has presented itself as the only realistic political-economic system.
Paperback: November 27, 2009 978-1-84694-317-1 $14.95 £7.99.
eBook: July 1, 2012 978-1-78099-734-6 $9.99 £6.99.

The Wandering Who? A study of Jewish identity politics
Gilad Atzmon
An explosive unique crucial book tackling the issues of Jewish Identity Politics and ideology and their global influence.
Paperback: September 30, 2011 978-1-84694-875-6 $14.95 £8.99.
eBook: September 30, 2011 978-1-84694-876-3 $9.99 £6.99.

Clampdown Pop-cultural wars on class and gender
Rhian E. Jones
Class and gender in Britpop and after, and why 'chav' is a feminist issue.
Paperback: March 29, 2013 978-1-78099-708-7 $14.95 £9.99.
eBook: March 29, 2013 978-1-78099-707-0 $7.99 £4.99.

The Quadruple Object
Graham Harman
Uses a pack of playing cards to present Harman's metaphysical system of fourfold objects, including human access, Heidegger's indirect causation, panpsychism and ontography.
Paperback: July 29, 2011 978-1-84694-700-1 $16.95 £9.99.

Weird Realism Lovecraft and Philosophy
Graham Harman
As Hölderlin was to Martin Heidegger and Mallarmé to Jacques Derrida, so is H.P. Lovecraft to the Speculative Realist philosophers.
Paperback: September 28, 2012 978-1-78099-252-5 $24.95 £14.99.
eBook: September 28, 2012 978-1-78099-907-4 $9.99 £6.99.

Sweetening the Pill or How We Got Hooked on Hormonal Birth Control
Holly Grigg-Spall
Is it really true? Has contraception liberated or oppressed women?
Paperback: September 27, 2013 978-1-78099-607-3 $22.95 £12.99.
eBook: September 27, 2013 978-1-78099-608-0 $9.99 £6.99.

Why Are We The Good Guys? Reclaiming Your Mind From The Delusions Of Propaganda
David Cromwell
A provocative challenge to the standard ideology that Western power is a benevolent force in the world.
Paperback: September 28, 2012 978-1-78099-365-2 $26.95 £15.99.
eBook: September 28, 2012 978-1-78099-366-9 $9.99 £6.99.

The Truth about Art Reclaiming quality
Patrick Doorly
The book traces the multiple meanings of art to their various sources, and equips the reader to choose between them.
Paperback: August 30, 2013 978-1-78099-841-1 $32.95 £19.99.

Bells and Whistles More Speculative Realism
Graham Harman
In this diverse collection of sixteen essays, lectures, and interviews Graham Harman lucidly explains the principles of

Speculative Realism, including his own object-oriented philosophy.
Paperback: November 29, 2013 978-1-78279-038-9 $26.95 £15.99.
eBook: November 29, 2013 978-1-78279-037-2 $9.99 £6.99.

Towards Speculative Realism: Essays and Lectures Essays and Lectures
Graham Harman
These writings chart Harman's rise from Chicago sportswriter to co founder of one of Europe's most promising philosophical movements: Speculative Realism.
Paperback: November 26, 2010 978-1-84694-394-2 $16.95 £9.99.
eBook: January 1, 1970 978-1-84694-603-5 $9.99 £6.99.

Meat Market Female flesh under capitalism
Laurie Penny
A feminist dissection of women's bodies as the fleshy fulcrum of capitalist cannibalism, whereby women are both consumers and consumed.
Paperback: April 29, 2011 978-1-84694-521-2 $12.95 £6.99.
eBook: May 21, 2012 978-1-84694-782-7 $9.99 £6.99.

Translating Anarchy The Anarchism of Occupy Wall Street
Mark Bray
An insider's account of the anarchists who ignited Occupy Wall Street.
Paperback: September 27, 2013 978-1-78279-126-3 $26.95 £15.99.
eBook: September 27, 2013 978-1-78279-125-6 $6.99 £4.99.

One Dimensional Woman
Nina Power
Exposes the dark heart of contemporary cultural life by examining pornography, consumer capitalism and the ideology of women's work.

Paperback: November 27, 2009 978-1-84694-241-9 $14.95 £7.99.
eBook: July 1, 2012 978-1-78099-737-7 $9.99 £6.99.

Dead Man Working
Carl Cederstrom, Peter Fleming
An analysis of the dead man working and the way in which
capital is now colonizing life itself.
Paperback: May 25, 2012 978-1-78099-156-6 $14.95 £9.99.
eBook: June 27, 2012 978-1-78099-157-3 $9.99 £6.99.

Unpatriotic History of the Second World War
James Heartfield
The Second World War was not the Good War of legend. James
Heartfield explains that both Allies and Axis powers fought for
the same goals - territory, markets and natural resources.
Paperback: September 28, 2012 978-1-78099-378-2 $42.95 £23.99.
eBook: September 28, 2012 978-1-78099-379-9 $9.99 £6.99.

Find more titles at www.zero-books.net